JEWISH FAITH IN
A CHANGING WORLD

REFERENCE LIBRARY OF JEWISH INTELLECTUAL HISTORY

ACADEMIC
STUDIES
PRESS

JEWISH FAITH IN
A CHANGING WORLD

A Modern Introduction to the World and Ideas of Classical Jewish Philosophy

Raphael Shuchat

Boston
2012

Library of Congress Cataloging-in-Publication Data:
A catalog record for this title is available from the Library of Congress.

ISBN 978-1-936235-68-1 (hardback)
ISBN 978-1-618112-16-3 (paperback)

Book design by Ivan Grave

Published by Academic Studies Press in 2012
28 Montfern Avenue
Brighton, MA 02135, USA
press@academicstudiespress.com
www.academicstudiespress.com

This book is dedicated to my mother,
Miriam (Bat Yaakov) Shuchat Z"L,
who at a great personal sacrifice let me leave home
at a tender age to pursue my dreams.

"Many daughters have done worthily but thou excellest them all"
(Proverbs 31, 29)

I miss you deeply and follow the beacon of
your light throughout my life.

My mother, Miriam Shuchat (Nee Sochet), was born in Bronx, New York to a religious family. She went to NYU to study education. Since her parents were not learned, she was determined to understand her Judaism more deeply. She took night classes in Jewish studies at the Jewish Theological Seminary in NY and studied weekly in a class given by Rabbi Shlomo Carlbach at the university. After marrying my father, Rabbi Wilfred Shuchat of Montreal, she created and taught the Bat Mitzvah class at the synagogue and was active in Emunah woman and other charity organizations. As we grew older she went back to school, earned an MA in Jewish studies and taught at Vanier College. She established the Jewish Studies program there and taught there for 25 years. She retired only to help my sister Elizabeth after her first bout with cancer. She had lost her brother just after her marriage so she was determined to help my sister recover. Unfortunately Liz passed away a year later and my mother never overcame the shock. In 2008 she developed symptoms of a debilitating disease which she endured bravely until she passed away on May 3th 2012(11 Iyar 5772). May this book honour her memory.

Table of Contents

Introduction

E ducation is a difficult task. It is not just theoretical ideas of information, but introducing an individual to new ideas by which to influence their lives, hopefully for the good. Jewish education is an even greater task, for it involves introducing one to an age old heritage whose ideas were formulated in times different from our own. Young children can be taught by role models, but adults, whether young or old, need an intellectual understanding of what they are doing. Without that, we are, as one Jewish educator put it, like a body without a head.[1] There is a negative tendency in religious education whereby teachers smother their student's curiosity by making the convenient claim that questions are forbidden. This is usually done to cover up for their lack of scholarship and understanding of the texts. Even more frustrating is the teacher who pretends that the answer is so deep and mystical that the student should wait 20 years before they ask again. Maimonides ridicules those who think that religious practice and belief must stand on illogical ground:

> There is a group of people, human beings who consider it a grievous thing that causes should be given for the law; what would please them most is that the intellect would not find a meaning for the commandments and prohibitions. What compels them to feel thus is a sickness....For they think that...if...there is a thing for which the intellect could not find any meaning at all...it indubitably derives from God.[2]

The way of questioning, of looking for reasons and logical explanations, is the way of the greatest rabbinic figures for over a thousand years.[3] They fearlessly asked the most intimate and "embarrassing" questions of every detail of Jewish life and beliefs, to understand the deeper teachings behind them. At Sinai, the Jews said "We will do and we will hear" (Ex. 24:7). Hearing—like "Hear O Israel the Lord is One" (Deut. 1:4), refers to understanding. It is true that Judaism requires observance even if there is not yet total understanding, but by all measures, understanding is the ideal way. The text in Deuteronomy says: "And you shall know today and bring unto your heart that the Lord is God" (Deut. 4:39) and King David says to Solomon: "know the Lord your God with a whole heart and an eager soul" (1 Chron. 28:9). Understanding is not only about knowing why God gave the Torah, but what it means to me. If I can find meaning in my life, make myself and my social environment a little better than it was before, then I have achieved something of worth. Jewish thought goes far beyond this, trying to make sense out of every nook and cranny of Jewish faith. Those who were the players in this intellectual arena were some of the greatest scholars the Jewish people have ever had since the second temple period. Unfortunately, today this area has been so neglected in study that contemporary Rabbis are unversed in these works, to the extent that even if they by chance happen to discuss philosophic issues, they will probably be oblivious to the fact that these issues were discussed in great length before them.

Those who do deal with issues of Jewish thought today, tend to follow the trend of explaining everything mystically. Far be it from me to belittle such an approach. Personally, I am a great lover of Jewish mysticism and kabbalah, but the intellectual basis has to be one of reason and logic, which is easier for one to swallow, before proceeding to mystical texts and ideas. It is like trying to build the second story of a house without a foundation. Even one of the greatest of kabbalists, R. Hayyim Vital, wrote that one cannot approach the secrets of Torah without a basis in the realm of philosophical inquiry.[4] The world of Jewish philosophy until now has been limited mostly to the marble halls of the academic world for the purpose of scholarly research and little attempt has been made to make these works relevant. The academic scholar often, presents these works in a scientific but rather dry fashion for the modern reader. In order to make the material more palatable I am consciously walking a fine line between writing popularly to an intellectual modern readership and attempting to be as faithful as possible to the works of academic scholarship. I update each idea with a modern discussion of its relevance to make it pertinent to the reader and have left all the academic discussion to the references at the bottom of each page, for the benefit of those who would like to pursue these discussions further. By this, I am attempting to open a window for the reader to gaze into this beautiful and profound world of Jewish philosophy, a world where even the most sacred of values is scrutinized in the pursuit of theoretical and moral truth; a world wherein Judaism becomes a real world view and life philosophy, as relevant today as then.

CHAPTER 1   *What is Jewish Philosophy?*

Chinese legend tells of an old man sitting by the river bank drawing a circle over and over again. A young man approaches him to figure out what he's doing. "I'm drawing the perfect circle," he says. "Well" says the young man, "that's easy enough!" So he picks a point on the river bank, sits down and begins to draw. The first circle looks good. He tries to improve some of its imperfections. However as he looks closer he finds more and more flaws. Frustrated, he erases it and draws it again and again. By the time he thinks he's as close as possible to drawing the perfect circle he looks into the water and sees the reflection of an old man.

As children, life seems rather simple. We just follow the example of others, however intellectually and morally poor or rich they may be, playing a sort of follow the leader. As adolescents we start to ponder the meaning of our lives and the values with which we grew up and try to make some sense of it all. That is when we become little philosophers.[1] However, asking too many questions can be not just a social nuisance but even intellectually dangerous. What if we discover that the values upon which our society seems to rest are devoid of value? Didn't Solomon say, "The greater our knowledge the greater our anguish" (Eccl. 1:8)? There are certain societies that limit human inquiry out of this fear. About 2250 years ago Socrates was arrested for corrupting the youth of Athens by asking them too many questions. The sentence was death. In Plato's book, *The Crito*, we are told that Socrates' students managed to make their way into the prison the night before the sentence was to be carried out and wanted to take Socrates with them. He, however, refused, arguing that after some thought, he had come to realize that the people of Athens were right to see him as a threat, for knowledge does take social values to task.

So the average person tends to "get over" their philosophic quest by their mid-twenties and just "fall into line" with the values of their parents, society, friends or all three.[2] Perhaps this is why this 'dangerous' dimension of thinking seems to always limit itself to a select few. In addition, these limitations may be due to the fact that it is easier to ask questions then it is to answer them. In any event, the role of the thinker has been somewhat elitist and even secluded from society.

In Hassidic lore, the arena for many of the good stories is the forest; the thick forests of the Ukraine and Poland where the tree tops are so meshed as to withhold the sun's light from the one who dares to cross below. When the wind blows, the crowns of the trees move, allowing for a ray of sunlight to enter the forest. As one approaches this ray of light, trying to grasp its essence, again the wind blows and the ray moves to another place. This is somewhat like the attempt to search for truth in this world. We can perceive the ray only for an instant, and only in the right time and place and even then only at infrequent times.[3]

Until now I have purposely used the term "thinker" and not philosopher. For "philosophy" is a Greek word with a specific meaning. There is a tendency today to use the term "philosophize" and "think about" synonymously. However, the Greeks did not invent thought and were not the first to try to figure out the world around them. The Chinese and the Indians as well as our own Hebrew ancestors predated the Greeks by many centuries in this field. So what is unique about the Greek contribution that we call them the founders of philosophy? To explain this we need to enter our first discussion of this book, namely, the meaning of three terms: "Philosophy," "Religious Philosophy," and

"Jewish Philosophy," for in order to understand what Jewish philosophy is, we need to see it in its proper context.

What is philosophy? The word is made up of two Greek words *philo*, meaning to love, and *sophon*, meaning wisdom.[4] This, however, is just an etymological explanation. What made philosophy a Greek invention, and differentiated it from earlier modes of thinking about the world, was the attempt to establish a universal basis upon which one could argue something about the world and prove or disprove it to another. For if one person believed that the Philistine God "Dagon" created fire, and another that the Greek God "Zeus" did so, there was little room for argument, for there was little common ground upon which they could have held the debate. You need some common ground for discussion and debate, whereas beliefs and emotions are not necessarily universal. The Greeks found human reason to be such a universal basis. If one can argue a point and prove it logically, then it must be true. So the art of philosophy is an attempt to make logical statements about the world. By doing so, one can create a framework whereby one can prove or disprove an idea. If it can be proven logically, then it becomes a universal truth.

Of course, before one can make a logical statement about the world, one needs to define what is meant by "logic." Therefore, already in the early days of Greek philosophy, Aristotle attempted to create a theory of logic. In this early stage of the study of Logic, he argued that logic is based on various forms of logical sentences called syllogisms. The most famous syllogism is the argument developed concerning Socrates' mortality. In answer to those students who wondered how such a great genius could warrant death, Aristotle said:

> *All Men are mortal*
> *Socrates is a Man*
> *Socrates is Mortal*

The syllogism is made up of two introductory sentences or statements and a conclusion.[5] The argument is that the conclusion is logically forced so that any reasonable human being should reach the same conclusion. Aristotle went on to explain the structure of the syllogism. After all, one must know how it is constructed in order to use it. For example if I say:

> *All dogs have tails*
> *All cats have tails*

What should be the conclusion? If I am to say "All dogs are cats," I have to figure out what went wrong with my syllogism's structure to have reached an erroneous conclusion. Similarly, if I am to conclude that "all dogs and cats have tails," I have not reached any new conclusion that was not stated in the opening sentences. The answer to this problem would be that in every syllogism I need a general statement and a particular statement with which I compare it. In the case above I have only two particular statements (about cats and dogs) and no statement about the generic species to which cats and dogs belong and therefore nothing can be learned from it.[6] The goal of this short discussion was to explain that logic needs to be defined before we can make logical statements about the world. Every serious philosophical school will adopt a theory of logic as a premise.

At this point one may ask what brought the early Greeks and Ionians to postulate this theory of philosophy based on human reason. Why didn't those who preceded them discuss such issues? This is a more complicated question touching upon a certain amount of speculation. However, it seems that the cradle of human culture, the Middle- and Far East, were societies deeply imbedded in beliefs based on revelation and therefore tended to belittle human reason in the face of Divine knowledge. Reason was there to explain life after revelation made its statements and not before. However, it is of interest that the early Greeks, like Pythagoras and his secret society as well as Socrates and his Daemon, were deeply involved in esoteric knowledge. It seems that there was a gradual universal movement away from Divine-based esoteric knowledge which started around 600 BCE, with the end of prophecy in the Middle East, the beginning of materialistic thought in India, the end of the Mayan rule in South America and the movement away from mythology in Greece, which enabled the path to human rational speculation to become legitimate. This is a movement from Theo-centricity to anthropocentricity, which brings human reason to the forefront.

Our next question is, "What is the meaning of the term religious philosophy?" Here we seem to be dealing with a paradox. After all, if philosophy is based on human reason, religion is based on revelation or on a belief in a specific revelation, so we have two distinct sources of knowledge that seem to have little in common. To understand this seeming oxymoron called religious philosophy we need to understand the history of its birth. When Alexander the Great captured the majority of the known world in 332 BCE, he brought Hellenistic culture to the

Middle East for the first time. This culture put philosophy on a pedestal. The need to prove things logically was a sort of novelty to this part of the world, which had held a religious world view from time immemorial. The dominance of Greek culture and the growing need for logic became somewhat of an embarrassment for the religionists, who felt the need to argue their religion from a logical point of view to show that it didn't fall from philosophic standards. These attempts to harmonize between reason and faith were the birth of religious philosophy and began specifically where Greek culture came in contact with the monotheistic religions. The religionists felt the necessity to prove that their faith was not contrary to logic. This was done in two ways: first and foremost by demonstrating that the seeming contradictions between faith and reason were solvable, and second by showing that the main principles of faith could be demonstrated logically.

One can say that religious philosophy emerged out of the interface between Western culture, with its Greek roots, and the three monotheistic religions of the Middle East: Judaism, Christianity and Islam. In simple terms, it is the attempt of the believer to understand how he looks from the vantage point of Western culture, which judges everything from a logical point of view. The earliest attempt of religious philosophy is found in the Epistle of Aristeas, written in the second century BCE, wherein the author attempts to give logical explanations for some of the Jewish practices. This is not to say that beforehand people thought that their practices were illogical, but just to say that they did not feel the need to argue them from a logical standpoint. The anonymous author, living in a world dominated by Hellenistic culture, is wondering "How do they see my people and our beliefs?" This happens under three conditions: a) when the dominant culture is not that of the faith of the believer, b) when the dominant culture allows the minority some type of religious and civil freedom, and c) when the dominant culture appears to be homogenous and not a multi-cultural conglomerate. By way of example, the Jews under Babylonian rule, a monarchy which controlled hundreds of varying cultures and religions, felt quite at home and did not feel that the Babylonian culture was a threatening entity compelling them to defend themselves or to write apologetical treaties to justify their faith. In fact, the Talmud is not embarrassed to express a feeling of superiority in relation to Babylonian pagan society. A different example would be the Jews of eastern Europe in the eighteenth century. Since Russian and Polish society were not very tolerant to Jews and forced them to live in the Pale of Settlement, keeping them out of the general society, Jews felt little desire to justify themselves in the light of that culture and again had little interest in it. Therefore, all three criteria are needed for a fertile ground for religious philosophy.

One can say that there are three main periods of Jewish philosophy: I) The Hellenistic period, from about 200 BCE to 115 CE (The fall of Alexandrian Jewry in the great revolt); II) The Golden Age of Spain, from about 1000 CE to 1492 CE (The expulsion of Jews from Spain); and III) The modern period, from 1800 (The Emancipation in Europe) until today.

I) The first period is dominated by Hellenistic culture. Alexandria, which at the time was the intellectual center of the Middle-East, was dominated by neo-Platonic thinking. Hellenistic culture influenced Jews as early as the beginning of the second century BCE, the time of the famous Maccabean revolt. As mentioned above, the first attempt to address Greek culture in a text is the Epistle of Aristeas, which tells the story of the Greek translation of the Bible, "The Septuagint," and shares the author's views of how he justifies Jewish practices rationally. However the first serious attempt to create some type of synthesis between the ideas of Plato and Jewish thinking was in the first century by Philo of Alexandria, who I will discuss later on.

II) The place and time of the most fertile development of religious philosophy was the Golden Age of Spain. After the Moors' conquest of Spain, this being the first entry of Muslims into Western Europe, they attempted to adopt Western culture as their own and asked the Jews to translate the major Greek works in medicine, astronomy and philosophy into Arabic.[7] This brought about a major attempt to synthesize between Greek philosophy, specifically the writings of Aristotle, and Islamic thought. This period begins with the Muslim conquest of Spain in 688 CE. However, the writings of this period go from around 900 to 1492 while the fourteenth century already marks the end[8] of classical Islamic philosophy, which produced monumental works by famous names such as Alfarabi, ibn Badja, Avicenna and Averroes. The Christians, who occupied Northern Spain, were nurtured by this fertile era, as is evident from the writings of Thomas Aquinas. This period, despite the fact that it entailed religious intolerance between the groups, exhibited a surprising tolerance in the realm of philosophy whereby religionists "borrowed" each other's arguments. So we find that Maimonides and Gersonides borrowed ideas from Alfarabi and Avicenna, and Aquinas borrowed from Maimonides and Alfarabi without any apologies. In fact, the works of religious philosophy written at this time were actually quite similar in their first few chapters. Usually the first few chapters of any book of religious philosophy, regardless of what religion the author was, would deal with the more universal issues of the religion, such as: belief in God, monotheism versus polytheism, the creation of the world, reward and punishment, prophecy, and the afterlife, and only towards the latter chapters would they deal with the particular issues of that specific religion. This would explain how a Latin work in the thirteenth century named "Fons Vitae," cited numerous times by the Christian thinkers Thomas Aquinas and Albertus Magnus and attributed to an Arabic philosopher called Aviceron, could have turned out to be a Latin translation of Rabbi Solomon ibn Gabirol's *Mekor Hayyim*.[9] It seems that the common challenges created a certain fraternity between the religious philosophers.

III) The third period, the modern period, is already post-Greek thinking and can be seen as having two parts: a) the nineteenth and early twentieth century, dominated by European philosophical thinkers like Kant, Kierkegaard and Husserl, who again created an environment in which Jewish thinkers had to show how one can synthesize these thinkers' ideas into the Jewish way of thinking; b) the later twentieth century, in which philosophy has lost its hold on the intellectuals of Western culture and instead scientific knowledge or scientism is considered the intellectual pride of Western culture. So even though there are still books written in religious philosophy, they tend to be dominated by questions that relate to science, such as creation and evolution, medical ethics, and even theoretical philosophic issues raised by science-fiction.

So we see that religious philosophy is an attempt first and foremost to harmonize between faith and reason, and secondly to build the main tenets of that faith on the basis of human reason to show that faith and reason can reach the same conclusions. Now that we have understood what religious philosophy is, we can understand that Jewish philosophy, as part of the realm of religious philosophy, has two goals: to harmonize between reason and Jewish faith, and to demonstrate that the basic tenets of Jewish faith are provable by reason. At this point it is imperative to mention two things: the first is that a religious philosopher is not the same as a religious theologian. Let me explain by way of illustration. If there is a contradiction between reason and faith, for instance, if I believe in Judaism, Christianity or the Islam which teaches that God created the universe in six days, and I attend the university of Cordoba in the twelfth century where I am taught that according to Aristotle the universe is eternal and never had a beginning, I have three options: A) to say that in light of the contradiction I must believe the Divine writ which is eternal and not in Aristotle who is human. (If I pick this option I remain a religionist but have turned my back to reason and am therefore not a religious philosopher). B) to say that Aristotle must be right because he proved his point logically. (In this case I remain a philosopher but have turned by back on faith and therefore am not a religious philosopher). 3) to say that there must be a way of harmonizing the two points of view, for example, by proving through the postulates of Aristotelian physics that the idea of the creation is no less valid than the argument for the eternity of the world.[10] Only if I attempt synthesis and succeed am I dealing with religious philosophy.[11]

The religious philosopher is one who believes that there are two sources of knowledge, revelation and human reason, and through both we understand the world. Both are equally important because God created both; so they cannot contradict each other.[12] The second stipulation involves understanding what religious philosophy is not. Often I have been asked the question of whether there is such a thing as Jewish philosophy. After all, didn't Maimonides draw from Aristotle, Saadia Gaon from the Kalam, and Herman Cohen from Kant? The assumption here is that they expected the religious philosophers to create a new philosophy. This is an erroneous understanding of religious philosophy. How can I create a synthesis between Aristotle and Judaism if I am creating another philosophy? This is not to say that there are no innovations, but the goal is synthesis; which means to show that the existing school of philosophy known to the intellectuals of the day can harmonize with that individual's belief system. Just as religious philosophy was born out of the meeting between East and West, so too its main goal is synthesis. This is its innovation. Anything else would miss the mark.

Having said this, I must add that if we are to say that Jewish philosophy is the attempt to harmonize reason and Jewish faith, then just as the philosophers must define what they mean by reason or logic, so too the Jewish philosopher needs to create a systematic understanding of what he means by Jewish faith. Therefore, we find a tertiary goal of Jewish philosophy, which is the attempt to offer a coherent understanding of Judaism and its major tenets as well as offer an explanation of the commandments. This is less a goal of Jewish philosophy than a byproduct of the discussions. To explain this point better we need to dwell for a moment on the question of what Judaism is for the Jewish philosopher. Until the modern period the answer to this question is quite simple. After all, Judaism is a tradition based on the biblical texts originally passed on orally and then written down from the second to sixth centuries of the common era in well-known corpuses called the Talmudic and midrashic literature of the sages (Hazal).[13] For after all is said and done, revelation and beliefs aside, the Talmudic period is the classic period of Judaism, and everyone who came later is dependent on these texts for their own knowledge of Judaism. If you understand this, you will understand that it is illogical that a later exponent claims that Hazal explained the text wrong, because, right or wrong, that is what Judaism has become. Therefore, no Jewish philosopher in the pre-modern period will say "Hazal said A but I think B." Instead, if they have a problem with a seemingly contradictory statement in Hazal, they will reinterpret it to show that this statement can be read differently. This is a crucial point to understand: that the Jewish philosophers used the rabbinic writings of the Talmudic period as their common ground to discuss Judaism, but sometimes re-interpreted these statements, thus creating different understandings of Judaism.[14] Most of the time, these understandings differ on minor issues, but we will give examples of more serious disagreements as well. Since every Jewish philosopher of the pre-modern period is interpreting rabbinic sources as well, you might say that each Jewish philosopher is also an interpreter of the rabbinic literature in one way or another. This of course would leave us with the question of what "Normative Judaism" might be. This is a complicated issue. On a simple level one might say that it is the "most accepted" interpretations of Hazal to be found in the writings of these thinkers. However, in each generation we see that certain writings have more influence and others less, so that a more detailed discussion of this topic goes beyond the scope of this book.

Getting back to our discussion, if Jewish philosophy is first and foremost the attempt to harmonize faith and reason, and assuming that there is a common ground for defining what Jewish belief is: we still need to ask what human reason is, for in every generation there is a different school of thought that captures the mind and hearts of the intellectuals of that period. Therefore, the Jewish philosopher, in most cases, instead of creating his own definition of reason, will adopt the prevalent philosophic school of his day, and harmonize it with his Jewish faith.[15] This is a necessity, for after all, the Jewish philosophical works were written (to borrow a term from Maimonides) for the perplexed

Jewish intellectuals of their day, who had difficulties living both with the philosophy of their day and Jewish faith. Therefore the solutions need to address the issues at hand.

I think that one can break up all of Jewish thought into three categories which I call: 1. Jewish Philosophers, 2. Anti-philosophic rationalists, and 3. Kabbalists and Mystics. The first two categories comprise Jewish philosophy. The third is not part of Jewish philosophy since by and large it does not involve harmonizing reason and tradition but rather developing the traditions further with the aid of a secret tradition or later revelations. However, this third category is definitely part of the legitimate realm of Jewish thought. In order to illustrate the categories I will mention some of the main exponents in each one.

JEWISH PHILOSOPHERS

The thinkers in this category usually adopt both elements of Jewish philosophy, i.e. to harmonize reason and faith as well as to prove the basic tenets of faith on the foundation of reason. However, for this discussion, the main aspect I want to mention is their use of the prevalent philosophic school of their day and their attempt to harmonize it with Jewish faith. As the philosophic schools changed over the ages, new books had to be written to deal with the new challenges.

It is not my purpose to mention all of the Jewish philosophers, but just to give examples to explain each category.[17] So I think that I should say a few words on the exponents of each category. Philo (or *Yedidyah* in Hebrew), the earliest Jewish philosopher, lived in the first century around the year 43 CE. It has been said[18] that in the study of history you have three categories of people: those who were born and died, those who died but were never born and those who were never born and never died. For famous people who lived in the past 500 years it's relatively easy to figure out the date of birth and death. However, for those who lived a thousand years ago it's easier to figure out the date of death than that of birth. For when Maimonides died, not only is there a tombstone, but many writers mentioned his passing. But when Maimonides was just little Moishele in diapers, he wasn't well known and few mentioned his birth. It is therefore not surprising to see that most of the great rabbinic figures of the Middle Ages lived exactly 70 years. In most cases the date of passing was known and the date of birth was assumed as being 70

Jewish Philosopher	Time Period	Prevalent Philosophic School
Philo of Alexandria	First century, CE	Neo-Platonism
Isaac ben Solomon Israeli	Ninth-tenth century	Neo-Platonism
Saadiah Gaon	Tenth century	Kalam (Muslim theologians)
(also Solomon ibn Gabirol, Bahya ibn Paquda, and Joseph ibn Zaddik, eleventh century)		
Abraham Bar Hiyya	Twelfth century	Neo-Platonic and Aristotelian
Abraham ibn Daud, Maimonides	Twelfth century	Neo-Aristotelian
(also Gersonides, early fourteenth century, Joseph Albo, fifteenth century, and many more)[16]		
Moses Mendelssohn	Eighteenth century	German Enlightenment
Samson Raphael Hirsch	Nineteenth century	Kantian Philosophy
(also Isaac Breuer, Hermann Cohen)		
Franz Rosenzweig	Twentieth century	Anti-Hegelian Existentialism
Joseph Dov Soloveitchik	Twentieth century	Phenomenology and Existentialism
(also Abraham Joshua Heschel)		

years earlier.[19] Once one goes back 2000 years, we usually do not know even the date of death. We know that Philo headed a Jewish delegation to Caligula, the Roman Emperor, in 43 CE to ask for a more lenient poll tax on the Jewish community. (He was turned down). Therefore, it is assumed that he was past his prime. Since we don't hear of him after this it's assumed that he died close to 50 CE (although of course he might still be alive, along with Jim Morrison and Elvis Presley). Take off seventy years and you have a birth date of 20 BCE.[20] Philo's commentary to the Torah, written in Greek, is an attempt to show how Platonic thought can be found in the Torah of Moses (or in Philo's words: to show how Plato "stole his ideas from Moses"). Wherever possible, the bible receives a Platonic interpretation. Abraham's name, according to Philo, is derived from the Hebrew root *Hemia* (sound), representing the Divine logos that created the world; and the Tabernacle shown to Moses on Mount Sinai becomes the transcendental ideal form of the tabernacle.[21] In Babylonia, where the thought of the Mutakalimum (Kalam) Islamic theological school was dominant in the eighth to eleventh centuries,[22] Saadia Gaon (meaning "Saadia the Exalted" and not "the genius"), born in 882, wrote his *Kitab Al-amanat wa al-l-tiqadat* in Arabic (called *Emunot v-De-ot* in Hebrew), which means the "book of [accepted] beliefs and [intellectual] convictions." Again, he tried to show the Jewish intellectual of his day how one can incorporate the prevalent way of thinking into Jewish tradition. Maimonides, in twelfth century Spain, is part of a number of Jewish scholars who again tried to show how the new school of thought, neo-Aristotelian thinking, prevalent among the Arab philosophers of their day, was in total harmony with traditional Jewish texts and faith. As the generations proceeded and Aristotelian thought subsided, new Jewish scholars arose to meet the challenge of the new schools of thought. Moses Mendelssohn wrote his *Jerusalem* to present a rational approach to Judaism in light of German intellectual thinking. Samson Raphael Hirsch, in his *Nineteen Letters to Ben Uziel*, rose to the challenge of the new Kantian philosophy that took Europe with a vengeance. In the twentieth century, when the ideas of philosophic existentialism became prominent, Franz Rosenzweig, Joseph Soloveitchik, and Abraham Heschel each in his own way tried to create a synthesis between the new way of thinking and ancient Jewish traditions. In a nutshell, this is the way of the Jewish philosophers in each generation, arising to meet the new intellectual challenges and attempting to reach synthesis.

However, one may ask, what happens if that Jewish intellectual differs with the prevalent school of thought of his day? What if he finds flaws with the scientific or philosophic thinking of his day and brings hard arguments to prove it? In this case, he cannot use that school of thought but can still harmonize reason and faith in arguments and discussions. This brings us to the second category of Jewish thought, which I call, anti-philosophic rationalists. The thinkers in this category are still dealing with Jewish philosophy for they are harmonizing reason and faith, but have a problem with some or even all of the philosophic thinking of their day. The best example of this category is the writings of Hasdai Crescas (died around 1412, so the official date of birth you can already figure out). In his magnum opus, *Or Hashem* (The Divine Light), Crescas criticized the 26 physical and metaphysical propositions of Aristotelian thought brought down by Maimonides in his *Guide*.[23] After criticizing the main tenets of Aristotelian physics, Crescas was left without Aristotle's metaphysics as well, which is heavily based on his physical conception of the universe. Therefore, Crescas created his own theory of Judaism based on the commandments and the love of God.[24] Another thinker that falls into this category is Judah Halevi (before 1075–1141). Despite his use of Aristotelian argumentation in the fifth part of his *Kuzari* (originally called "The Book of Argument and Proofs for a Despised Faith"), Halevi is extremely critical of Greek thinking in general (he actually claims that real wisdom bypassed them)[25] and begins his treatise with an anti-philosophic, historio-existential approach to Judaism. A third thinker that can be found in this category is Judah Loew of Prague (the Maharal, sixteenth century). As Judah Halevi, the Maharal has a strong mystical element to his writings. However, in his book *Nezah Yisrael*,[26] he presents a historiosophical approach to Judaism, with a great contempt for Greek philosophy.

The third and last category is already not part of the tradition of Jewish philosophy, but is an important and integral part of Jewish thought. These are the writings of the mystics and kabbalists. A detailed description of these thinkers would be beyond the scope of this book. Let it suffice to say that these writings were not an attempt to adopt any philosophic school of thought, or to harmonize reason with faith, but to enhance the tradition with esoteric knowledge. In most cases the kabbalists did not claim personal revelation but that they had received (hence the Hebrew word *kabbalah*, to receive) a secret esoteric tradition of knowledge passed on from the time of the prophets up to their day.

In this book it is not my intention to write a history of Jewish philosophy. This I hope to do at a later date. It is rather my intention to present the reader with the main issues of early Jewish philosophy, explain the problems, present some of the solutions, compare some of the main thinkers of each of the three categories on these issues and update the main ideas in light of how things are seen in the twenty-first century. My anchor will be Maimonides, whose systematic thinking made him the dominant thinker of the first category. I will at times compare his ideas with Gersonides and others of this category. I will enhance the discussion by comparing the three categories on each issue. From the second category I will use the ideas of Judah Halevi and Crescas, and for the third category, that of the kabbalists, I will use the thinking of Moses Hayyim Luzzatto, (the Ramhal) of eighteenth-century Italy. Influenced by the Italian Renaissance, he tends to present kabbalistic ideas in a coherent and reasonable dress, facilitating a comparison with other modes of thought. Even though the third category is not "philosophy" per se in the sense that it is based on revelation (or a revelation-based tradition) alone and does not try to combine reason with revelation, these views have nonetheless influenced traditional Jewish thought over the generations and therefore cannot be ignored in any serious exposition of Jewish thought. I purposely put the kabbalistic-based discussions in separate chapters, so if you are more inclined to the rationalist discussion, you can skip these chapters in the first reading and return to them at a later time.

These issues of Jewish philosophy and thought, despite being raised close to a thousand years ago, deal with the crucial issues of life and therefore have eternal value to them. I will of course offer a certain amount of comparison to modern thinking, updating the issues as we discuss them.

CHAPTER 2

What is Man 1: A Rationalist Approach

The Bible introduces Man as a being created in the Divine image: "And God created man in His image, in the image of God He created him; male and female He created them." (Gen. 1:27). There seems to be an intuitive beauty to this passage, stemming from the Divine concern with man, but technically it is quite a problematic statement. How can God create Man in His image? Does God have a body? How does one deal in general with the anthropomorphic terms in the Bible? Does God have a hand,[1] eyes,[2] legs[3] or ears[4]? The midrash explains that the Bible talks in human terminology ("*dibra torah belashon benei adam*"). This might explain Moses' saying to Pharaoh: "Then the hand of the Lord will strike your livestock in the fields" (Ex. 9:3), but how does it explain the verse that mankind was created in "the image of God"? Philosophically we are up against an immense problem, for anything with an image is corporeal, and anything corporeal has a beginning and an end, which would defy God's being eternal and bring up the absurd question of who created God. To add to our problem, it seems that even the Bible itself is ambivalent, for it states that God has no image or body: "The Lord spoke to you out of the fire; you heard the sound of words but perceived no shape (*temuna*)." (Deut. 4:12) and "Be very careful for you saw no shape (*temuna*) when the Lord your God spoke to you at Horeb" (Deut. 4:15). Isaiah added: "To who, then, can you liken God, What form compare Him to?" (Isa. 40:18). So if the Bible itself claims that God has no body, what are all the anthropomorphic terms doing there? Maimonides (*Rambam* in Hebrew) dedicates the whole first part of his *Guide* to explaining that each corporeal term concerning God in the Bible is a metaphor. He begins by dealing with the most difficult term, the "*Zelem Elohim*" (image of God) mentioned above. He states that the Bible uses two words: "image" (*zelem*) and "likeness" (*demut*) (Gen. 1:26). Rambam tries to show that likeness (*demut*) can be used to describe a non-physical trait as well:

> As to the term "likeness" [*demut*], it is a noun derived from the verb *damoh* [to be similar] and it signifies likeness in respect of a notion. For the scriptural dictum, "I am like [*damiti*] a pelican in the wilderness," [Ps. 102:7] does not signify that its author resembled the pelican in regards to its wings and feathers, but that his sadness was like that of the bird.[5]

Maimonides argues that the term *Damoh* can mean a likeness in a certain respect, and not necessarily a physical image. But how does he explain "image" (*zelem*)? Rambam writes that due to this term in the Bible, there were those who thought that God must have a body:

> People have thought that in the Hebrew language "image" denotes the shape and configuration of a thing. This supposition led them to the pure doctrine of the corporeality of God...They accordingly believed in it and deemed that if they abandoned this belief, they would give lie to the biblical text.[6]

In refutation, he argues from biblical text that the word *Zelem* (image) can refer to either physical or internal characteristics. The actual term for physical form alone is *to'ar*:

Now I say that in Hebrew the proper term designating the form that is well known among the multitude, namely, that form which is a shape and configuration of a thing, is *to'ar*. Thus scripture says: beautiful in form [*to'ar*] and beautiful in appearance (Gen. 39:6)...Those terms are never applied to the Deity...the term image, on the other hand, is applied to the natural form, I mean to the notion in virtue of which a thing is constituted as a substance and becomes what it is. It is the true reality of the thing.[7]

His proof that image [*zelem*] can be incorporeal is from a verse in Psalms (73:20) "Thou contemptest their image." "For contempt has for its object the soul... not the shape and configuration of the parts of the body."[8] Since textually *Zelem* (image) may refer to an inner trait, and since logically we cannot attribute physicality to God, Rambam comes to the conclusion that the image of God referred to is "this intellectual apprehension that is said of man: In the image of God He created him (Gen. 1:27)."[9] The reference is to: "the specific form,[10] which is the intellectual apprehension, not the shape or configuration." In other words Rambam is saying that the Bible claims that man was created in *demut* (likeness) and *Zelem* (Image). *Demut*, which comes from the root *damoh*, means a similarity. We are similar to God in a sense. In what sense? The word *Zelem* comes from the word *zel*, which means a shadow. We reflect Godliness in a sense. This is through our intellectual capacity to choose right and wrong, and control our lives; the capacity that enables us to control our environment and create new technology to enhance our comfort. This intellectual capacity makes us a cut above all the natural world and gives us a Godly edge and dominion over the world.[11] King David hints to this in the Psalms when he says: "thou hast made him a little lower than the angels, thou dost crown him with glory and honor. Thou makest him to have dominion over the works of thy hands; thou hast put all things under his feet: all sheep, and oxen, and also the beasts of the field; the birds of the sky, and the fish of the sea" (Ps. 8:6-9). To paraphrase R. Joseph Albo, we cannot fly like birds or run like horses and we do not have armor like a turtle, but we can build planes that fly better than birds, build cars that run faster than horses and build tanks that protect us better than the turtle's armor. This is due to our intellectual capacity.[12]

This sounds like a rather convincing argument. The notion, of the Divine Image in man as being reason and free will, was a popular explanation in all classical works in the Middle Ages from philosophy to Bible commentary.[13] Its popularity is obvious. We just need to analyze its meaning and implications. In Western thinking, Man is referred to as a Homo Sapiens, which means thinking man. This is a direct continuation of the Aristotelian world view which described man as a being endowed with the power of speech, "logos," from which is derived the word "logic." The natural world as described in Aristotle's physics was built on a hierarchy. The lowest rung, that of inanimate objects like minerals, rocks and dirt, have no life, do not grow or move. Above this is the vegetative world, made up of plants that have the power of growth. Above this is the animal kingdom, equipped with the power of inherent motion. The reason they have motion is due to their soul ("anima" in Greek, hence the word "animal") which propels them. Above the animals we have mankind whose unique power is the power of speech, representing the intellect. This is a definition of Man as an intellectual being. If this is so, it would appear that the goal of Man is to develop this intellect and shun anything that might hinder that capacity. The Greeks took this idea to the extreme, claiming that the true philosopher needs to be apathetic to his emotions or any non-intellectual aspect of Man's being. Rambam had his own understanding of this as we will see in the next chapter. However he did adopt the viewpoint that the intellect is the highest capacity in Man and one that is of a defining character. That is the meaning of his statement above that *Zelem* refers to "the natural form...It is the true reality of the thing." The term "form" is an Aristotelian term. Aristotle saw all things in this world as having "matter" and "form." Matter means the substance of the thing, but by form he does not mean the outer contours of the object, but the defining character. For example: if we want to describe a knife, its matter can be of metal, wood or plastic, but its form is the ability to cut. A knife that has no ability to cut is not a knife. A chair has matter consisting of either wood, plastic, metal or any other matter; its defining form, however, is the ability to have someone sit on it. If you cannot sit on it, it is not a chair. There is of course a relationship between the outer form and the defining form, because a chair has to have a certain structure to be able to support someone sitting on it. We are dealing with a concept that originates with Plato and was used by Aristotle to describe the defining character. In Man, then, the matter would be his or her body, whereas the form would be the intellectual capacity, which defines man. This understanding of Man has been the Western tradition ever since.

With the development of the computer world and artificial intelligence, some criticism has arisen, pondering the question of what might be the difference between man and a computer. In Hollywood, Gene Roddenberry, in his "Star Trek: The Next Generation," created an image of an android, Lt. Data, who is defined as a non-human due to his lack of emotions. The movies "Bi-Centennial Man" and "AI" followed with the same argument. Is this an attempt to redefine man in the twenty-first century? Is Man, as defined in the late twentieth century, a predominantly emotional being? The interesting thing is that in the realm of psychology, there arose new definitions of human emotions. The latest theory, presented by Schacter and Singer, is that human emotions are a result of three influences: thoughts, bodily reactions (like adrenaline) and feelings.[14]

In 1962, Schacter and Singer gave 184 college students one of two types of injections: adrenaline or saline injection. All experimental participants were told that they were given an injection of a new drug called Superoxin to test their eyesight. The adrenaline injection caused a number of effects including increased heart rate, rapid breathing, and increased blood flow to the muscles and brain. The saline injection had no such effects.

Some participants were told about the expected effects of the adrenaline; two other groups were misled and told either that it would produce a dull headache and numbness, or told nothing at all.

After the injections the students waited in a room with another participant who was actually a confederate of the experimenter. The confederate behaved one of two ways: playful (euphoric) or angry.

Those subjects who had received the adrenaline injection were more emotional by both measures, showing that the first factor in emotion, intensity, resulted from visceral arousal.

Participants who were misled or naïve about the injection's effects behaved similarly to the confederate, while those who were informed of the expected effects of the adrenaline showed no emotional pattern.

This suggests that participants who were informed cognitively attributed their feelings to the physiological effects of the adrenaline, while the uninformed or misinformed groups could perform no such attribution and so interpreted the feelings as emotion.

What about the hierarchical relationship between emotions and reason? Is the intellect the highest conceivable element as Aristotle thought? The Neo-Aristotelian thinkers of the Middle Ages assumed that even the heavens must be populated by higher intelligences. Is there no spirituality conceivable beyond intellectual definitions? In addition, what is the relationship between the intellect and human behavior? Is there an intellectual way of life? How does this relate to morality? These are the questions we must now face in the coming chapter in trying to understand the message of the Garden of Eden story according to Rambam, the meaning of the first human responsibility and blunder.

CHAPTER 3

The Place of Moral Judgment and the Garden of Eden Story

Maimonides wrote in his *Guide*:

> Years ago a learned man propounded as a challenge to me a curious objection....It is manifest from the clear sense of the biblical text that the primary purpose with regard to man was that he should be, as the other animals are, devoid of intellect, of thought, and of the capacity to distinguish between good and evil. However when he disobeyed, his disobedience procured him as its necessary consequence the great perfection peculiar to man, namely his being endowed with the capacity that exists in us to make this distinction. Now this capacity is the noblest of the characteristics existing in us; it is in virtue of it that we are constituted as substances. Now it is a thing to be wondered at that man's punishment for his disobedience should consist in his being granted a perfection that he did not possess before, namely, the intellect. This is like the story told by somebody that a certain man...disobeyed and committed great crimes, and in consequence was made...a star in heaven.[1]

The question is one that many of us have asked as children in Hebrew school. If Adam and Eve were devoid of knowledge before eating from the Tree of Knowledge, and if knowledge is good and virtuous, doesn't that mean that God gave them a prize for their disobedience instead of punishing them? Often I have students who will counter argue that intelligence is not necessarily good. However, we do tend to take pity on the mentally challenged and raise funds to help them in life, therefore it appears that we see knowledge as a benefit. (We all know that what you don't know can hurt you.) Besides, if they had no knowledge, being as animals, why were Adam and Eve to blame for their actions at all? Rambam, at this point, proceeds to demonstrate that Adam and Eve had knowledge, meaning, reason and free will, even before partaking of the Tree of Knowledge. He offers two arguments. The first is based on his commentary in chapter one on the "image of God." Rambam explained above that the image of God (*Zelem*) mentioned in Genesis 2 refer to the intellectual capacity of Man. If this is true, then the text says that Adam was created with this *Zelem*. This means that he had an intellectual capacity before eating from the Tree of Knowledge. The second argument is textual. Since you cannot verbally command beings devoid of knowledge, the very fact that God commanded Adam and Eve to eat from any tree but not to eat from the Tree of Knowledge assumes that they already had knowledge. We all know that to put a steak on the table and ask your hungry dog to refrain from eating it until you return is a useless endeavor. The very act of command assumes an intellectual being who is being commanded.

After proving that Adam and Eve had knowledge prior to partaking from the Tree of Knowledge, Rambam must now proceed to explain what happened when they ate from this tree. What did they have which they did not have before?

> Through the intellect one distinguishes between truth [*haqq*] and falsehood [*batil*], and that was found in [Adam] in its perfection and integrity. Fine [Good, *Hasan*] and bad, [*qabih*] on the other hand, belong to the things generally accepted as known, not those cognized by the intellect. For one does not say: it is fine that heaven is spherical, and it is bad that the earth is flat; rather one says true or false with regard to these assertions.[2]

This chapter contains one of the most difficult and misunderstood passages in Rambam's writings. First I will explain what he is saying and then explain the inherent problems within. Rambam distinguished between two basic levels of awareness. Adam and Eve before the sin had knowledge of Truth and Falsehood. After partaking from the tree they had knowledge of Good and Evil. What is "knowledge of Truth and Falsehood"? By way of example, Ramban says that if one says that planet Earth is round this is not good or bad, it is either true or false. This seems to describe scientific knowledge. Unfortunately this is the only example he gives. As usual Rambam has us guessing the meaning of what he is saying. What does this mean? Is the level of truth and falsehood the level of scientific knowledge and the level of good and bad the level of moral knowledge? If so, that would mean that Adam and Eve understood factual concepts of science without understanding the moral implications. However if this be the explanation, that would mean that when God told them not to eat from the tree of knowledge they didn't understand the moral implications of disobeying God, so why punish them? A second problem with this explanation is that Rambam, as a neo-Aristotelian, follows the Socratic belief that knowledge and morality go hand in hand. For Socrates, the wise man knows to do good. (This is debatable, considering how many intelligent criminals you have out there, but this was the thinking then.) Therefore, the more knowledge, the more chance of doing the right thing. (Even today it is thought that better education for the masses lowers crime.) Therefore, Rambam would never claim that there is knowledge devoid of morality. To solve this problem Shlomo Pines in his rendition of the *Guide* translated as follows: the tree of knowledge of "Fine and Bad," meaning esthetic perception versus objective knowledge.[3] In my opinion this misses the mark as well. Is the reason that Adam and Eve covered themselves with fig leaves due to not finding each other esthetically pleasing? To understand what Rambam is really saying we must be aware of his perception of morality.

MAIMONIDEAN MORAL JUDGMENT

From Socrates up to Kant morality was seen in absolute terms: what is bad is universally bad and what is good is universally good. This type of thinking, which has been challenged over the centuries, lies at the basis of the moral way of thinking. Ethical thinking is related to rational capability. For Socrates, as for Aristotle, wisdom and virtue go hand in hand.[4] For Rambam as well, wisdom and virtue are synonymous to such an extent that the Bible sometimes uses the term wisdom to denote the acquisition of moral virtues.[5] Kant in eighteenth-century Germany argued that moral cognitions work in a different way than regular logic. They are logical statements which are not proven but understood universally by all human beings. They are a priori forms of knowledge, i.e. notions that all reasonable people can understand without having to prove them; sort of like the axioms of linear geometry, which claim that the shortest distance between two points is a straight line. This is an axiom which cannot be proven but is self-evident. So too, the basic notions of morality, i.e., not to steal and not to murder, are self-evident notions that we understand prior to being taught (a priori). In fact, moral ideas are such that the attempt to prove them logically actually lessens their value. For instance, if I were to say that I don't steal because I don't want others to steal from me, that would mean that if I could be certain that others would not steal from me then it would be okay. This we call "burglar's ethics." A thief will prefer not to steal from another thief in order to keep the status quo concerning the mutual respect of territory. All attempts to rationalize ethical conduct take away from its essential value until one understands it as self-evident a priori knowledge. In the twentieth century as well the question of morality and human cognitive development was researched by Lawrence Kohlberg. Based on the ground-breaking research of the Swiss psychologist Jean Piaget in the field of cognitive development, Kohlberg formulated a comprehensive stage theory of moral development.[6] In a sense this type of thinking is a continuation of the Socratic tradition with a new twist. Kohlberg's stage theory is based on universal issues of morality usually relating to issues of life and death or theft. Grey areas of socially accepted issues were purposely avoided to sharpen the point.

For Maimonides there are two types of morality: 1) Absolute universal morality and 2) relative universal morality. If this latter concept sounds like a paradox it will clear up in a moment. Absolute morality includes notions like: the value of human life (not to kill, not to commit suicide, not to injure, etc), the respect for other's property (not to steal, damage or use others' property), and proper sexual conduct towards others (not to commit adultery, etc., which can be seen as being related to respecting others' property). However, there are moral notions that exist because we are human beings and not because they are universal. These Rambam refers to here as "Well known ideas" (*mefursamot*). The *mefursamot* are ethical values that originate not in a universal logical notion but in the fact that we were created human. This discerning of two categories clears up many questions related to moral research.[7] By way of illustration: the prohibition to steal is a universal logical notion which implies that taking what is not mine is wrong. Even if I were not human or if I were to steal from a Martian the logical notion of stealing applies. Therefore it is a universal and objective moral value. However there are things which we consider wrong only by virtue of the fact that we are human. The clothing I wear protects me from the cold in winter and from the heat in summer. This is logical. However there is another task for clothing: to create a social barrier between the sexes, so that I do not look at the other human being as a sexual object but rather as a person. The physical attraction between men and woman necessitates some form of dress to help us control and modify our social behavior. This is what Adam and Eve discovered when they ate from the Tree of Knowledge. Before eating from the tree, they were naked "and were not embarrassed." They did not understand the problem of being naked and felt no urge to sexually dominate one another. The clothing they made of fig leaves was not to protect themselves from the elements but to cover themselves up from embarrassment. What is the embarrassment? It is looking at a human being, created in the image of God, as a sexual object to satisfy your own desires. Therefore the two Hebrew words denoting clothing reflect this biblical story. The first is "lebush" with the root of "bushah" or embarrassment, and the second is "begged" from the root "boged" meaning to betray, or to rebel against God's command. The idea of covering one's sexual organs is universal, but it is something that only humans understand. Animals feel no need to do so. I assume that if a Martian were to descend to planet earth he too would have difficulty understanding why human beings spend so much time on fashion. The whole idea of clothing being both a defense mechanism and a form of enticement through fashion would be totally foreign to them since they do not feel the sexual attraction that humans feel to the opposite sex. This form of ethical conduct Maimonides refers to as mefursamot. It is subjective since it applies only to human beings, but it is universal in the sense that it applies for all human beings. Adam and Eve before the partaking of the Tree of Knowledge were not aware of the mefursamot. They were naked but did not see why they should be embarrassed. How is this possible? I once heard someone explain this point as follows. It is a matter of your personal reference point of identity. Adam and Eve before the sin did not see themselves as bodies; they saw themselves as human souls which were clothed in bodies. Therefore even though they were aware that their bodies were attracted to each other this did not mean that *they* were attracted to each other. If I am riding a male horse and my friend is on a female horse and they are drawn to each other I might see this as cute but I will not be part of the attraction. Adam and Eve before the sin saw themselves as human souls riding on a physical body, so to speak. They knew that their bodies were attracted to each other but they did not see why that should influence their thinking. After the sin, they identified themselves first as bodies and only afterward as souls, as we do today. Therefore the feeling of attraction between the bodies meant that *they* were attracted, and made them embarrassed. This explains then why the Bible talks of the immediate embarrassment after partaking from the Tree of Knowledge of Good and Evil. We can now offer a new explanation of why it is called the Tree of Knowledge of Good and Evil. Before partaking from this tree, Adam and Eve know what good and evil were and make rational decisions about life; afterwards, good and evil were not just theoretical issues to decide upon but part of their own psyche. In Genesis, the word "to know," "*la-daat*," means "to connect" as it says: "And Adam knew his wife Eve and she was impregnated and bore a son" (Gen. 4:1). After eating from the tree, Adam and Eve now connected to good and evil equally. Both are now part of their psychological makeup. Evil, like good, is now not just on the tree but in the heart. There is a midrash which claims that the serpent actually copulated with Eve,[8] stressing this point of the evil inclination now entering the human psyche and heart and not just a theoretical idea of the mind.

Where does this leave us? For Maimonides, it appears, the level of Adam and Eve before the sin is one of Truth and Falsehood, which means a level of objective judgment in scientific as well as moral issues. The level of good and evil is a level where good and evil are part of the human psyche. It is a level full of inner conflicts and dilemmas between what we should do (truth and falsehood) and what we would rather do.[9] It is filled with personal interest, inclinations and desires that cloud the real moral issues. I am reminded of a story in *Huckleberry Finn* by Mark Twain. Huck and Jim enter a watermelon field in the heat of the summer. In his thirst, Huck takes one of the melons. Jim scolds him, saying that it is stealing, but Huck answers that the field is so big that by the time the owner gets to this melon it will probably be rotten, so that he is actually do him a favor by getting rid of it. This desire to rationalize our desired conduct in light of what we know is right and wrong is a constant dilemma for the moral human being. Let's get back to Adam and Eve. I will illustrate the move from the level of truth and falsehood to the level of good and evil through a theoretical example. Eve was walking in Manhattan and came across a fancy women's clothing store on Fifth Avenue. As she was trying on a rabbit tail fur coat she noticed that the salespeople had all stepped out due to a toast they were invited to in honor of the new calendar year. January can get cold in the Big Apple (pardon the pun), and Eve really likes the coat. The problem is that she was created without money or even a credit card. (No creation is perfect.) She now thinks to herself: "Should I take this coat to cover me in the cold of winter?" However, being on the level she was at before the sin, she wouldn't. She knows that stealing is wrong and she will just walk out of the store (and get arrested for indecent exposure). Eve after the sin may think: "This coat is beautiful and it's cold outside. I could freeze to death and nobody cares. Besides, who will miss this coat anyway? This is a rich store. In addition, maybe the environmentalists will protest selling furs and no one will be willing to buy it. I deserve at least one coat, don't I?" Will she steal it? Not necessarily, but on the level of good and evil it is now a real dilemma. The struggle between what she knows to be right and want she wants to be right is a difficult one.

We can now see that Maimonides' interpretation of the Garden of Eden story presents it as a metaphor for human moral decision making. In this world, we are all on the level of Adam and Eve after the sin. We know what is right but have difficulty living up to it. It is even harder to do the right thing in face of ethical conflicts. What happens when two moral values coincide? How does this affect our decision making? After all, there can be moral dilemmas even on the level of truth and falsehood. For example: The Talmud tells of the case of two people crossing the desert. One of them is carrying a canteen with water enough for himself. The question is whether he should drink this water to survive and let his friend die of thirst or split the water with his friend. This might, of course, gain time, but he takes the risk that they might both die.

> If two are traveling on a journey [far from civilization], and one has a pitcher of water, if both drink, they will [both] die, but if one only drinks, he can reach civilization, — The Son of Patura taught: It is better that both should drink and die, rather than that one should behold his companion's death. Until R. Akiba came and taught: "that thy brother may live with thee: thy life takes precedence over his life."[10]

Rabbi Akiba taught that we are responsible for the lives of others but not at the cost of our own lives. This water that I am carrying in the desert is my life support. It is like giving a vital organ to my friend. Am

I obligated to remove my heart, resulting in my own death, in order to save someone else who might need it? Even if R. Akiba came to a conclusion, the argument is still a legitimate argument and Ben Petura's position is legitimate as well. This is an example of a dilemma on the objective level of truth and falsehood.

What happens if the dilemma is not on the objective level but rather on the subjective level of our personal interests? Years ago, L. Kohlberg created a test to measure the moral development of children and adults. It was called the Heinz test.[11] Putting Kohlberg aside, I use a similar test with a variation to demonstrate Maimonides' point of how the subjective issues of our lives cloud the objective moral issues. I have done this test in my classes for over 16 years. The results are always the same. I offer the class two stories about which they have to state their opinion. Half the class is given one story and half is given the second. The question is the same.

> Story one: You hear of a man who is sick in the hospital with a terminal disease. A cure is found but it is very expensive and neither you nor he has the money to buy it. Would you be willing to steal in order to save his life?

A simple question. The first thing that usually happens is that students ask me who the person is. I say: no one you know. Then they start to explain that it depends on A or B, to which I add, "There are no circumstances to remedy the situation. It is you and him alone." After, the class has written a "yes" or a "no" (no "maybe"s or "it depends"s or "abstain"s), we proceed to analyze the story. The dilemma is two-fold. On the objective level, which Maimonides calls Truth and Falsehood, there is a real collision of two opposing values: Not to steal versus saving a life. These are real values that are in a contradicting position. A person would have to weigh which is more important to them: to steal the medicine, thereby saving a life, or not to steal, thereby letting the person die. Often we might see stealing as being active and not letting this person die as being passive, and we might choose to be passive. However, alternatively we might feel that saving a life overrides the moral prohibition of stealing. However, there is of course another consideration which is unrelated to the moral question but will affect my decision. I am referring to not wanting to go to jail. After all, if one is caught stealing the drug they might be sent to prison. I'm sure the judge has heard many a thief rationalizing their actions by claiming they are stealing for a higher cause. Would one then take the chance even if they thought that saving a life overrides stealing? As you might have guessed, the majority of the students I asked (and possibly the honest ones) said that they would not take the chance of stealing to save the unknown person. (Besides, we rationalize by saying that they are in the hospital and the State should take care of them.)

Diagram 1:
The Sick Man in the Hospital
Objective dilemma: Not to steal vs. saving a life
Subjective issue: Going to jail
Outcome: No

The second story which I give out simultaneously to the second part of the class goes like this:

Your mother is sick in the hospital with a terminal disease. A cure is found but the pharmacists have hiked up the prices to make more money and neither you nor she has the money to buy it. Would you be willing to steal the cure in order to save her life?

Again, as in the first case, the objective moral dilemma consists of not to steal versus saving a life. The fact that she is your mother does not change the objective moral issue at hand. Just as before there is a subjective issue that I prefer not to go to jail. This of course may sway me in the direction of not stealing. However, the relationship I have with my mother, which of course is a subjective issue, and the desire to have my mother alive, might sway me in the direction of stealing in any event. If this overrides the other desire not to go to jail, the outcome will be different than the previous case. As you have probably guessed, the overwhelming majority of students write that they would be willing to steal in such a case (unless of course they don't like their mothers).

Diagram 2:
The Sick Mother in the Hospital
Objective dilemma: Not to steal vs. saving a life
Subjective dilemma: Going to jail vs. relationship to mother
Outcome: Yes

As we can see, in two cases where the objective moral dilemmas are identical but the subjective issues are changed, the subjective influences will change the outcome of our moral decision. This is Maimonides' point, that we are all on the subjective level of good and evil after the sin. One should add at this point that if the object level is clear with no dilemma then the subjective influences will have less of an input on our decisions.

In conclusion, Maimonides has demonstrated the far-reaching effect of subjective influences on our moral decision-making and the necessity to remain objective in our moral decision-making.

CHAPTER 4   *What is Man 2:*
A Kabbalistic Approach
and an Alternate
Explanation of the
Garden of Eden Story

As I mentioned above, the Aristotelian perspective adopted by Western philosophy and culture saw Man as a being wherein the intellect is the defining form. This perception has been challenged in the late twentieth century by the development of various forms of artificial intelligence that have brought people to wonder if maybe our defining form as humans is more emotional than intellectual. The mystical Jewish tradition, better known since the twelfth century as the kabbalah, sees the intellect as an essential part of the human psyche but not as the highest point within our psyche. Within conscious Man, the intellect, or more specifically wisdom, is the highest point of our awareness, but essentially the inner "I" transcends the intellect. It is the inner self, the defining subconscious core which the kabbalists sometimes referred to as the "inner will." Therefore, we can say "our" intellect just as we say "our" emotions, but "we" are above them. The idea of the inner will, in this tradition, is not compatible with our external desires and wishes, but is a more fundamental element of our being. It can be compared to the "will to survive"; similar to that aspect in the old brain that cannot be directly affected but only indirectly influenced by our thoughts and actions. So too the inner will is our essential core upon which all the rest of the self is built. In early kabbalistic literature this inner will was sometimes referred to as the "crown" (Keter), since a crown sits above the head, defining the body but transcending it, and in the same way, the inner will define our being but transcend our consciousness.

MAN CREATED IN THE IMAGE OF GOD

The next question which of course arises is: If the intellect is not the defining form of mankind, then how do the kabbalists explain the term Zelem or image of God in which man was created according to the Bible? Maimonides' explanation of the Zelem Elohim as human intellect and choice was widely accepted by the rationalist commentators of the Bible. However, this was not the sole approach. R. Solomon Ben Isaac, of France, better known as Rashi, a commentator with both a pragmatic and a mystical bent, solved the anthropomorphic problem of the Zelem by explaining that the image referred to in Genesis was actually a tool through which God created man. As a cookie-sheet is used to make the form of the baked cookies, so too the Zelem was used by God to make the human form. According to this explanation, in the words (Zelem Elohim), image of God, the word "of" represents ownership and not comparison.[1] This is a unique commentary. Kabbalists of the eighteenth century, like Joseph Irgas of Italy, explained the Zelem in an alternate way, in a way that would be a motif in kabbalistic literature. Irgas' explanation can be explained as follows: what was Maimonides' problem with the term image of God? It is the same problem that we have with all the anthropomorphic terms in the Bible, like: God's hand, (Ex. 9:3) God's eyes, (Deut. 11:12) or God's chair (Is. 66:1). Does God have a hand and an eye? Does he have any human form? Isn't it philosophically impossible for an eternal being to have finite corporeal features? This type of thinking assumes that a hand and an eye in the Bible refers to our form of a physical hand and a physical eye. Therefore we ask how it can be that God has such a thing. However, says Irgas in his Shomer Emunim, what if the Bible was not referring to a physical hand or eye? Maybe the Bible is referring to a spiritual hand and eye which represent a concept and our human hands and eyes are just a physical representation of these non-physical concepts. This idea, which reminds us of neo-Platonic philosophy, is a major theme in kabbalistic thinking. The anthropomorphic terms in the Bible in connection with God represent Divine attributes through which God runs the universe. Therefore the human body in its physical design parallels this non-physical world of Divine attributes. To illustrate this idea, consider a map of New York City. Through the map one can get an idea of the streets, parks and sites of the city. The map, despite being a two-dimensional representation of a three-dimensional city, can help us understand the layout of the city. So too, the human body, created in the image of the Divine reality, is a three-dimensional physical map of a non-dimensional and non-physical world.

THE GARDEN OF EDEN STORY TAKE TWO: A KABBALISTIC APPROACH

As I mentioned in the introduction, even though kabbalistic thought is not part of Jewish philosophy, it is part of traditional Jewish thought and therefore cannot be ignored in any serious discussion of traditional Jewish thought. The rationalist approach looks to solve apparent logical contradictions through the use of metaphors, as well as to show the central position of the human intellect in biblical thinking. The kabbalists, as we have seen already, have a lot in common with the rationalists concerning Man but define the hierarchy within the human psyche differently. We will now see as well that they have a different take on many aspects of the Garden of Eden story.

What happened in the Garden of Eden? For Maimonides, even if the Garden of Eden was a real place, the story in which a snake is talking must be metaphorical since snakes do not talk. The metaphor, as we explained, is to be understood as a teaching in the realm of human moral decision-making. The kabbalists see the story differently. R. Moses Hayyim Luzzatto (Ramhal), the Italian kabbalist from the early eighteenth century, following his predecessors, explained that the Garden of Eden was a real place but not in the dimensions of time and space. It represented a microcosm of our world in a sort of primordial spiritual state. Since Adam and Eve are the first man and woman from whom all mankind will be derived, they are like the seed. Whatever happens to the seed affects the whole tree. God takes Adam and Eve, the microcosm of mankind, and places them in the Garden of Eden which is the microcosm of the world to be created. What they do there will affect all that comes after them. To understand this further we need to delve deeper into the biblical story of the creation.

THE SIX DAYS OF CREATION

On day one God created light. This is confusing, since God created the sun, moon, and stars on day four. Why then did the world need light on day one? Alternately, we may ask why He needed the sun and the moon if light was already created? The sages of the Talmud pondered this question and explained that the light created on day one was an unusual light. Through it one could see from one side of the world to the other. (Who this person might be is confusing, since mankind was created on day six.) When God saw that the world was not worthy of this light He hid the light; storing it for the righteous in the time to come.[2] This midrash, brought by Rashi in his first comment on the Torah, seems puzzling. Why doe God create a unique light just to take it away? What is the meaning of the riddles in the midrash? Luzzatto explains that the light on day one is a metaphor for a perfect world. God creates a perfect world and then removes perfection from the world. Why? This is to suit mankind since we are not perfect beings.

Creation Story					
Day One	Day Two	Day Three	Day Four	Day Five	Day Six
Light	Firmament	Land, water, grass, and trees	Sun, moon, and stars	Fish and fowl	Animals and mankind
God's World	Division between perfect world and imperfect world	First imperfections	Imperfect lights		
Perfect world	World of Eden, to be perfected.				

The creation of the firmament, the *Rakia*, on day two, represents the division between the perfect world God created and the imperfect world eventually given to man.[3] You might say that day one is God's world and day two on describes the world that eventually evolves into our world, but which was still in the primordial state of the Garden of Eden. It is our world in a less physical state. The next question would be, why would God create a perfect world just to make it imperfect? Two answers can be given. The first is that God wants there to be a perfect state of the world at least for a moment in order that there will be something to strive for in the subconscious collective world memory. Secondly, this is a necessity, since a perfect being must create a perfect world before making it imperfect, for the world comes from God's infinite being. Being produced from such, it must first mimic God's perfection before being flawed for mankind. This imperfection gives mankind something to perfect in the world, making us partners with God in creation. By perfecting the world, it becomes, as it were, our world as well.

The flaws after day one are hinted to in the midrashic interpretations. The midrash says that on day three there is a difference between what was commanded and what actually happened.

And God said: Let the earth bring forth grass, herb yielding seed, and *fruit-trees bearing fruit*" (Gen. 1:11). However in actuality what came forth was: "And the earth brought forth grass, herb yielding seed after its kind, and *trees bearing fruit*" (Gen. 1:12). Why in the command does it say: "Fruit tree bearing fruit" but in actuality the earth brought forth only "trees bearing fruit"? The midrash explains: "Said the Holy One Blessed Be He 'Let the earth bring forth grass... [fruit-trees bearing fruit]' [meaning] just as the fruit can be eaten so can the tree itself, but [the earth] did not do so, but 'the earth brought forth grass... [and trees bearing fruit' of which] the fruit can be eaten but not the tree.[4]

The act of the earth bringing forth imperfect trees on day three does not mean that it rebelled or that God fouled things up, it means that it was the imperfection of an imperfect world. To understand this better we must assume that Ramhal is basing himself on Rashi's interpretation of the creation story. Rashi writes: "All the multiplicity of heaven and earth was created on the first day but each one was put in its place on its appropriate day."[5] This means that God gave all the commands to create things on day one, but each individual item came into being only on its appropriate day. Based on this understanding we can say that God gave the command on day one, the day of the perfect world, to bring forth fruit trees bearing fruit, but in reality they appeared on day three in an imperfect world and therefore did not taste like the fruit they bore. So too God created a perfect light on day one but it was already imperfect by day four. Therefore, the luminary bodies on day four are referred to as "me'orot," spelled without the letters *vav*, as "*m'erat*" which also means a curse.[6] The curse was the evolving of the world from a perfect to an imperfect state. We now can understand that according to this explanation the six days of creation are on two levels. Day one, which is the world God created. This I refer to as God's world. It is a perfect world, and the difference between it and its maker is that it is the created and He the creator. The second level, from day two on, is the world made for humans. This is the world that Adam and Eve will enter on the sixth day. This world in theory is ready for human beings but it too represents our spiritual side at its best even if it is less than the world of day one. Eventually Adam and Eve will demonstrate that they are not as yet ready for such a lofty world. The world they will enter after the sin of the Tree of Knowledge of Good and Evil will be our physical world as we know it today. After this overview we can now proceed to the details of the Garden of Eden story according to Ramhal.

The word in Hebrew for tree is *Etz*. This has the same root as the word *Etza* which is advice. God put Adam and Eve, the root of mankind, into the microcosm of our world at its highest spiritual point. This world, despite its high level, was still incomplete and awaited their acts of completion. Therefore the text says that God put them into the garden "to work and to keep it" (Gen. 2:15). In the garden were two trees representing two forms of advice or two options: the Tree of Life, the tree obtained after completing the world of Eden, or the Tree of Knowledge of Good and Evil. Knowledge in this context means connection (see for example: "And Adam knew his wife Eve and she conceived a child," Gen. 4:1). The eating of the fruit of the Tree of Knowledge of Good and Evil did not refer to obtaining knowledge. This they had beforehand, as Maimonides had demonstrated. However, for the kabbalists it was not a new type of knowledge either. It represented the possibility of connecting with a world on a lower plane then the sterile world of Eden. A world in which evil will not just be represented by a serpent on a tree but be part of Adam and Eve's psyche. Adam and Eve in Eden knew what good and evil were but they had never experienced them before. The garden was a sort of laboratory where they could understand all human events, feelings, successes and failures, goodness and evil, but from a theoretical point of view. The Tree of Knowledge of Good and Evil represents a world of experience. A world in which Adam and Eve and all their descendents will connect with good and evil not from a theoretical point of view, but by experiencing it themselves. It is like the difference between reading about this world in an encyclopedia and experiencing it. God tells Adam and Eve: I give you two options. The better one is just to know about the world and make your decisions from afar. Once you opt for the experience of the Tree of Knowledge, the choice will be harder because you will now be in this world and experience it from within your psyche. The midrash says that the serpent cohabitated with Eve. This means that it entered her being. In Hebrew history is written "*historiyah*" which can comprise the letters of the words "*seter yah*," meaning, "God is hidden." In Eden, God and Man conversed openly. In our world of experience, of history, God is hidden even when human beings suffer. God knows that Adam and Eve will eat from the tree. He knows that the world of Eden is too lofty for them, but He had at the least to give them the chance not to partake of the tree. Mankind has an urge to experience. We teach children in school not to use drugs. We send in lecturers, show films, and introduce them to rehabilitated addicts and dry alcoholics hoping that they will choose to keep away. So why do many of them still try these substances anyhow? There is a strong human urge to experience things. Experience is a form of knowledge. The one who studied the dangers of narcotics will know a lot, but he who took them will really understand the problem (assuming that he or she was able to get over them). Therefore experience is a double-edged sword. It is a deeper form of knowledge but much more dangerous. So God says: "Let me give you some sound advice, keep away from the tree of knowledge." But humans as humans have the urge to experience and find their way into our reality. There is more to say on this topic and we will return to it in Chapter Ten. For now, after explaining the Garden of Eden and the trees, it's time to return to our philosophical discussion of Man.

CHAPTER 5

Free Will vs. Determinism, Divine Pre-Knowledge vs. Human Free Will, Divine Knowledge of the Present

In order to better understand human morality we need to deal with the central issue upon which all this is based; the idea of human free will and choice. Human intuition and maybe common sense as well inclines us to believe that we are free agents making our own choices in life. However, this seemingly logical deduction has been challenged time and again. In the middle-ages, the challenge came from theologians. The argument was that if we are to assume that God is all-knowing and knows the future as well as the past and present, how could there be human free will? After all, if God knows in advance that Mr. Cohen will be righteous then can Mr. Cohen really have the choice not to be righteous? Conversely, if we are to say that Mr. Cohen still has a choice whether to be righteous or not, this would mean that God did not know this idea absolutely. However, the assumption is that God has absolute knowledge of the future. After all, didn't he share this knowledge periodically with the prophets? Therefore it is illogical to assume human free will. This argument was so central to religious thought in the Middle Ages that it brought early Islam (the Kalam) and the Church fathers (such as St. Anselm) to argue that human free will is nothing but a delusion. The Jewish stance taken in the Ethics of the Fathers was that there is human free-will despite Divine foreknowledge. We will discuss this further a bit later. In modern times science has returned us to the same dilemma. When Newton demonstrated that the world works according to universal mechanical laws, again the question was asked: if everything works by blind laws, why should human beings be any different? Isn't mankind part of nature as well? It is said that when Newton discovered that the planets revolve based on gravitation and inertia he was perplexed. After all, what then is God's task in all this? But when he discovered that his theory did not fully explain the revolving of the planets around the sun (since he was unaware of the existence of three planets: Pluto, Neptune and Uranus) he died a happy man as he found an ongoing task for the Creator of the world.

The Judeo-Christian answer to this problem was that Man is unique since he has an intellectual soul which accords him free will. This makes Man the exception to the rule. In modern times as well, the question again arose: if biology and psychology can explain behaviour based on parts of the brain, who is to say that Man's free will is not just an illusion and that our decisions are merely programmed by the same super computer that controlled our existence in the evolution of life? This reductionist position sees the human self as the sum total of the synapses of the brain.

It is hard to offer proofs for or against free will. In fact it might be easier to argue against free-will than for it. Don't people tend to mimic others? Don't children follow their peers' and their parents' ideas and dreams? Couldn't it be that I wanted to be a doctor since my father was? Why do socio-economic conditions determine the level of crime in a community? In favour of free will we can argue that if there is no free will, then why do we punish criminals? After all, they had no choice. In fact, what exactly would be the whole point of the judicial system without free will? And who would ever believe in rehabilitation without free will? What about education? What is the point of trying to change character traits if there is no free will? The best argument for free will is from its negation. If there is no free will, why did I have to get up this morning and go to work? I will get the salary anyway if that is how my life was determined. The same goes for school or any goal in life. The complexity of the arguments shows how real the issue is. In order to delve deeper into this issue we can state that there are at least four possible positions concerning human free will.

A) Total Free will
B) Total Determinism
C) Mostly Free Will
D) Mostly Determinism

Over the centuries there were groups of people who held each one of these opinions. We mentioned before the Kalam and the early Christian theologians who felt that free will would endanger the idea of Divine foreknowledge. Many of the early astrologers felt that life was controlled by the constellations. In the realm of mostly determinism we might place the Buddhist perspective with its doctrine of the karma, which believes that what we do in this world cannot change our position here but only in the next incarnation. This is a sort of mostly determinism stand. Within Judaism, the only position which cannot be considered legitimate is total determinism. The reasons for this are obvious: for one, Judaism is filled with commandments, and what would be the point of the commandments if there were no human free will? Second, the Bible actually mentions this idea clearly and by inference. "Behold I set before you today life and good, death and evil....and you shall choose life" (Deut. 30:15) "Who would give that their hearts would fear me all the days" (Deut. 5:29) etc. Also the rebuke of the prophets and the idea of Divine reward and punishment—all these point towards free will. Therefore there must be some idea of human free will. However, positions differ as to how much free will we have as human beings. The Jewish astrologers, such as Abraham Bar-Hiyyah, Abraham ibn Ezra, and Gersonides, tended to limit free will by claiming that the circumstances of life are decided by the constellations but each individual can choose within these set circumstances. For instance, if according to the stars Simon will fall off the bridge on Tuesday, if Simon is righteous, he will fall off the bridge but at that moment a banana boat will pass under and he will be saved. Alternatively, Simon might decide to stay at home that day. This type of thinking can draw support from Talmudic sources as well.[1] The Hassidic thinkers can also be found in this category of mostly determinism. Contrary to the Jewish astrologers, they taught that it is God, rather than the constellations, who controls the circumstances of our lives. Even if I go to buy a house, God might test me to see if I buy the house near the school which is good for my children, and which is near the synagogue and has good neighbours, etc. In the category of mostly free will we find many of the Jewish rationalists, such as Saadiah Gaon, who believes strongly in free will but admits that at times there are things that are beyond our free will: for instance, the Talmud relates that it is God who brings people together in wedlock, and that what we will earn during the year is decreed on the New Year. In the category of total free will, we can find Maimonides. As we shall soon see, Maimonides takes a radically absolutist stand on human free will, since he feels that it is an essential element of the Jewish faith:

> Permission is given to all men: whether they want to incline towards a good path and be righteous, the choice is theirs; and whether they want to incline to an evil path and be wicked; the choice is theirs. This is what the Torah says: "Therefore has Man become as one of us to know good and evil (Gen. 3:22), meaning; therefore has this genus called Man become the sole being in the world in this aspect, that he by himself, in his mind and thought knows good from evil and does whatever he pleases and nothing can stop him from doing good or evil; therefore [we are worried] "lest he extend his hand to eat from the Tree of Life and live forever (Ibid).[2]

In his discussion of the laws of penitence, Maimonides stresses that mankind has total free will. Without this free will there would be no possibility of accountability for wrong human action. Therefore if we have done wrong we must mend our ways between Man and Man and between Man and God.

> Do not think that which the ignorant of the nations or the unlearned of Israel say; that it is by Divine decree that a Man be righteous or wicked. This is untrue. Anyone can be as righteous as Moses[3] our teacher or as wicked as Jeroboam, or studious or frivolous[4] or compassionate or cruel or stingy or generous as well as any other character trait. Neither is there someone who forces him or decrees that he do this or that—only he by himself and by his own mind inclines to any way he sees fit. This is as Jeremiah said: From above does not emerge the evils or good (Lam. 3:38). This being so, it is the sinner who has brought damage upon himself and therefore he should lament his sins and whatever evil he has done to himself."[5]

The idea of human free will is the basis of the Divine reward and punishment as well as the idea of self improvement and *teshuvah* (penitence). Without this free choice we are but puppets in a cosmic theater. Since Man is judged by his or her actions, and ethical action is the basis upon which human beings are judged, the idea of free will is the most basic concept in the Torah.

> This idea [of human free will] is a great principle and is the pillar of the Torah and the commandments, as it says: Behold I have given to you this day life and good, death and evil (Deut. 30:15) and it says: Behold I have set before you today the blessing and the curse (Ibid, 11:26), meaning, the choice is in your hands, and all a man wants to do in human action, he can, whether good or evil. Therefore does it say: May it so be that their hearts should revere me all the days (Deut. 5:26) meaning, that the creator neither forces people nor decrees that they do good or evil but it is all in their hands.[6]

The terms used by Maimonides in this paragraph are unusual. Human free will is the pillar of the Torah and its commandments. It is interesting to note that Maimonides wrote that there are thirteen principles of Jewish belief[7] but did not include free will as one of them. This would mean that free will is the pillar upon which all other principles rest. Without it there is no Torah and commandments and no room for human moral decision-making. Maimonides' belief in the centrality of human free will is so strong that he is not willing to limit it even in light of rabbinic sources which seem to imply otherwise. We mentioned before that the Jewish-astrologers limited human free will to decisions taken within the given circumstances. For Maimonides there cannot be any limitations of free will between birth and death. Therefore he goes to great lengths to reinterpret any rabbinic or Geonic source which might seem to imply otherwise.[8] In his letter to Obadiah the Proselyte we see evidence of this relentless approach concerning human free will.

Obadiah asked Maimonides how one can reconcile his position of total human free-will with rabbinic sources that seem to limit human free will. The first source Obadiah brings is from the Talmud in Brakhot which says: "All is in the hands of heaven except for the fear of heaven."[9] This of course seems to imply that human free will is limited to just a few areas and the rest is in God's hands. Maimonides is at his intellectual best here and with astonishing exegetical skills interprets the statement to harmonize totally with his position:

That which you have said that all human action is not predetermined by the creator, may He be elevated, is the flawless truth. Therefore one receives reward if he has gone in the path of goodness and is punished if he chose the path of evil; and all human action is included [in the term] "fear of heaven." For all of human activity brings one to a *mitzvah* or to a transgression. [Therefore] what the sages of blessed memory said: "all is in the hands of heaven," [refers to] the laws of nature and all the derivatives therein like trees, animals, souls [*nefashot*], upper intellects, the planets, angels; these are all in the hands of heaven. [10]

Maimonides claims that the rabbis in the Talmud were not discussing the human arena alone. In the cosmos as a whole, many things are devoid of free will, including the laws of nature, plants, animals, stars and even the angels and higher intellects (a neo-Aristotelian concept) but mankind is totally free in its ability to choose. The reason this is referred to as "the fear of heaven" is since all of human action can be seen as relating to moral choices, whether directly or indirectly. For instance, if we buy a house, did we buy in a good neighborhood where our kids will be influenced for the good? Is it near a school and a house of prayer? Did we pick the rich area just to impress our friends? Did we do the business transaction honestly? Since human action can be seen in such a way, it is right to call human action the realm of "the fear of heaven." Maimonides, after answering the query, goes on to say something that gives us insight into his way of understanding the issue.

Anyone who puts aside these ideas which we explained, which are based on eternal foundations, and goes off to look in the *aggadah*, the *midrash* or the sayings of one of the *Geonim* of blessed memory, to find a word to contradict our ideas which are based on reason and knowledge, is basically committing [spiritual] suicide and it is [bad] enough [the damage] which he has already done to his soul.[11]

What makes Maimonides so convinced of the truth of human free choice? It is true that there are verses in scripture which speak of human free will, but its importance we know mostly due to rational inference. It is illogical that the Torah demand human action through specific commandments and through specific prohibitions as well as talk of reward and punishment if there is no human free will. This is an example of human logic deducing an idea from scripture and the notion being just as important as revelation itself. This in a nutshell is how Maimonides sees human reason. It is God-given, just like scripture. After all, didn't God create human beings "in his own image" and instill within them the faculty of reason, the Divine aspect within us? Therefore, if human reason infers a notion from the Divine-based scripture through logical deduction which is beyond doubt, then that notion becomes part of the intent of scripture. The notion of human free will is so obviously important that Maimonides says that there is no point in looking for rabbinic statements which might contradict it. If such statements exist, they would have to be reinterpreted.

The second Talmudic source brought by Obadiah the proselyte to challenge the notion of total free will concerns the question of human business transactions and marriage. The Talmud says: "Every day a heavenly voice (*Bat Kol*) announces: the daughter of so and so will wed the son of so and so and the field of so and so will be acquired by so and so."[12] This of course implies that human monetary transactions as well as choosing a mate are predestined by heaven. Doesn't this assume that there are limitations to human free will? Maimonides answers: "That which your Rabbi said to you [that a heavenly voice announces daily] 'the daughter of so and so to so and so and the money of so and so to so and so,' if this is a general rule and [we are to understand these] words by their simple meaning, why does the Torah say 'lest he die in battle and another man wed her' or '[lest] another man reap [his vineyard]'?"[13]

Maimonides offers quite a clever answer. The Torah in *Devarim* says that there are three people who are exempt from army duty in a non-obligatory war (*milhemet reshut*).[14] The three are "the man who has built a house and has not entered it yet, he shall return to his house lest he die in battle and another man enter it... the man who has planted a vineyard and has not yet reaped [its produce]... the man who has betrothed a wife and has not as yet wed her, he shall return to his house lest he die in battle and another man wed her." (Deut. 20:5-7). In short, what Maimonides is saying is that if we are to assume that one's spouse is predestined by God, then why does the Torah say "lest he die in battle and another man marry her"? What does it matter? If they are destined to be together, then he will surely return from battle, and if they are not destined to be together then it shouldn't matter if another man weds her. Therefore, we can conclude that according to the Bible, marriage is not predestined by heaven:

Is there someone in the world who would doubt this [that marriage is not predestined] after it is written in the Torah? Therefore, this is how one who understands and is ready to take the truth in hand [should act]; that he put the Torah based idea as his main principle...and if he finds a verse in the prophets or in the words of the sages of blessed memory, that contradicts this...he should try to understand the words of the prophet or of the sage. If they can harmonize with the words of the Torah—fine. If not, he should say: these words of the prophet or of the sage, I do not understand. They must be metaphorical.[15]

Maimonides creates a rule of thumb. If the Torah brings an idea which seems to contradict the prophets or the sages, one must follow the principle of the Torah and reinterpret the idea of the sages. This sounds like a sound proposition. The problem with this rule is that Maimonides himself does not seem to follow it. Many times he reinterprets the Torah to avoid conflict with a logical dictate.[16] This then would mean that for Maimonides, both the torah and reason are the principles upon which Divine will is understood. This is quite an insight into his thinking. In the end, though, no traditional Jewish philosopher can say that the sages (*Hazal*) say A but he says B. For in the end of the day, without the words of the sages of the oral tradition we would be in the dark about most of Judaism. Therefore Maimonides does not stop here but attempts to reinterpret the Talmudic statement.

That which the sages said: "The daughter of so and so to so and so," [refers] to reward and punishment. If this man or this woman did a good deed that deserves reward, they receive a good mate from the Holy One Blessed Be He. If they deserve punishment, they receive a mate who battles and quarrels with them...but this is not a general principle.[17] (Moed Katan 18b)

Maimonides claims that in general, marriage is not predestined by God, however, in certain cases there is Divine intervention in the way of reward or punishment.

This is quite a surprising conclusion to anyone who might have been present at a traditional Jewish wedding today. The most popular wedding pastime is always trying to show how the marriage was predestined in heaven. Actually, the Talmud itself states that from the Torah, the prophets, and the later writings it can be proven that marriages *are* predestined by heaven. The Talmud itself raises the question from Devarim 20 and answers differently than Maimonides. We can see, therefore, how important the principle of human free will is for Maimonides. It is so important that even if it appears that the sages held the opinion that free will has limitations, we must reinterpret.

Maimonides is quite unique among Jewish philosophers in his unbending position on total human free choice. This position however has a major educational implication. Maimonides' staunch belief in the centrality of human free will creates a sense of moral responsibility. If I am the one choosing, then I must bear the responsibility of my actions. This is a healthy way to relate to moral choices in life. However, despite Maimonides' claim of the centrality of human free will in Jewish faith, there is a tendency among religionists to act in almost a fatalistic manner in many scenarios of life claiming that God had proclaimed the outcome of the situation in advance. I have witnessed this type of attitude in relation to automobile accidents. Sometimes we forget that it was a human being at the wheel and not just God who decreed the outcome. About this Solomon said in Proverbs: "The foolishness of man distorts his way but in his heart he blames God [instead]." (Prov. 19:3) Therefore one can understand the importance of teaching the Maimonidean view on free will from the point of view of moral responsibility. However, the question still remains: why does popular religion tend to be so fatalistic if human free will is so central to the idea of Judaism? To understand this we must enter the next arena if our discussion; the idea of Divine fore-knowledge and human free will.

DIVINE PRE-KNOWLEDGE AND HUMAN FREE WILL

The theologians of the Kalam, an early Islamic school that developed in the eighth century, as well as the early church fathers, came to the logical conclusion that if God knows the future, i.e., events before they take place, then there cannot be human free will. In other words, if God knows that Robert will be saintly, then Robert will have to be saintly. If you say that there is still the possibility that Robert will not be saintly that means that God did not know this in absolute terms. If God knows for certain what the future holds, there is no room for human free will. Now since the prophets appear to receive knowledge of the future from God, and since Isaiah 41:4 also says that God knows the future, we are left with the realization that human free will cannot really exist from a biblical point of view. However, if we say that human free will is an illusion, then why does the Bible tell us to do good and keep away from evil and promise reward and punishment? This is a seeming biblical paradox and was a major theological problem in the early Middle Ages among religionists. Early Christian thinkers, such as St. Anselm, used this logical paradox to prove that God predestines human action. The Kalam, who believed the same, needed to explain how the Koran can require human actions if there is no free will. After all, what is the point of the five major commandments of Islam if free will is an illusion? The Kalam developed an idea called the "principle of acquiring." The idea was that the righteous man, even though predestined by God, could not reach eternal reward without actually doing the good deed. Therefore, by doing the good deed, even if pre-destined, it becomes ours. This doesn't give us free will, but is an attempt to solve the paradox even if in a limited way. By the twelfth century, Persian Islamic thinkers such as Avicenna had developed new ways of solving the problem. At this point it is appropriate to say that from a Jewish point of view the problem had to be reconciled in some way, for the Mishnah in the Ethics of the Fathers states that: "All is known [by God] but [human] free choice is still given."[18] This paradox was an attempt to hold both ends of the cord. Maimonides, influenced by Avicenna, tried to reconcile this and wrote:

> If you should say: Doesn't the Holy One Blessed Be He know all events before they happen and therefore knows whether one will be wicked or saintly? If He knows that one will be saintly it cannot be otherwise and if you shall say that He knows he will be saintly but he can still be wicked, that means He did not know this absolutely. Know that the answer to this question is lengthy and broad and many great and lofty principles are connected to it. But you must understand this which I say: We have already explained in the second chapter of Yesodei Torah, that God does not know through a knowledge that is separate from him as humans do, for they and their knowledge are two things. God and his knowledge are one and no man can understand this fully. For just as man cannot grasp God's essence as it says: for a man cannot see me and live, so too he has not the ability to understand God's knowledge. This is what the prophet says: "For my thoughts are not your thoughts and my ways not your ways." Therefore we cannot understand how God can know all the creatures and their actions [in advanced knowledge], but we do know for certain that one's actions are their own and not forced by God.[19]

How does Maimonides reconcile free will and Divine pre-knowledge? He adopts Avicenna's idea, as follows: When we say that Divine pre-knowledge contradicts human free-will this is since we equate Divine knowledge with human knowledge. We assume that God knows the future as we know the present and the past. Now since human beings know only events that have already happened, we then assume that God's knowledge of the future must be of events that have to happen. But what if God's knowledge is totally different from our knowledge? Then we could not make any comparison and the assumption could be wrong. To prove that God's knowledge is different than human knowledge Maimonides gives an example. With human beings we can differentiate between themselves and what they know. In fact, as Maimonides states in chapter 8 of the eight chapters, with Humans we talk of the knower (us), the known (the idea we discovered) and knowledge (our intelligence). We cannot speak of God and His knowledge as two things. For one could ask if God had this knowledge previously. If not, then he was missing this knowledge and was not perfect and if we are to say that he always had this knowledge since time eternal we have just argued that there are two separate eternal beings, God and this knowledge of his; which would be impossible. Therefore we must say that God and his knowledge are one. Maimonides states in the *Guide* that God is the Knower, the knowledge and the known, for He is one. Having said this, Maimonides sees this as a demonstration that God's knowledge by definition must be essentially different than ours.[20] This being the case, we now see that Avicenna's argument that God's knowledge and our knowledge must be different is a sound argument. Therefore we do not know in which way God knows the future. We only know the two logical imperatives: that God knows the future and that we have free will.

This does not explain how God knows the future, of course, but just that it must be in a very different way from how we perceive the past and present.

This of course is still hard to understand. I sometimes like to explain this through the example of sight. I see what is in the room but I did not cause it to be there. Somehow, God can see the future without having caused the actual event to happen. To our minds this is incomprehensible since we do not perceive things in the same way. This position is the dominant view in Jewish philosophy and seems to be the simple meaning of the Mishnaic saying: "All is known but Free will is given." However, as in every issue, there is a dissident view; that of Levi Ben Gershon, referred to as Gersonides.

THE DISSIDENT VIEW

Judaism has always been quite tolerant to the plethora of ideas, even some unorthodox ones, but less so to unorthodox actions. A good example of this tolerance would be Gersonides' book *Milkhamot Hashem*, or *Wars of the Lord*, which his critics called the "Wars Against the Lord." Despite this, they not only tolerated him but held him in good repute. Gersonides takes Maimonides to task on the issue of God's pre-knowledge. Since we cannot logically assume that there can be human free will and Divine pre-knowledge without assuming Divine predestination, we must assume that God does not know the future. Differing from Maimonides and Avicenna, Gersonides takes the view of Averroes:

> That the knowledge of God, may He be blessed, is not different from our knowledge in the way that the Master [Maimonides], may his memory be blessed, maintained. This is because it is clear that we derive matters that we affirm of God, may He be blessed, from matters that are (affirmed) of us. I mean to say that we affirm of God, may He be blessed, that He has knowledge because of the knowledge found in us.... Now it is self evident concerning any predicate when it is affirmed of a certain thing on the basis of its existence in another thing this it is not said of both things in absolute nominal equivation. That is because between things which are absolutely equivocal there is no analogy.[21]

In other words, if we did not have intellect, we would not know that God should have intellect. Therefore, this intellect must resemble ours in some way. Therefore we must say that God's intellect is like ours, just greater.

> Therefore, it is clear that there is no difference between the knowledge of God, may He be blessed, and our knowledge except that the knowledge of God, may He be blessed, is immeasurably more perfect and this kind of knowledge is truer in level and clarity.[22]

Now, since God's knowledge is like ours but just greater, and since human free will is a sin qua non from biblical literature, it would be illogical to state that God knows the future. However, this is not an imperfection in God since the future does not exist.

This is all fine and dandy, but how does Gersonides explain prophecy, which is God's sharing his knowledge of the future with the prophet? Gersonides' answer is that God shows the prophet both the future and its contingent possibilities.

Scripture says, "Surely the Lord God does nothing without revealing His secret to His servants the prophets" [Amos 3:7] But it does not follow necessarily from their testifying to a certain evil that it will be actualized. As [Joel] said, peace be unto him, "For the Lord is gracious...and repents evil" [Joel 2:13].[23]

In other words, the prophet is shown that evil could befall the people but if they repent it will not happen. In the same way, prophecy for the good can change if the people go on the path of evil. Therefore God is showing the prophet the possibilities that the future holds. To understand this better, we need to remember that Gersonides is a believer in astrology.[24] Gersonides states that God does not know the future in exact detail, however since He created the world, and since He knows exactly how the world works according to the various constellations and times, He knows exactly what choices will be available in any given future date. In fact, since He knows human nature as well, He also can guess with a 99% probability as to how each human being will choose in these given circumstances. This is what he reveals to the prophets. This can be compared to a statistician who can say that next Labor Day weekend, based on past statistics, 400 people will die in road accidents in the US. However he will not know who. God has 99.99% probability knowledge of the future with only the slightest margin of error produced by human free will.[25] This differs immensely from Maimonides, who claims that God has perfect knowledge of the future. Maimonides also states that if God shows the prophet the future, it has to happen. Only in the event of an evil decree can repentance change the outcome, but a positive prophecy has to come about if it is true.[26]

GOD'S KNOWLEDGE OF THE PRESENT VERSUS HUMAN KNOWLEDGE

Since we are discussing issues of God's Knowledge I would like to complete this discussion with a famous argument between the Rationalists and the kabbalists concerning how God perceives the present.

At this point we can ponder how God perceives the present. Is it as we do or can He see things in the here and now that we do not? To state it in different terms: if human reason is universal, does that mean that the way we understand a rational concept is the same way that God does?

For instance, if one and one is two and I state that I know that for certain, does that mean that for God one and one can only be two as well, or is it possible that God might one day point out that one and one can come out to something else other than two in another scenario? Maimonides as a rationalist who believes in the universality of human reason would argue that God knows things that I do not. However, in the limited realm of human understanding, what we know as absolute truths even God would perceive in an identical way. If I don't say this, I am basically claiming that all logic is subjective, which in an absolute sense would render it untrue. Rambam as a rationalist assures us that this cannot be. "We cannot ascribe to God the power of doing what is impossible,"[27] and therefore what we perceive as true in this world is universally true. On this point Maimonides agrees with Aristotle. However, he makes one exception. God can create the universe ex nihilo, which seems to be impossible from the point of view of human reason.[28] This creating of something from nothing is a miracle which God performs even though it is not understood by human reason how this can be possible. But wait: if God cannot do things generally impossible to fathom, how can He perform miracles? Is that why Maimonides claims that all miracles were created in advance by God in the moment before the end of the sixth day of creation just before nightfall?[29] Is it an attempt to give a rule to that which breaks the rules of nature? Is the miraculous an anomaly of nature that God created to be part of nature, therefore giving it a sort of logical status?[30] Joseph Albo tried to answer this problem by differentiating between things logically and innately impossible which cannot change, and things that are impossible due to the laws of nature and therefore are subject to a miracle.[31] God can break the rules of nature, since he set them. This is what we call a miracle. However, God cannot do something which we understand as logically impossible.[32]

GOD'S KNOWLEDGE OF THE PRESENT —
THE KABBALISTIC APPROACH

The Rashba [R. Shlomo Ben Abraham Adret 1235-1310] was one of the first to argue with Rambam on the scope of Divine knowledge. In a famous letter concerning the negative influence of philosophic Judaism on the masses, Rashba addressed what he perceived to be the major causes of confusion in Jewish thought. One of them was this issue of God's ability to enact the impossible.

What we were told and taught, to allow [the idea] that some of the [logical] impossibilities have a stable nature [even for God], specifically among those certain ideas that are needed for Torah [faith] for they are the root and base that all the rest depend upon. They are for example: that God make another God like Himself or that He incarnate Himself or cause any change in Himself for we do not believe that the blessed God can be described as capable of such a thing as the great Rabbi [Maimonides], of blessed memory, wrote. Enumerated among these impossibilities are other necessary ideas [of faith] making it impossible to explain it all in writing.[33]

As mentioned above, Rambam limits God's ability to perform the logically impossible to one instance, creation ex nihilo,[34] whereas Rashba enumerates what impossibilities God cannot do, and gives a rule of thumb, i.e., those items necessary for our belief; suggesting that all other humanly logical impossibilities are possible for Him. The exceptions, for Rashba, seem to revolve around the main theological tenets of Judaism those ideas concerning the being of God. Therefore, where Maimonides made an exception for creation ex nihilo and took the point of view that rational impossibilities cannot exist from God's perspective, Rashba took the opposite view, making the exceptions all the theological issues relating directly to God's being. Obviously we can ask why according to Rashba, there should be exceptions. Apart from what I stated above, this is too involved a question to delve into here. I would rather like to focus on these two positions and their implications. The Rashba's stance is that logical impossibilities are a human condition. There are certain things that we will call impossible for God for reasons of belief, but in general, there is no reason to limit God by human boundaries. If we extend this idea to the realm of logic, then this discussion has implications for the understanding of human logic. For if God can perceive our world differently, how can we know if logic is really universal outside our own perception? This type of thinking is every rationalist's nightmare. However, it is also a very different perception of God vis a vis creation than that of the rationalist. By way of illustration, I remember in my late teens taking a bus from Kiriat Malakhi to Ashkelon. Two teens approached and asked me if I believed in God. Upon hearing an affirmative answer they proceeded by asking me if I believed that God was all-powerful. They then asked me if this God could create a stone which He could not lift. Being a devout rationalist at the time, I explained to them in accordance with the *Guide* III:15, that logical limitations do not take away from God's perfection. Therefore, by answering in the negative to their question concerning such a stone, I was merely establishing that God could pick up everything for there is nothing He cannot pick up. Therefore, I claimed, it is illogical to imagine Him creating such a stone. Today, after reading Rashba, I would offer them a second explanation (if I could find them. At the time they seemed impressed that I was willing to offer an answer). Based on the assumption that God has no logical limitations, since He cannot be defined by human logic except for those which we need for our understanding of the tenets of faith, I would say: "Can God create a stone that He cannot pick up? Yes, and He can pick it up as well." You might point out the flawed human logic here, but this is according to the opinion that logical contradictions are possibilities as far as God is concerned.[35]

FREE WILL AND SCIENCE

In the ancient world view, God had a constant role in the natural world. Since according to Aristotle, nothing could move without some force acting upon it, it seemed puzzling that the planets moved in an endless circular motion. Since no notion of inertia existed this was a great puzzle. The solutions offered were twofold; what I call the religious and the secular solution. The secular solution was that if the planets move and no one is moving them, then they must have a soul which enables them to move just as animals and humans do. The religious answer was that God moves them constantly.[36] Since the time the Western world adopted the views of Isaac Newton, nature was seen as numerous laws governing a mechanical universe. The idea of universal gravity as well as inertia rendered the old explanations unnecessary. This is not to say that Newton was very happy with the new situation. As I mentioned earlier, he wondered, as did others of his generation, what exactly God's role in nature was. If we live in a universe governed by blind laws of nature, in a sort of clockwork of things, why should humans be any different? As Paul Davies put it: "Newtonian mechanics permits, in principle, the accurate prediction of everything that will ever happen on the basis of what can be known at one instant. There is a rigid network of cause and effect, and every phenomenon, from the tiniest jiggle of a molecule to the explosion of a galaxy, is determined in detail long in advance."[37] Maybe our actions are governed by hidden laws as well, yet to be discovered? The religious response was that human beings are endowed with free will which is their Godly trait, and this separates them from the rest of the universe. However, scientists, especially since the French revolution, when religious values were replaced with secular ones, wondered if maybe there was no free will after all. Pierre Laplace (1749-1827) declared that if one were to know at one instant the positions and motions of every particle in the universe he could compute the entire future history of the universe.[38] The discoveries in biology, especially in neurobiology, as well as theories of behavior in psychology called these old assumptions into question again. However, the new physics, particularly nuclear physics, has again swung the pendulum back by analyzing the building blocks of matter and asking anti-Newtonian questions such as: do electrons have free will? "According to the basic principles of quantum theory, nature is inherently unpredictable. Heisenberg's famous uncertainty principle assures us that there is always an irreducible indeterminism in the operation of subatomic systems. In the micro world, events occur that have no well defined cause."[39] Heisenberg showed that it was impossible for scientists to achieve an objective result because the act of observation itself affected their understanding of the object of their investigation. As one thinker put it: "Heisenberg has liberated us from the seventeenth-century mechanics, when the universe had seemed like a giant machine made up of separate components, whereas this new generation of scientists was revealing the deep interconnectedness of all reality."[40] This shift in thinking paved the way again for the legitimacy of the idea of free will in humans even in relation to the physical universe. This does not mean that there are not complications. Free will is a complicated topic. Despite the questions in Newtonian physics, the idea of human free will over a blind mechanical world is easier to swallow for us than thinking that there are other non-human free agents working simultaneously in our universe. However, it does shed new light of the old idea of a blind mechanical universe.

"Many physicists these days are inclining towards the so-called Everett many-universes interpretation of the quantum theory. This view has bizarre implications for the subject of free will. According to Everett, every possible world is actually realized, with all the alternative worlds coexisting in parallel. This duplication of worlds extends to human choices. Suppose you are faced with a choice—tea or coffee? The Everett interpretation says that the universe immediately divides into two branches. In one of the branches you have tea, in the other coffee."[41]

Young's Two-Slit Experiment

"The famous Young's two-slot experiment is ideal for exposing the bizarre wave-particle duality of light. The small hole in screen A illuminates the two narrow slits in screen B. The image of the slits is displayed on the screen C. Rather than a simple double band of light, there appears a sequence of bright and dark bands (interference fringes) caused by the light waves from each slit arriving successively in step or out of step, depending on position. Even when one photon at a time traverses the apparatus, the same interference pattern builds up in a freckled fashion, though any given photon can only go through either one slit or the other in screen B, and has no neighbouring photons against which to gauge its step." The question of how this can be was a major debate between Neils Bohr and Einstein and raises questions as to the relationship between the experimenter and the experiment being done (P. Davies, God and the New Physics, NY 1983 p. 109) For a graphic representation of the experiment see:

http://www.colorado.edu/physics/2000/schroedinger/two-slit2.html

"The essential dichotomy can be illustrated with the aid of the humble television. The image on the television screen is produced by myriads of light pulses emitted when electrons fired from a gun at the back of the set strike the florescent screen. The picture you perceive is reasonably sharp because the number of electrons involved is enormous and by the law of averages, the cumulative effect of many electrons is predictable. However, any particular electron, with its inbuilt unpredictability, could go anywhere on the screen. The arrival of this electron at a place, and the fragment of picture that it that it produces , is uncertain. According to Bohr's philosophy, bullets from an ordinary gun follow a precise path to their target , but electrons from an electron gun simply turn up at the target." (Davies, p. 103).

CHAPTER 6

*The Human Soul
and Personality: Plato,
Aristotle, Hippocrates,
Al-Farabi
and Maimonides*

The Greek philosophers did not differentiate between the various disciplines. Philosophers were scholars learned in all the sciences. (It was a bit easier to do in those days.) Therefore, psychology was considered a part of philosophy just as physics and metaphysics were.[1] Psychology as a science is less than 200 years old. The Greeks dealt with these matters in a more intuitive way. Remember that psychology means the study of the psyche, which means soul in Greek. For the Greeks, the soul was a force within the body and not exactly a metaphysical concept. For both Aristotle and Plato, the human soul transcended physicality even though it existed within the body. However, only Plato spoke of the soul in terms of something continuing after death. For Aristotle, even though the soul was not physical, it needed the body to survive, so that after the body died, the soul ceased to exist as well. Therefore, it is not surprising that the Jewish rationalists who normally followed an Aristotelian line incorporated Platonic notions of the afterlife into their thinking. Plato compares the human soul to a rider with two horses. The rider, standing in his carriage, is called the intellect and the two horses are called the spirited horse and the appetitive horse. This is a division of the soul into three powers: the intellectual, the vital and the physical desires and needs. The driver needs to keep the horse under control. Sometimes one horse wants to go one way and the other another way and sometimes they both go against the rider. Therefore the intellect has to control the various elements of the psyche. One can also deduce from this paradigm that the intellect is the most defining aspect of the psyche. It is a human rider, whereas the other aspects are compared to horses. The ninth century Muslim philosopher Al-Kindi tried to deduce from this parable that the rider (the intellect), being separate from the horses, continues after death as we mentioned above. Maimonides follows the Aristotelian model of the soul as brought down in Aristotle's *De Anima* and as explained by Al-Farabi in his work on the State. Maimonides discusses the aspects of the soul in the first two chapters of his *Eight Chapters*, which are an introduction to his commentary on the ethical Mishnaic work, the Ethics of the Fathers. Maimonides opens the discussion by saying that just as a Doctor needs to know anatomy before learning how to cure the ailments of the body, so too does one need to understand the aspects of the soul before one can discuss moral improvement.

> Know that the human soul is one but it has many diversified activities. Some of these activities have been called souls, which has given rise to the opinion that Man has many souls, as was the belief of the physicians, with the result that the most distinguished of them[2] states in the introduction of his book , that there are three souls: the physical, the vital, and the psychical (intellectual). These activities are called faculties and parts, so that the phrase "parts of the soul" frequently employed by philosophers, is commonly used. By the word "parts" they do not intend to imply that the soul is divided into parts as are bodies, but they merely enumerate the different activities of the soul as being parts of a whole, the union of which makes up the soul.[3]

This opening remark is important to Maimonides. The human soul is indivisible. It has various functions but they all stem from the same root. The need to reiterate this idea seems to fit in with Maimonides' claim that the human soul is unique. As we mentioned above, in Aristotelian thinking, the natural world has four levels: minerals, plants, animals and mankind. The levels are considered quite distinct and represent a hierarchy. This is different from modern biological thinking which sees mankind as a sophisticated animal. For Maimonides, therefore, mankind is distinct from any animal. Even if our digestive tract might resemble that of a horse or a dog, the source of the human soul is the intellectual human soul whereas the source of the horse's soul is an animal soul.

Maimonides proceeds to describe the functions of the soul.

The Maimonidean Model of the Functions of the Soul	
The Rational Faculty	a. Theoretical knowledge b. Practical knowledge
The Vital Faculty	a. The appetitive faculty (motion and emotion) b. The imaginative faculty c. The five senses
The Natural or Vegetative Faculty	a. Bodily functions (digestion, growth, and reproduction)

Maimonides explains them in ascending order:

The nutritive or vegetative faculty is in charge of the bodily functions, particularly growth, the digestive tract, and the reproductive organs. This is an involuntary faculty which works even while we sleep.

The five senses—"include the five well known capacities: sight, hearing, taste, smell and touch—[the latter] is found throughout the body without being associated with any particular limb as the others are."[4]

The Imaginative faculty—"This is the ability to remember physical impressions after they have disappeared from the [5] senses."[5] This is an interesting definition of the imaginative faculty. Imagination is the ability to remember what the senses perceived. This can be from any of the five senses. We can remember an image, a symphony, a smell, a hug, or the taste of our favourite dish. This is not all of memory, since we can remember ideas as well, but is related to an aspect of memory. This discussion brings Maimonides to a fascinating argument with the theologians of the Kalam.

[This faculty can] combine some [of these images] and can divide some [of these images] resulting in combinations of that which one perceived together with things which were not perceived and cannot be perceived — like imagining: a metal ship flying in the air; or a man whose head is in the heavens and whose legs are on the earth; or an animal with a thousand eyes, for example, for many of these impossibilities can be formed by the imagination. This is where the Kalam made their terrible mistake upon which they built many a mistake by speaking of the necessary, the possible and the impossible. They thought or brought others to think that all which is imagined is possible and did not know that this faculty can conceive of things that are impossible [to be found in reality].[6]

Maimonides argues that not everything imagined is possible. After all, we can imagine a fish with the head of a woman or an animal with a thousand eyes. These of course are things that do not exist outside our imagination. The Kalam's argument is quite interesting. They argue that we cannot imagine things that we have never seen or perceived through our senses, such as God, the human soul, or the angels. If we can imagine something it is because we perceived it or its parts in some combination in this world. Therefore, if we can imagine something, it is at least possible even if at this moment it does not exist. Today we can argue the point on their behalf. Maimonides claimed that there cannot be metal ships flying in the air, but today we have planes. (I guess Maimonides could counter that planes are not boats flying in the air, but it might be just a matter of time until we have those as well.) For the Kalam, therefore, the category of the impossible would only be things that are logically impossible, such as that God exits and does not exist, or that the creator can also be the created (their argument with Christianity, of course).

The Appetitive faculty: "This is the faculty through which one desires something or despises it. From this faculty is derived: the wish for something and fleeing from it, the choosing of something or avoiding it, anger and appeasement, fear and courage, cruelty and compassion, love and hatred, and other affections. The vehicles of this faculty are all the limbs of the body: as the power of the hand — to take or touch something, the power of the foot — to walk, the power of the eye to see, the power of the heart to be courageous, or to fear in fearful events. All other limbs of the body, as well, whether seen or not, they and their powers — are all vessels for the appetitive faculty.[7]

The appetitive faculty is quite interesting. It is not identical to what we would today call the emotions. It contains the seat of human will, the emotions, but also the control over the bodily limbs. It includes both motions and emotions. Emotions were seen in a more active way then they are seen today. Love is a movement towards something in a positive way whereas hate is a movement towards something in a negative way. Fear is a movement away, etc. You might say this faculty includes emotions that are inner movements of the heart, as well as motion which is an external movement of the bodily limbs.

As I mentioned above, Maimonides follows the Aristotelian perspective as interpreted by the tenth-century Muslim philosopher Al-Farabi. Al-Farabi in his book on the State devotes the tenth chapter to the faculties of the soul. Concerning the appetitive faculty he writes:

> The appetitive faculty — by which desire or dislike of a thing occurs — has a ruling faculty and subordinates. It is the faculty which makes the will arise; for will is an appetite towards or away from what has been apprehended either by sense perception or by representation or by the faculty of reason...Appetition is brought about by the ruling faculty of appetite only. Bodily acts are brought about by faculties which are subordinate to the appetitive faculty.[8]

The similarity to Maimonides is obvious. Al-Farabi adds that will is also a form of appetite. He claims as well that the appetitive faculty's control over bodily movement is a secondary function. There are still unclear issues in Maimonides' description. What is the difference between the appetitive's power of the eyes to see and the five senses? Is there an idea here that the senses work through the appetitive faculty? What about hearing? As I mentioned above, there is clearly a different perception of the five senses from what we know today.

The rational faculty — Maimonides divides the rational faculty into theoretical knowledge and practical knowledge. Theoretical knowledge is pure intellectualization which Maimonides refers to as "the discussion of eternal entities" — meaning, fields of knowledge that are totally disconnected from anything dependent on this world. This definition seems to limit this category tremendously and includes both fields of pure reason, such as mathematics, geometry and logic, as well as fields whose objects of discussion are purely metaphysical, such as theology and metaphysics. All other fields of study are contingent on data from this world and fall into the category of practical intellect. Maimonides identifies two types of practical knowledge as well: the theory of studying the theory of the practical, but if I am programming a computer at this moment I am involved in the practical of the practical intellect.

This description of the intellect, differentiating between pure intellectual subjects and worldly subjects, differs from the standard medieval categories of primary and secondary subjects of study found in early university departments called the quadrium and the trivium. These latter categories acted more as pedagogical tools than as statements about pure reason and were therefore considered a lesser level of study. Today we remember this through the word "trivia" which still connotes less important matters.

The oldest university in the FSU was the school of the Grand Duchy of Lithuania. It was called Vilnius University in 1579.

"This preparatory faculty was renamed the Philosophy faculty with Latin as the main language of instruction. Students studied seven liberal arts subjects consisting of the trivium of Grammar, Rhetoric and Dialectics, followed by the quadrium of Arithmetic, Geometry, Astronomy and Music. Students became Bachelors of Arts after finishing their trivium course. On completing the quadrium, students were awarded a master's degree."[9]

As was stated earlier, for Maimonides there is nothing above intellect in the human psyche.

THE HUMAN SOUL AND ETHICAL CONDUCT

The discussion in chapter two of the eight chapters revolves around the role of the various aspects of the human psyche in the act of a good or bad deed.

Know that transgressions and good deeds [mitzvot] will be found, however, only in two parts of the soul which are: the [five] senses and the appetitive; in these two will be found all transgressions and good deeds [mitzvot]. However, the nutritive faculty and imagination — have neither mitzvah nor transgression ascribed to them, for they are not under free will and one cannot willfully stop them or slow them down. After all one can see that these two faculties: the nutritive and the imagination carry out their activities while one is asleep contrary to other faculties of the soul.[10]

Out of the various faculties of the soul Maimonides rules out the possibility of transgression and good deeds ascribed to the nutritive faculty or the imagination since both are involuntary faculties. This he proves from the fact that they work as we sleep. Digestion and growth happen while we sleep, as do dreams. Does this mean that ethical action must be ascribed to voluntary faculties? The answer would appear to be in the affirmative. Therefore he ascribes ethical actions to the appetitive which is the seat of human will. This means that if one has a stomach ache (nutritive), this would not reflect badly on them as showing bad character, rather we would say that their digestive tract acts poorly. Subsequently, if one gets angry often, we will not say that their appetitive faculty is malfunctioning, rather that they show bad character traits and therefore we will see them negatively.

However, what seems puzzling is that Maimonides includes the fives senses in the list of faculties that control ethical conduct. Aren't the five senses involuntary faculties? Don't the eyes work like a biological camera? Where is human volition in this picture? It seems that Maimonides is following the Talmud, which states: "The eye beholds and the heart covets and the faculties of action finish the work." This would imply that one sees the desired object (through the five senses), the heart desires it (appetitive) and the human limbs finish the work (appetitive). These then are the two faculties which Maimonides refers to. Even so, it is difficult to comprehend according to the modern understanding of human sensory-perception, where there can be a voluntary element here. Possibly one could say that there is a concept of selective seeing and hearing. Sometimes we hear only that which is pleasing to our ears and muffle out the rest. This might represent an element of volition within sensory-perception. Alternatively, it is known that there can be psychosomatic effects on the senses. There were documented cases of American pilots flying in the Korean War at night who developed night blindness. However, it is possible that in Maimonides' day, the five senses were perceived as having a voluntary aspect to them. This needs to be researched further.

In any event, Maimonides finds transgressions and good deeds in the faculties of the senses and the appetitive.

CAN THERE BE TRANSGRESSIONS OR GOOD DEEDS IN THE FACULTY OF REASON?

Maimonides continues:

Concerning the intellectual capacity — uncertainty prevails, However, I say that this faculty can also commit a transgression or a *mitzvah*, through a true or false doctrine concerning one's faith. Although, there is no deed which can be called a *mitzvah* or a transgression.[11]

At the end of the paragraph, Maimonides states that even if there can be a transgression or a *mitzvah* done by the intellect, since there is no action attached to these, they are transgressions in the eyes of God alone and cannot be punished by a human court. This follows a basic Talmudic principle that a transgression devoid of action, whether intellectual or passive, cannot be punished by a human court. Therefore, if in the Decalogue there is a prohibition to covet thy neighbor's house, this transgression, done by the mind, is punishable by God only. In fact, even passive transgressions cannot be punished by a human court. The Talmud[12] brings the example of the paschal offering. Exodus states: "You shall not leave any of it over until morning and if any of it is left until morning, you shall burn it in fire" (Ex. 12:10). The Torah says that one cannot leave over any of the paschal offering, which is a negative command, and then adds a positive command to burn whatever is left over. Therefore, if one were to leave over some of the paschal offering, they have transgressed a negative command and not fulfilled a positive one. However, since they were passive and did no action, this cannot be punished by a human court. This idea is quite unique to Judaism. Many religions persecuted heretics for their unorthodox ideas. Thousands were burned at the stake of the inquisition for the wrong theological beliefs. Many holy Muslim wars were fought against infidel Muslim nations (as Sunni and Shiite). In Judaism no punishment can be enacted for wrong theological beliefs. The person can be condemned, but not harmed or punished. In general, punishment for wrong beliefs can always be abused since it is hard to prove what someone thinks. Therefore, Jewish law took the more logical path, which also displayed great tolerance to dissenting views. Even those in the thirteenth century who disagreed with Gersonides' ideas on Divine Providence in his *Wars of the Lord* and nicknamed the book "Wars Against the Lord" never thought of calling for his excommunication.[13]

Concerning the first part of Maimonides' quote above we find an interesting point. Even if there is no human punishment, can there be a transgression done through the intellectual capacity? Maimonides replies in the affirmative. After all, one can hold a true or false doctrine about one's faith. This then would be a transgression carried out by the faculty of theoretical intellect. He does not give any example of a transgression done by the practical intellect.

The next question would be: Isn't this obvious? It says in the Decalogue: "Thou shalt not have any Gods beside me" so obviously any belief in another god would be a transgression against the Torah. So what then is the "uncertainty" that prevails here according to Maimonides? It seems to me that when Maimonides mentions uncertainty, he does not refer to whether there can be a transgression done by the intellect, but rather to the question of whether there can be a *mitzvah* done by the intellect. As we will see in Chapter 11, there is a major dispute in the Middle Ages whether there is a *mitzvah* to believe in God or not. I believe this is the uncertainty Maimonides refers to.

CHAPTER 7   *The Human Soul:*
A Kabbalistic View

Ⅰt is somewhat beyond the scope of this book to present the kabbalistic view on the human soul in its entirety since this is quite a lengthy discussion and a major topic in Jewish mysticism. However, I would like to mention the points of departure from the rationalists' perspective in the middle-ages.

In the Maimonidean view of the human soul three main aspects were discerned: the Intellectual, the Vital (Appetitive, Imaginative and sensory-perception) and the nutritive. The seat of the will was unclear. Al-Farabi put it in the Appetitive, but for Maimonides in chapter one of the *Guide*, human free will is considered an intellectual exercise. Moreover, if for Maimonides there can be transgressions and *mitzvot* in the intellectual faculty, this would imply a degree of volition as well.

For the kabbalists, the point of will is the highest point of the human psyche. It is above the human intellect which is a lower expression of the human psyche.[1] There are two points of will. The first is the inner point of the subconscious will which can be compared to the will to live, which stands at the highest point of the psyche; the second is the outer will, or the conscious will, which represents human volition and choices. The inner will is above human consciousness originating in a higher spiritual realm and resides above the intellect, whereas the outer will works with the intellect.[2] In Hassidic thinking the human psyche is divided into: intellect, emotions and actions. Above the intellect is faith and above faith is the inner will. The Talmud in Eruvin claims that the average person is three cubits high,[3] therefore the ritual bath, Mikveh, must contain enough water to cover 3 cubits of height and one square cubit in width.[4] In addition one may carry in a public domain on the Sabbath up to 4 square cubits in area since if one were to lie down their body would cover three cubits and their hands could reach an additional one.[5] In Hassidic thinking the three cubits of height represent the intellect, the emotions, and the action (also referred to as the brain, the heart and the liver) and the outstretched hands over the head represent faith, as it is written about Moses that when his hands were raised the Israelites were successful over the Amalekites, "And his hands were faithful until the sun shone." (Ex. 17:12) .Will is called the crown beyond the head. It originates from above. In kabbalistic thinking the intellect is described as a process. There are three levels: wisdom (hokhmah), intelligence (binah), and knowledge (daat). This is based on the verse concerning Bezalel, the architect of the tabernacle, who received Divine insight in order to form the temple vessels, "And I shall fill him with Divine spirit, with wisdom [hokhmah] and with understanding [tevunah] and with knowledge and with all [creative] work." (Ex. 31:3). "Wisdom" is seen as the first spark of an idea, what comes into the mind from nowhere when the light bulb over our head (so to speak) turns on with a new idea. "Understanding" refers to analytical knowledge; the ability to derive new teachings from the idea. "Knowledge" is the idea after it has been internalized into our minds and we understand it fully. The emotions are made up mainly of the three major emotions: Love (kindness), fear (or judgment) and mercy. All these elements are a vital force working within the body. There is some similarity to the rationalist model. The intellect parallels the intellectual capacity, the emotions parallel the appetitive (to an extent) or even the whole vital aspect, and the level of action or liver parallels the vegetative faculty. For the neo-Aristotelian rationalist however, there is nothing above intelligence. Even the spiritual realm is described as higher levels of intelligence. For the kabbalist, the human psyche with its three levels (cubits) is only the lowest expression of our soul. It is our outer soul. However we have an additional fourth level to our inner soul which binds us up to the Divine spark which created us.

CHAPTER 8

A Theory of Morality –
Maimonides' take on
Aristotle's Golden Mean

Socrates claimed that the wise man knows the good and will behave accordingly. (For sure he knows the good; behaves accordingly can be disputed, but that's what Socrates said.) Therefore knowledge leads to good moral conduct. Aristotle continued this line of thinking, adding that personal virtue is a balanced state. "Actions then are called just and temperate when they are such as the just and temperate man would do."[1] He goes on to develop a whole theory of virtue claiming that "Virtue, then, is a state of character concerned with choice, lying in a mean, i.e. the mean relative to us, this being determined by a rational principle, and by that principle by which the man of practical wisdom would determine it."[2] Maimonides, following Al-Farabi, describes the theory in its entirety.

Good deeds are such deeds which are equibalanced; maintaining the mean between two equally bad extremes: one being too much and the other—too little. Virtues—are character traits and acquired [habits] which are midway between two reprehensible extremes, one characterized by an exaggeration, the other by a deficiency. Good deeds are the products of these dispositions. To illustrate: abstemiousness is a disposition which adopts a mid-course between inordinate passion and total insensibility to pleasure…likewise liberality is the mean between miserliness and extravagance; courage, between recklessness and cowardice; dignity, between haughtiness and loutishness; humility, between arrogance and self abasement.[3]

The idea of the golden mean is that the best character traits are the balanced ones. Two things have to be said here as an introduction. First of all, the theory of the golden mean is a theory of morality concerning character traits. It does not apply to ideologies, or political views. This reminds me of a discussion I had years ago with an ultra-orthodox friend of mine from Baltimore. He said, "Concerning Zionism I take the position of Maimonides' golden mean. I am not anti-Zionist like some in my community and I don't make aliyah to Israel either. I remain here and therefore have found the golden mean." To that I replied that according to his thinking he should be a Conservative Jew. Since the Reform do not accept the authority of the commandments and the Orthodox feel all is binding without exception, he should have taken the middle road according to Maimonides. In any event, Maimonides is referring solely to character traits. Second, the middle way for Maimonides, as for Aristotle, is the optimal way of behaving. It is not a compromise. You might even say that one must be extremely devoted to the middle trait. Maimonides gives examples:

Diagram 2a:
The Golden Mean

Extreme (too little)	Mean	Extreme (too much)
Insensibility to Pleasure	Abstemiousness	Inordinate Passion
Cowardice	Courage	Recklessness
Miserliness	Generosity	Extravagance
Self-abasement	Humility	Arrogance

The idea here is that too much and too little are equally bad traits. Being over-courageous when unnecessary, or giving away all your money to charity, is just as bad as being a coward or a miser. The one who gave away their money will now have to look for ways to feed their family and become needy. The reckless one is endangering his or her life for nothing. The mean is considered the optimal way of behaving. Maimonides realizes that often there are social norms which bring us to deviate from this type of thinking.

> It often happens however that men err as regards these qualities imagining that one of the extremes is good and is a virtue. Sometimes the extreme of the too much is considered noble as when temerity is made a virtue and those who recklessly risk their lives are hailed as heroes. Thus when people see a man reckless to the highest degree, who runs deliberately into danger intentionally tempting death, and escaping only by mere chance, they laud such to the skies and say that he is a hero.[4]

Society has a tendency to laud those who take great risks. If someone gets into a barrel and throws themselves over Niagara Falls, coming out alive by chance, we laud them as brave heroes. When we see major car races with drivers zooming at high speeds and every now and then one of them gets killed in an accident, we see them as heroes; when we pay money to watch boxing matches where two grown man cause each other brain damage by trying to knock each other out, we are giving out a message. Young people pick up on it. Kids love to feel the rush of living on the edge. They can play street roulette, where they stand in the middle of a highway attempting to evade oncoming cars, or playing chicken by tossing a knife at the other guy's feet, or, as was done in Mexico, standing on top of trains and ducking when meeting an oncoming tunnel. They see this as brave, since the adults are willing to pay money to see it on TV. So what is the difference between courage and recklessness? Why, when a soldier goes into a mine field to save a friend, risking his life, do we call this courage, and when another person goes into the same minefield after the war just to prove that he isn't chicken, we call this recklessness? Maimonides answers: What makes the former courage and the latter stupidity is the weight of the moral issue involved. One can only risk a life to save a life. No one can send someone into a minefield even to save a life. However, if someone decided of their own volition to do so there was moral logic here. They are taking a risk on one life in order to save another. However, the one going through the minefield just to show he isn't scared is simply acting stupid in order to impress his friends (or to commit suicide). The reason for the risk has to be as weighty as what is being jeopardized. The same can be said about extravagance. If someone gives away all of his money we tend to think of him as saintly, but what about their family members who will now suffer? The Mishnah says that one should not give more than one-fifth of one's money to charity or one might become needy as well.

> At other times, the opposite extreme, the too little is greatly esteemed, and the coward is considered a man of forbearance, the idler as being a person of a contented disposition, and he who by dull senses of his nature is callous to every joy is praised as a man of moderation.[5]

Society has a way of wrongly praising the misguided. Not everyone who seems disinterested in making money is "satisfied with their lot"; sometimes it is an excuse for laziness. It's easy for a young man to say he keeps away from woman for religious reasons when he knows that the ladies are not interested in him. It's only a challenge when they are. The bottom line is that balanced actions are preferred actions and need to be guided by reason.

IMPLANTING VIRTUE
AND CORRECTING A BAD TRAIT

Maimonides goes on to explain how one can instill the concept of the middle way in children:

> Know moreover, that these moral excellences or defects cannot be acquired or implanted in the soul except by means of the frequent repetition of acts resulting from these qualities, which practiced during a long period of time, accustoms us to them. If these acts performed are good ones then we have gained virtue; but if they are bad, we shall have acquired a vice.[6]

Children are born a tabula rasa. They acquire character traits through education; through assimilating new ideas and actions into their world view. Maimonides takes a sort of behaviorist approach to character education, saying that through the repetition of the middle way one can teach a balanced life. If, for example, we want to teach children liberality with money we can give them three dimes in class and teach them to use one to buy milk and cookies, one to put into the class bank and one for the charity box. This would teach liberality, saving and cautious consumerism. However, since we often follow the wrong role models, whether among our family, friends or social icons, we need to know how to mend a wrong character trait.

> Since no man is born with an innate virtue or vice…and as everyone's conduct from childhood up is undoubtedly influenced by the manner of living of his relatives and countrymen, his conduct may be in accord with the rules of moderation; but then again, it is possible that his acts may incline toward either extreme, as we have demonstrated, in which case, his soul becomes diseased. In such a contingency, it is proper for him to resort to a cure exactly as he would were his body suffering from an illness. So just as when the equilibrium of the physical health is disturbed and we note which way it is tending in order to force it to go in exactly the opposite direction until it shall return to its proper condition, and just as when the proper adjustment is reached we cease this operation and have recourse to that which will maintain the proper balance, in exactly the same way must we adjust the moral equilibrium.[7]

Maimonides, the physician, gives an example from the medical practice of his day. Just as one who caught cold outside in the winter needs to be inside and near the fire and only after he has warmed up a bit to be drawn away, so too if one is a miser with great avarice, depriving him- or herself of every comfort of life, if we wish to cure this person we need to induce them to squander often enough to break out of his old habit, but before they actually fall into the trait of squandering, to bring them back to the middle point and have them practice this balance from now on.[8] So too, the squanderer is taught actions of miserliness, the coward — recklessness, the arrogant — self abasement, etc.

However the question that arises here is: How does this work in a practical sense? How realistic is it to ask a coward to go bungee jumping off the San Francisco Bay Bridge or the miser to donate a million dollars towards the research of children's diseases? Therefore, I think we have to understand this idea of moral therapy in a subjective way. One can heal the coward by asking him to take steps that in his mind are reckless, like getting up in front of 500 people to ask a question at a public lecture, or doing things they consider reckless which are within their range or just slightly beyond it. The miser as well needs to be helped in stages.

An additional point to mention is that just as in the Maimonidean concept of penitence (*teshuvah*), one needs to recognize that one sinned before being able to repent, so too, only if one sees him- or herself as a miser will a person think to try to fix the problem. The miser thinks himself cautious with money, the coward, cautious with security, the reckless — brave, the indulgent — moderate, etc. Consider the miser-minded parent: buying games for their kids that they keep high up on the top shelf so that they should not be damaged (or used too often); a game they buy only if the kid had a birthday, so it needs to last for the year; this personality type sees itself as cautious more than stingy. People who experienced verbal aggression in the home as children often grow up in a like manner, developing callousness to the problem. "What does it matter if I called him names, or shouted in his face, I didn't hit him, did I?" It is the need for self-realization of the problem that is a prerequisite for this type of personal therapy.

MAIMONIDES' GOLDEN MEAN UNDER CAREFUL SCRUTINY

Until now we have understood from Maimonides that the mean is the optimal form of behavior. I will now proceed to demonstrate the problems with this understanding. The first problem arises with Maimonides' claim that there is one side of the equation which is easier to fix. Further explaining how to mend a bad attribute, Maimonides writes:

> If on the other hand a man is a squanderer, he must be directed to practice strict economy and to repeat acts of niggardliness. It is not necessary however for him to perform acts of avarice as many times as the mean man should those of profusion. This subtle point, which is a canon and secret of the science of medicine, tells us that it is easier for a man of profuse habits to moderate them to generosity, than it is for a miser to become generous. Likewise it is easier for one who is apathetic (who eschews sin) to be excited to moderate enjoyment, than it is for one burning with passion to curb his desires.[9]

This of course seems problematic. Why is one side easier to fix than the other? What is the rule of thumb here? One cannot say that it is necessarily the deficient or the over-abundant side since it changes according to the issue. Recklessness is easier to fix and it is an over-abundance of courage; however self-abasement is easier to fix and is a deficiency of humility. What then is the rule? The second question is: is this side which is easier to fix a better character trait to have than the other extreme? If the answer is in the affirmative, then how can we explain Maimonides' opening remarks that the mean is the optimal course of action and the extremes are equally bad? At this point the second question seems easy to answer. Obviously both extremes are equally negative. However, technically speaking, there is one extreme which is easier to mend. What is the rule? It is the side that includes the middle attribute that is easier to fix. A reckless person has too much courage, whereas the coward has none. The extravagant person is too generous whereas the miser is not at all. Self-abasement is too much humility whereas arrogance is the opposite. This seems like a plausible explanation, but now we will see that this explanation is not water-tight. Maimonides continues to explain the golden mean and adds:

On this account the saintly ones were not accustomed to cause their dispositions to maintain an exact balance between the two extremes, but deviated somewhat, by way of (caution and) restraint, now to the side of exaggeration, now to the side of deficiency. Thus for example, abstinence would incline to some degree toward excessive denial of all pleasures; valor would approach somewhat toward temerity, generosity to lavishness, modesty to humility and so forth. This is what the Rabbis hinted at in their saying, "Do more that the strict letter of the law demands" (Bava Metzia 35a).

Why does Maimonides bring this addition? Who are the "saintly ones" (hassidim)? Maimonides explains that the saints purposely deviate a bit from the mean towards the side which is easier to fix. We are supposed to understand by this that they do this in order to avoid falling into the extremity which is harder to fix. This appears again to be a technical decision, but it is quite puzzling. If the mean is the optimum, why would the saintly ones not want to do the maximum possible? Doesn't saintly (hassid) refer to a person who does more than the letter of the law? Why then in this case is "more" achieved by doing less? Secondly, it would seem that the saintly ones are the last people we have to worry about. They are very cautious about their actions. It should be the average person who we should tell to go a bit towards the extremity which is easier to fix if we are worried about one falling into bad traits. Therefore, the statement about the saintly ones seems to contradict the theory of the golden mean.

To answer this we could propose that the mean is not a small road but rather a major highway in which a slight deviation right or left is still on the mean course. This is what we would have to explain according to the simple understanding of the text. However, there might be a whole other story going on here.

THE PROBLEM OF THE *HASSID* AND THE GOLDEN MEAN THEORY

In biblical writings there seem to be four levels of saintliness:

Yashar
Zadik
Hassid
Kadosh

Yashar—refers to one who is innately good. The patriarchs were referred to by our sages (*Hazal*) as *yesharim* or righteous. The book of Genesis is called Sefer Hayashar (The Book of the Righteous) since it speaks of the patriarchs, and when Balaam said: "may I die the death of righteousness (*yesharim*)" (Num. 23:10) the rabbis saw it as referring to the patriarchs. About the patriarchs the Mishnah says: "Morality (*derekh eretz*) came before the giving of the Torah." The *yashar,* then, is one who is innately moral even without receiving instruction.

Zaddik—refers to one who knows the law and follows it. In the Bible, a *zaddik* refers to one who is innocent in a court of law, whereas a *rasha* (evil doer) is one who is found guilty. The verse says: And they shall justify the righteous one (*zaddik)* and condemn the evil one (*rasha)*" (Deut. 25:1). The zaddik is one who does the letter of the law and therefore will be found innocent in a court of law.

Hassid—refers to one who does more than required. The root is the word *hessed,* or loving-kindness. The *zaddik* keeps the law out of fear of punishment but the *hassid* out of love.

Kadosh—holy, or removed. This refers to a certain level of ascetic lifestyle where one removes oneself from the physical comforts and pleasures of this world. (This is a level, we will see, that Maimonides has a difficulty with conceptually.) These four levels are mentioned in the Sabbath morning prayer service.

Getting back to Maimonides, the *hassid* who acts out of love wants to do more, so he or she moves slightly to one of the extremities, in order not to fall into the side which is harder to fix. Why? How can one do more than the maximum? Is it possible that the *hassid* does not need the theory of the golden mean? Secondly, why is Maimonides telling us this? Concerning the second question, it is possible that Maimonides is pre-empting our questions. Upon reading his theory of moderation, the average reader probably asks himself how it is that Maimonides talks of moderation and the mean, when there are so many righteous individuals who practice an ascetic lifestyle; staying up all night learning, fasting on Mondays and Thursdays, depriving themselves of comforts, living like monks and hermits, etc. Maimonides wants us therefore to know that these things exist and that they are positive only as temporary measures. This he spells out clearly.

> When at times, some of the pious ones deviated to one extreme by fasting, keeping nightly vigils, refraining from eating meat or drinking wine, renouncing sexual intercourse, clothing themselves in woolen and hairy garments, dwelling in the mountains and wandering about in the wilderness, they did so partly as a means of restoring the health of their souls, as we have explained above, and partly because of the immorality of the townspeople...when the ignorant observed saintly men acting thus, not knowing their motives, they considered their deeds virtuous in and of themselves, and so blindly imitating their acts, thinking thereby to become like them, they chastised their bodies with all kinds of afflictions, imagining that they had acquired perfection and moral worth, and that by this means man would approach nearer to God, as if He hated the human body and desired its destruction.[10]

Maimonides is known as one who teaches moderation in general. It's of interest that he takes the golden mean theory of attributes and uses it as a springboard to preach moderation in general. This is Maimonides' belief and this approach has dominated Jewish thinking ever since, even if not exclusively. Actually, ascetic groups always existed within the Jewish fold. In days of old there existed Nazirites and ascetics, and even in the modern era, the Mussar movement of nineteenth-century Eastern Europe praised self-abasement and an ascetic lifestyle. Is Judaism then a moderate religion, as Maimonides teaches, or one that praises self denial?

The answer to these questions is twofold. Concerning moderation as a Jewish expression one can say as follows: yes, Judaism is a religion that despite limiting consumption of certain animals, and having regulations concerning marriage and relationships, is a religion that believes in moderation as well as control. As Maimonides writes:

> The perfect Law which leads us to perfection — as one who knew it well testifies by the words, "the law of the Lord is perfect restoring the soul; the testimonies of the Lord are faithful making wise the simple" (Ps. 19:9) — recommends none of these things (such as self torture, flight from society, etc.). On the contrary, it aims at man's following the path of moderation in accordance with the dictates of nature, eating, drinking, enjoying legitimate sexual intercourse, all in moderation, and living among people in honesty and uprightness, but not dwelling in the wilderness or in the mountains or clothing oneself in garments of hair and wool, or afflicting the soul. The law even warns us against these practices if we interpret it according to what the tradition tells us the meaning of the passage concerning the Nazirite, "and he (the priest) shall make an atonement for him because he has sinned against his soul" (Num. 6:11). The Rabbis asks, "Against what soul has he sinned? Against his own because he has deprived himself of wine...If one who deprives himself of wine must bring an atonement, how much more incumbent is it upon one who denies himself every enjoyment (Nazir 19a).[11]

However the question here is not just a general one. The question is how one relates to those unique individuals who, without preaching to the general populace, prefer a restrictive and ascetic lifestyle in order to reach holiness. Maimonides is against any form of asceticism even for individuals. He even has his own explanation as to why these individuals are practicing what they do. This of course seems ironic. After all, if one were to ask these ascetics if their practices are just temporary measures to cure themselves of vices they would probably answer either in the negative or claim that all of life is temporary. However, in order to sell his theory of the golden mean to the general reader, Maimonides must have an explanation for these individuals as well, forcibly molding them into the golden mean theory. He does the same to the biblical discussion of the Nazirite, viewing it as a paradigm for all asceticism and deeming it negative. It is of interest that the Talmud as well sees the Nazirite as a paradigm for the ascetic lifestyle; however the Talmud brings two opinions. One, which Maimonides quotes, that deems the Nazirite unacceptable for having depriving himself of something that the Torah allows, and one that sees the Nazirite as holy and positive. These two trends of thinking reflect the issue of asceticism for the populace versus the individual. What is wrong as a general rule is not, without exception, for individuals. Ascetics existed all along Jewish history, but Maimonides in portraying the golden mean is interested in the masses and not the individuals and therefore needs to give them a neat explanation for those whose lives seem to be exceptions to the rule.

THE HIDDEN RULE OF THE GOLDEN MEAN

Having said this we can now go back and again try to understand the answer to our first question above. How can the *hassid* do more than the letter of the law? How can one deviate from the mean even a little and still do the maximum? In order to answer this we need to understand the basis of the golden mean. Let us examine again the above diagram 2a. When Maimonides states that generosity is the mean, who decides this? Who decides that humility and courage and caution are the middle? Let us again look at the diagram and consider changing the description of the mean.

Diagram 2b:
The Golden Mean with Alternatives

Extreme (too little)	Mean	Extreme (too much)
Insensibility to Pleasure	Abstemiousness (Moderation)	Inordinate Passion
Cowardice	(Prudence) Courage	Recklessness
Miserliness	(Caution) Generosity	Extravagance
Self-abasement	Humility (Self-Respect	Arrogance

The above proposal of an alternative mean offers one which is closer to the opposite extreme than that proposed by Maimonides. Assuming the middle is wide, which Maimonides does, we can then ask why he proposed abstemious behaviour and not moderation, which is closer to inordinate passion. Why did he propose courage rather than prudence?

Why humility and not self respect? The answer would appear to be that even though technically both options can be theoretically considered the middle, only one option is the moral preference. It is preferred since it tends to be more altruistic and better for society at large. Prudence is okay but courage is more altruistic. Caution is fine but generosity is more altruistic, etc. This being stated, we have now discovered the secret of the golden mean. The middle is chosen not by its being in the middle alone, but rather by understanding which point of the middle is morally preferable. If this is so, then we can now explain the *hassid*. The *hassid* who understands the concept of the mean does not really need the theory at all. He therefore can deviate slightly according to his understanding. It is the general public who needs the golden mean as a rule of guidance.

Understanding the Afterlife and Messianism: A Rationalist Approach

Even though Messianism deals with this world and the afterlife with the World to Come, the Greek term used to denote all such issues was "eschatology." The term eschatology assumes an *eschaton*, or an end of days. For Maimonides, however, as for many Jewish thinkers, this concept does not exist. Even if the apocryphal book of Jubilees seems to refer to a destructive end of the world,[1] no such concept was adopted by Jewish philosophers. Maimonides went as far as claiming that the world will have no end.[2] The term closest to the "end of days" in the Bible is from Isaiah: "And it shall come to pass in the last days [*aharit hayamim*] that the mountain of the Lord's house shall be firmly established on the top of the mountains, and shall be exalted above the hills and unto it shall flow all the nations"(Isa. 2:2). For this famous passage I used a regular translation which I will now proceed to demonstrate as faulty. The term *"aharit"* does not mean the end or the last, but rather is from the root *ahar*. This can be clearly seen from Genesis: "And he put the handmaids and their children foremost, and Leah and her children after (*aharonim*), and Rachel and Joseph hindermost (*aharonim*)" (Gen. 33:2). Here we see clearly that the term *aharon* means something that comes later. Therefore, it is clear that *aharit hayamim* in Isaiah 2, in reference to the messianic period, refers to a future time period and not to an "end of days."

We have to distinguish here between two concepts: Messianism or redemption, which is a concept dealing with the collective in this world, and the afterlife or the eternity of the soul, which refers to the individual reward and punishment. Let us begin with the individual. In Maimonides' writings, the idea of the eternity of the soul and the reward in the World to Come is the goal of the individual.

DOES BIBLICAL JUDAISM BELIEVE IN AN AFTERLIFE?

Before we enter the discussion of the afterlife, we need to ask a few questions. First, does Judaism actually believe in an afterlife? After all, the twenty-four books of the Bible seem to give no indication of such a concept. It might not even be clear if the Bible believes in the resurrection of the dead in this world. After all, the prophecy of the valley of the dry bones in Ezekiel 37 can be understood as a metaphor regarding the ingathering of the exiles. Immanuel Kant, the eighteenth-century German philosopher who was friendly with Moses Mendelssohn, though somewhat his younger, could not understand Judaism, since after reading the Old Testament he assumed that it had no concept of the afterlife. There are places in biblical scripture which allude to an afterlife idea, but this is never stated clearly. R. Joseph Albo in his book of *Ikkarim* mentions some of these hints. The first regards the idea of the resurrection of the dead.

In Deuteronomy the Torah says:

"See now that I, I am He, and there is no God with Me;
I alone **put to death** and **bring to life**;
I **wound** and I **heal** and there is none that deliver from my hand."
(Deut. 32:49).

In this verse we have a parallel structure, of a sort often found in biblical texts. "Put to death" and "bring to life" are compared to "wound" and "heal." Just as healing comes after wounding, so does bringing to life follow being put to death. A similar but even clearer hint to the resurrection of the dead can be found in the book of Samuel. Hannah says in her prayer, "God putteth to death and bringeth to life; He bringeth low and also lifteth up" (I Sam. 2:6). The parallel here is similar to the one in Deuteronomy. Just as bringing low is before lifting up, so is putting to death followed by making alive. However, the term in Hebrew for bringing low is "brings to *sheol*," which in biblical text often refers to the grave. Therefore, the "lifteth up" becomes that much more significant.

The Book of Daniel has the strongest statement concerning the resurrection of the dead, saying: "And many of those sleeping in the dirt of the ground will awaken, some to eternal life and some to eternal suffering" (Dan. 12).

The idea of the afterlife has fewer biblical references. The clearest one is from the book of Ecclesiastes: "And who knows the spirit of man arising upwards and the spirit of the animal descending downwards" (Eccl. 3:21); and again "For the body shall return to the dust from where it came and the spirit shall return to the Lord who gave it" (Eccl. 12:7). Another hint to the afterlife is the statement by Abigail to King David: "And may the soul of my master be bound up in eternal life with his God and let the souls of his enemies be cast away by the slingshot" (I Sam. 25:29). Both Maimonides and Nachmanides claim that the biblical term *Karet* (To be cut off, E.g. Lev. 23:29), used to describe a form of punishment, refers to a soul that does not merit the afterlife. If this is correct then there is no doubt that the Bible refers to the afterlife. Nachmanides adds that the Bible does not need to discuss such concepts, since for the Israelites, living in an environment with prophets and immanent Divine presence, the spiritual realm was a given that did not need any proof. Rabbi A. I. Kook writes that the Bible purposely left out any direct discussion of the afterlife since this type of talk robs human deeds of their moral significance. If I tell someone that the reason they are doing a *mitzvah* or keeping away from a transgression is in order to receive a reward in the World to Come, that means that the deed has become a means to an end and not an end in itself. If morality is not an end in itself, it loses its meaning. It becomes a mere tool to get the prize, as it may be, the place in the World to Come, and not an end in itself. Therefore the sages said

"The reward for a good deed in the good deed itself," and "Do not be as those servants who serve the master in order to receive reward" (Ethics of the Father chapter 1).

THE AFTERLIFE IN THE WRITINGS OF MAIMONIDES

Maimonides opens his discussion on eschatology claiming that many faulty views can be found in this area and the confusion seems to be greater than the clarity. The confusion is understandable, since there are differences of opinion even among scholars concerning how to understand the rabbinic writings concerning the end of days and the afterlife.

> I must now speak of the great fundamental principles of our faith. Know that the masters of Torah hold differing opinions concerning the good which will come to a person as a result of fulfilling the commandments which God has commanded us through Moses, our teacher. As a consequence of their different understanding of the problem, they also held widely different opinions concerning the evil which the transgressor suffers. So much confusion has invaded their opinions that it is impossible to find anyone whose opinion is uncontaminated by error.[3]

The confusion has created various groups of people in their understanding of what the afterlife holds. Maimonides lists five groups and their different understanding of the concepts Garden of Eden, Gehinom, the messianic era, and the resurrection of the dead. As a general rule, when Maimonides states various opinions without siding with any particular opinion it means he disagrees with all of them. For Maimonides, the main concept is the idea of the World to Come, which he will explain later in his treatise.

Before elaborating on the concepts of the afterlife and the end of days, Maimonides offers us three cautious introductions. The first, similar to what we brought above from Rabbi Kook, is the educational problem with talking too much about a spiritual eternal reward for human moral deeds. After all, if one is to do the good deed just for the sake of reward, this dwarfs the value of ethical conduct.

> I would like to share an analogy…Let us assume that a young child were brought to an educator with the intent that he teach the

child knowledge. This is the ultimate good and will lead the child to perfect his [character]. Nevertheless, because he is young and immature, he will not appreciate that this is good, nor will he see how it will bring him to perfection. Therefore it is necessary for the educator, who is himself a more developed personality, to encourage the child by offering something he will appreciate according to his childish conceptions of things. And so the educator will tell him: study and I will give you nuts, figs or a piece of sugar. This promise will make the child study and try. It is not that he is interested in the study itself—he does not comprehend the value of that at all. He wants to gain the food [he has been promised]. Eating that food is more important for him than the study and undoubtedly more satisfying...When he grows older and develops his mind, he will view lightly the things he previously thought were important and instead will consider other things to be valuable. Then...his teacher will tell him: Study and I will buy you attractive shoes or clothes that look like this. Then also he will not be studying for the sake of study, but instead to receive the promised garment. When his mind becomes more developed, and he understands enough to regard these things as negligible, he will be encouraged to study [by promises of] things that are more valuable. His teacher will tell him: study this passage or this chapter and I will give you a dinar or two dinarim. Even at that stage, he will regard obtaining the money as more important than the study itself....And when he reaches a deeper level of understanding, and knows to appreciate even this matter [money] as having little importance, he will be encouraged by something that is of even greater eminence. He will be told: Study so that you will become a Rabbi or a judge and others will honour you. They will stand before you, endeavour to uphold your words, and enhance your reputation, both in your lifetime and afterwards, like so and so. And so he will study to reach this position; the ultimate goal in his mind will be that other people will honour him, elevate him and praise him. All this is shameful.[4]

Just as it is improper for one to study wisdom for the sake of any other goal aside from attaining wisdom itself, so too it is improper for one to do the commandments in anticipation of the ultimate reward. This empties the *mitzvah* of any value by rendering it a means to an end. We excuse children who do not understand the value of education and try to entice them to learn, but it would be strange to have to do the same with an adult. If you cannot see the value in learning, then maybe you should pursue a different field. In the study of Torah, we actually say that "what starts off not for its own sake may end up for its own sake" which could be an argument in the realm of the *mitzvot* as well. However, the goal is to do it for its own sake.

There is a rabbinic statement that says: "If a man says: this selah (amount of money) is for charity on condition that my children live [a long life] or on condition that I merit the World to Come: He is (considered) a perfect Saint." Wouldn't this contradict what we just said above concerning the importance of doing something for its own worth and not for an ulterior motive? The answer is simple: the money he already gave to charity and the condition is something he cannot guarantee; therefore what he did was on an act of faith and is meritorious. This reminds me of a children's story about the comic, mythical people of Chelm. Once Yankel was in the office of the Rabbi of Chelm and saw his name on the list of the town's fools. "Rabbi, why am I on the list?" The Rabbi answered: "Remember the stranger who came to town and asked you for a loan of 500 rubles?" "Yes," retorted Yankel. "He said he would pay me back upon returning next summer." "That's why I put you on the list of the town fools," replied the Rabbi. "Well," said Yankel. "What would you say if he came back and repaid the loan to me?" "No problem," answered the Rabbi. "Then I would remove your name from the list and put his instead."

Maimonides then offers a second introduction in which he discusses the role of the aggadic and midrashic literature in the Talmud. He takes great care to explain that if one sees a rabbinic explanation that appears to run contrary to logic, it should be understood as an allegory. The Rabbis used allegories and metaphors in explaining metaphysical matter. That was their literary technique.

Maimonides' third introduction to his discussion of the afterlife concerns the difficulty in discussing an afterlife or any spiritual reward. As human beings living in a material world, we cannot fathom anything which does not have physical dimensions.

Know that just as a blind man cannot image color, as the deaf person cannot experience sounds, and as the eunuch cannot feel sexual desire, so bodies cannot attain spiritual delights. Like fish who do not know what the element of fire is, because they live in its opposite, the element of water, so are the delights of the spiritual world unknown in this material world. Spiritual delight does not come in to our experience at all. We enjoy only bodily pleasures which come to us through our physical senses, such as the pleasures of eating, drinking and sexual intercourse. We neither recognize them nor grasp them at first thought. They come only after great searching.[5]

Here we have an example of Maimonides' pedagogical stategy, as I have discussed elsewhere. Maimonides tends to make an unequivocal statement and then retreat slightly from his position. He first states that mankind cannot understand spiritual delights in any sense, like a blind person who has no sense of color. He says that spiritual delight does not come into our experience at all. Then he proceeds to add that, "We neither recognize them nor grasp them at first thought. They come only after great searching," meaning that they can be understood to a certain extent through intellectual searching. This is the Maimonidian style. He makes a point by making a black and white statement concerning a complicated issue and then proceeds to retreat to a lesser position after making his point. The idea is to stress the difficulty in really understanding what we mean by spiritual delight. No matter how much we speak of spiritual pleasures, we really do not understand what we are saying. After we have admitted this, we can then proceed to try to fathom such an idea.

"It could hardly be otherwise, since we live in a material world and are therefore able to achieve only inferior and discontinuous delights."[6] Maimonides states that by definition the delights of this world must be inferior since they are discontinuous, whereas the pleasures of the spiritual can be continuous. This is an intellectual definition but still does not teach us what these delights are.

Those men who choose to purify themselves will reach this spiritual height. They will neither experience bodily pleasures nor will they want them. They will resemble a powerful king. He would hardly want to go back to playing ball with children as he did before he was a king. Such games attracted him when he was a child and was unable to understand the real difference between playing ball and royal power. Like children, we now praise and glorify the delights of the body and do not understand the delights of the soul.[7]

Here Maimonides claims that when the time comes that we understand what spiritual pleasures are, we will lose all interest in physical ones. Just as a king who in his childhood loved to play ball but as he grew up learned to love the power and sophistication of diplomacy more, so too when one experiences the delights of the spirit, the delights of the body seem trivial in comparison.

Until now, the analogies have been intellectual. Now, however, Maimonides retreats again from his opening statement and claims that even from human experience one can partially understand the meaning of non-physical delights, for one can see examples of non-physical pleasures, whether positive or negative, in day to day life, such as: fame, a good name, and vengeance, which many are willing to forfeit all physical pleasures to attain. This is another example of Maimonides' educational method. First he states the position he wants us to think about, and then he recedes slightly from his clear-cut position into a more complex one.

> If you consider carefully the nature of these two kinds of delight, you will perceive the inferiority of the first and the superiority of the second even in this world. Thus, you find that most men will exert extraordinary amounts of intellectual and physical energy laboring at ordinary tasks in order to acquire honor or be exalted by their fellowmen. The pleasure which honor brings is not of the same sort as the pleasure derived from eating and drinking. Similarly, many men pursue vengeance over their enemies more intensely than they pursue any bodily pleasures. Many others deny themselves the keenest of bodily delights because they fear shame and public disgrace or because they seek to acquire a reputation of virtue. If this is the case even in this material world, how much more must it be so in the spiritual world. That world is the World to Come.[8]

There are non-physical pleasures in this world which people desire more than physical ones. These can be positive or negative. Some desire vengeance and are willing to forgo all pleasures and comforts to achieve this goal, others seek fame and a good reputation. The politician, while running for office, will forgo good meals, sleep and comfort, in order to obtain that office or fame or position of power. The examples here are just to demonstrate that there are non-physical delights which people will forgo the physical ones in order to attain. This analogy can be helpful in understanding how one could lose interest in the physical delights of this world upon experiencing the spiritual delights of the next.

THE AFTERLIFE: A MODERN VIEW

How can modern man understand the idea of an afterlife? Can one describe something never attained by a live human? Why talk about this type of subject at all? In the end we all will go down that road, so can't we just wait and see? The issue at hand is really how the concept of the afterlife influences how I live life. The view that sees material life as the beginning and end of all human life tends to be a view of life and man which in its extreme form can preach egotism, narcissism, or nihilism and in its milder forms makes people wonder why they should be moral if they're not hurting anyone. An afterlife is supposed to teach us about the spiritual side of man and the moral development of the soul. If it fails to do so it seems redundant. As Maimonides argued above; if the idea of doing a good deed is just to merit a portion in the World to Come, did I really see it as a good deed?

But how can one prove the existence of anything that cannot be measured or described? Recently, there has been ample research on near-death experiences (NDE). This research, which started with the work of Raymond Moody and Elisabeth Kubler Ross in the 1970's and now fills internet sites with detailed cases, has aroused interest and definitely affected the popular view of things. Moody summarizes his own findings from his famous book *Life After Life* in a sequel, *Reflections on Life After Life*:

A man is dying and, as he reaches the point of greatest physical distress, he hears himself pronounced dead by his doctor. He begins to hear uncomfortable noise, a loud ringing or buzzing, and at the same time feels himself moving very rapidly through a long tunnel. After this, he suddenly finds himself out of his own physical body, but still in the immediate physical environment, and he sees his own body from a distance, as though he is a spectator. He watches the resuscitation attempt from this unusual vantage point and is in a state of emotional upheaval. After a while he collects himself and becomes more accustomed to his odd condition. He notices that he still has a body, but one of a very different nature and with very different powers from the physical body he left behind. Soon other things begin to happen. Others come to meet and help him. He glimpses the spirits of relatives and friends who have already died, and a loving, warm spirit of a kind he has never encountered before—a being of light—appears before him. This being asks him questions, non-verbally, to make him evaluate his life and helps him along by showing him a panoramic, instantaneous playback of his life. At some point he finds himself approaching some sort of barrier or border, apparently representing the limit between earthly life and the next life. Yet, he finds that he must go back to the earth, that the time for his death has not yet come. At this point he resists, for by now he is taken up with the experiences in the afterlife and does not want to return. He is overwhelmed by intense feelings of joy, love and peace. Despite his attitude, though, he somehow reunites with his physical body and lives. Later he tries to tell others but has trouble doing so. In the first place he finds no human words adequate to describe these unearthly episodes. He also finds that other scoff, so he stops telling other people. Still the experience affects his life profoundly, especially his views about death and its relationship to life."[9]

Some of the most fascinating examples of such tales are those near-death experiences (NDE) in which the person describes events seen from their out-of-body vantage point.

A woman recalls: About a year ago I was admitted to the hospital with heart trouble, and the next morning, lying in the hospital bed, I began to have a very severe pain in my chest...I was quite uncomfortable lying on my back so I turned over and as I did I quit breathing and my heart stopped beating. Just then I heard the nurses shout, "Code pink! Code pink!" As they were saying this, I could feel myself moving out of my body and sliding down between the mattress and rail on the side of the bed—actually it seemed as if I went through the rail on to the floor. Then I started rising upward, slowly. On my way up, I saw more nurses running into the room—there must have been a dozen of them. My doctor happened to be making his rounds in the hospital so they called him and I saw him come in, too. I thought, "I wonder what he's doing here." I drifted up past the light fixture—I saw it from the side and very distinctly—and then I stopped, floating right below the ceiling, looking down....I watched them reviving me from up there! My body was lying down there stretched out on the bed, in plain view, and they were all standing around it. I heard one nurse say, "Oh, my God! She's gone!" while another one leaned down to give me mouth to mouth resuscitation. I was looking at the back of her head while she did this....Just then I saw them roll this machine in there, and they put the shocks on my chest. When they did, I saw my whole body just jump right up off the bed, and I heard every bone in my body crack and pop. As I saw them below beating on my chest and rubbing my arms and legs I thought, "Why are they going to so much trouble? I'm just fine now."[10]

The Indian-American spiritualist, Deepak Chopra, in a chapter comparing near-death experiences with Indian delogs, writes:

In a 1991 Gallup pole, 13 million Americans, roughly 5% of the population, reported that they had such an experience. Near death is a momentary brush with another reality, or so it seems to those who report the experience…Dr. [Pim] Van Lommel who conducted the Dutch study of near-death experiences…screened 344 patients whose hearts had defibrillated in the hospital. Talking to them within days of being revived, van Lommel discovered that anesthesia or medications didn't affect their experiences. What he marvels at the most, however, are those reports of consciousness in the absence of brain activity…They can think extremely clearly, have memories going back to their earliest childhoods and experience an intense connection with everything and everyone around them. And yet the brain shows no activity at all.[11]

However, the counter-argument is that these people never actually died. They only experienced near-death encounters. The rebuttal to the materialists by the NDE enthusiasts is that many of the people studied described events that they could have seen only from an out of body vantage point or described things that occurred while their eyes were closed as well as at times when no brain activity was in evidence. The controversy will continue, however, only among the living. Another interesting study was done by the psychologist Cherie Sutherland, attempting to understand how these NDE affect those who experience them and transform their lives. Sutherland summarizes the NDE experiences as having certain similarities: feelings of peace and well being, entering the darkness and seeing the light, the life review, spiritual contact with a voice or a light, and entering the light. These experiences have a profound affect on the people experiencing them. Moody wrote: "Many [NDErs] have told me that they felt their lives were broadened and deepened by their experience, that because of it they became more reflective and more concerned with the ultimate philosophical issues."[12] Sutherland adds:

"To family and friends, some near death experiencers appear to be changed from the very moment of their 'return.' However it may take many years for the transformation to become fully manifest....Such profound personality changes have been noted by other researchers and authors. Noyes reports that twenty percent of the sample people who survived an encounter with life threatening danger...spoke of their lives taking on a sense of mission. Raft and Anderson comment on the changed motivations of their subjects, and Moody remarks on the way they feel more in control and responsible for their lives. Inherent gifts and talents that have lain dormant are often awakened in near-death experiencers, and inner potentials actualized to an astonishing degree. Changes in self-concept are marked according to Ring. Other researchers have commented on the near death experiencer's acceptance of themselves. Their growth in self confidence enhanced self esteem and drive to self understanding. They are said to have become less judgmental and less self righteous, less prejudiced and less in need of other's approval or social success."[13]

In her summary Sutherland writes:

The entire sample of fifty near-death experiencers said they no longer had any fear of death...many changes were also reported by this sample of experiencers in terms of religious beliefs, attitudes and practices. They overwhelmingly considered their experiences to be spiritual rather than religious in nature...there appeared to be a general feeling among this group that during their NDE they had a direct contact with God, or a higher power.[14]

There are actually interesting parallels in rabbinic and Zoharic literature to the aspects described by those who went through NDE's. In the wake of the beginnings of the research on NDE's, Rabbi C. D. Halevi, the former Chief Rabbi of Tel Aviv, looked for parallels in Jewish literature. He brings parallels for the meeting with the souls of relatives after death, and other elements described in NDE's.[15] However, what I find of particular interest is his understanding of the being of light who greets the dying person after they feel themselves drawn through a long and dark tunnel. Drawing on a source from the Zohar I, 57), "When the soul leaves this world, it enters the cave of Makhpela [where Abraham buried Sarah (Gen. 23:20) and according to our tradition where Adam and Eve were buried as well], which is the opening of Eden, and meets Adam and the forefathers. If they are happy they open doors for him and if not they send him away." (Zohar I, 81a). In addition it says, "No one leaves this world until they meet the first Man [Adam] and he [Adam] asks them why they departed from the world and what happened." (Zohar I, 57b). According to this interpretation, the light would not be God or an angel, but Adam, that first primordial Man whose offspring we all are, drawing the later generation of souls to their source for self-evaluation.

MAIMONIDES' UNDERSTANDING OF THE CONCEPTS RELATING TO THE AFTERLIFE AND MESSIANISM

There are various aspects of eschatology which can be found in biblical and rabbinic literature. They are: the World to Come (oral tradition); the messianic era (biblical and oral tradition); the day of judgment (biblical); wars leading up to the messianic era (biblical); the ingathering of the exiles (biblical); the messiah king (biblical); Divine reward and punishment after death (oral tradition); and the resurrection of the dead (biblical). Maimonides attempts to make sense of all these concepts by taking the biblical and rabbinic sources and explaining them in a rational way. Therefore I call this the rational approach to Jewish eschatology. Maimonides begins his discussion with the famous pair of concepts from rabbinic literature "The Garden of Eden and Gehinom," the symbols of Divine reward and punishment. However, he quickly surprises us by explaining these concepts in a most unconventional way:

> The Garden of Eden is a fertile place containing the choicest of the earth's resources, numerous rivers and fruit-bearing trees. God will disclose it to man someday. He will teach man the way to it and men will be happy there. It is possible that many exceedingly wonderful plants will be found there, plants which are far pleasanter and sweeter than those which we know now. None of this is impossible or improbable. On the contrary, paradise would be possible even if it were not written in the Torah. How much more sure then is it since the Torah specifically promises it.

Gehenna is the name for the pain and the punishment which will come upon the wicked. No specific description of this punishment is contained in the Talmud. One teacher says that the sun will come so close to the wicked that it will burn them...Others say that a strange heat will be produced in their bodies...[16]

This is a puzzling passage. In rabbinic literature, Gan (The Garden of) Eden refers to a heavenly paradise after death representing the ultimate Divine reward, and Gehinom, or hell, represents Divine punishment after death. Therefore we have a pair. Maimonides discusses them as a pair but they seem to have little in common: 1. Gan Eden he describes as a physical place on the globe which mankind may or may not discover and Gehinom he describes as a form of punishment for the wicked. To make things more complicated it appears that Gehinom must be punishment after death. For if one is to say that it's in this world we could then ask when does this occur? If on a certain date, then what about the evil people who lived before or after this date? Are they absolved of punishment? Therefore, the only way to understand this as a universal idea of Divine punishment is to assume that it is after the death of the individual. If that is the case, Maimonides is describing Gehinom as a concept of Divine retribution after death; Gan Eden, however, he is rendering void of any eschatological value since it is merely a nice vacation spot somewhere, which we should be able to find "even if it were not written in the Torah." What then is going on here? Why speak of a pair of terms which according to your explanation have no connection to each other? In Genesis chapter 2, Gan Eden is a physical place near the Euphrates and the Tigris rivers. Depending on how one understands the verses, (whether the rivers flow from Eden or into Eden) Eden would either be north of Iraq or in Bahrain. Is this the Eden that Maimonides is referring to or is it a metaphor for any beautiful place; say in the Caribbean islands under a nice palm tree facing a sandy beach? In any event, what eschatological meaning does this term have? The answer is: none. Maimonides has just dropped a philosophical bombshell right at the beginning of his discussion on the afterlife. He is aware that his audience lives in an Islamic culture in which the idea of Eden, based on Koranic reading, has been interpreted as a physical reward after this world. This idea Maimonides finds reprehensible. There is no body after death, therefore there can be no bodily pleasures after death. If Maimonides would assure the reader that Judaism has a concept of Eden which represents reward after death, right away the reader would assume the Islamic take on this concept. There is no point arguing that, "we have a different take on the same term." Instead, he decides to tell the reader that Gan Eden is a term devoid of any meaning in Judaism. Maimonides believes in a spiritual reward in the afterlife but he refers to this as the World to Come (*olam habah*) and not as Gan Eden.

Returning to the term Gehinom, there is no biblical mention of a hell. The term "sheol," mistakenly associated with the Greek "Hades," probably refers to the grave site. The rabbis referred to the punishment after life as Gehinom. This word is found in the book of Joshua as two words, "Gei Hinom," or "Gei Ben Hinom" (Josh. 15:8), meaning, the valley of Hinom. This valley, found just outside Jerusalem's Jaffa gate, is one of the two valleys surrounding Jerusalem. Jeremiah refers to this valley as the valley of the destruction (tofet) (Jer. 19:2-6), where children were offered to the pagan worship of molekh. This might be the root of the connotation Gehinom (or Gehenna) for hell, i.e., some sort of Divine punishment after life. Maimonides calls this: "the name for the pain and the punishment which will come upon the wicked." He then goes on to say that there are a few opinions concerning how this punishment happens. As I mentioned earlier, as a general rule, when Maimonides brings a few opinions without deciding between them, it means he disagrees with all of them. He disagrees since he understands the punishment of Gehinom as something devoid of physical dimensions.

The World to Come — For Maimonides the ultimate goal of this world is to achieve the World to Come, which is the reward of the afterlife. This is an individual goal which one achieves through good action. "The world to come is the ultimate end toward which all our effort ought to be devoted. Therefore, the sage who firmly grasped the knowledge of the truth and who envisioned the final end, forsaking everything else, taught: All Israel has a share in the world to come (Sanhedrin 10:1)."[17] This is an afterlife where the intellectual soul continues without the body. "This spiritual delight is not divisible into parts, nor can it be described, not can analogy explain it. It is as the prophet said when he was awe-stricken at the lofty magnificence of that good: 'How great is your goodness which you have hidden away for those who fear you' (Ps. 31:30)."[18] It appears, therefore, that for Maimonides, the pair of terms representing Divine punishment and reward are: Gehinom and the World to Come. This spiritual realm cannot be explained by words, on the other hand, as Maimonides said before: it does not behoove a righteous person to do the good deeds in order to receive a reward, even the reward of the World to Come:

> Nevertheless, even though this is the end we seek, he who wishes to serve God out of love should not serve Him to attain the world to come. He should rather believe that wisdom exists, that this

— 93 —

wisdom is the Torah; that the Torah was given to the prophets by God the creator; that in the Torah He taught us virtues which are the commandments and vices that are sins. As a decent man, one must cultivate the virtues and avoid sin. In so doing, he will perfect the specifically human aspect which resides in him and will be genuinely different from the animals. When one becomes fully human, he acquires the nature of a perfect being; there is no external power to deny his soul eternal life.[19]

One should not do good in order to reach the World to Come, but the very art of seeking the good actualizes our potential as human beings, attaching us to the eternal life of the World to Come.

THE MESSIANIC ERA IN MAIMONIDES' THOUGHT

What is the messianic era? Messianism has gotten bad press in Judaism in the past three hundred years since Sabbatianism, since we right away think of false messiahs and other megalomaniacs. However, the concept of redemption in Judaism is really the profound belief in the ability to make the world a better place. If the idea of God is the deepest collective human idea, then the idea of redemption is the ultimate belief in human optimism concerning the world we live in. The mistake of the false messianic movements was, among other mistakes, the over-emphasis on the personae of the messiah. The very term "messianism" coined by researchers of Sabbatianism over the past 100 years, has created a false impression of Jewish messianism. Therefore, as I wrote in a previous work, it's time to go back to the term "redemption," which stresses the period more than the particular leader. We all like heroes, but Jewish redemption starts with the individual and continues with the collective without over-emphasizing the messiah king. In Maimonides' thinking, there is a messiah king, who is a political leader; however, we shall see that the actual identity of the messiah is secondary to the occurrences which must happened in the course of this time period.

What is the origin of the term messiah? In Hebrew the root is from *mashiah* referring to one who was anointed (*mashuah*) by oil. To be anointed is to be appointed for a specific public task. The kings were anointed either by a flask of oil[20] or by a horn full of oil.[21] The prophets[22] and priests[23] were anointed as well. Anointing can represent both appointing one for a task[24] and purification.[25] In the prophets, the term *mashiah* became synonymous with a public servant even without the actual anointing with oil; therefore the *mashiah* is the one chosen by God for a specific task.[26] In the later writings, the term already refers to the elect of the people.[27] The longing for the ideal king of Davidic descent is described as the longing for the *mashiah*, meaning God's chosen King.[28] The term "messianic era" is a later theme describing events surrounding the return of the ideal leader to Israel. These events, however, have biblical roots as well. The Bible speaks of the returning of the exiles in the time to come (Deut. 30:1-5), the return of law and order (Is. 1:26; 11:3-5), of world peace (Is. 2:1-5; 11:6-9) and of punishment for the wicked (Is. 2:12-19). Maimonides' explanation of the messianic era is close to these biblical sources. In Maimonides' thinking, we find the messiah king as a specific political leader. However, the emphasis is on his ability to bring about the goals of the messianic era.

> The "days of the messiah" refers to a time in which sovereignty will revert to Israel and the Jewish people will return to the land of Israel. Their king will be a great one, and his royal palace will be in Zion. His name and his reputation will extend throughout all the nations in even greater a measure than did Solomon's. All nations will make peace with him and all countries will serve him out of respect for his great righteousness and the wonders which will occur through him. All those who rise against him will be destroyed and delivered into his hands by God. All the verses of the Bible testify to his triumph and our triumph with him. However, except for the fact that sovereignty will revert to Israel, nothing will be essentially different from what it is now. This is what the sages taught: "The only difference between this world and the days of the messiah is that oppression by the other kingdoms will be abolished" (Brachot 34b).[29]

We can enumerate already a few essentials comprising Maimonides' understanding of the messianic era:

> 1. A Jewish-run State will be set up in the land of Israel: "Sovereignty will revert to Israel."
> 2. The ingathering of the exiles: "The Jewish people will return to their land."
> 3. A messianic king who is the political leader: "Their king will be a great one."

4. World peace: "All nations will make peace with him."

5. A leader victorious in battling the evil nations: "All those who rise up against him will be destroyed and delivered into his hands by God."

6. Nature will not change and nothing supernatural has to occur: "Nothing will be essentially different from what it is now."

In the laws of Kings, Maimonides adds:

7. The building of the temple: "The messiah king will return the kingdom of David to its original stature, will build the temple and return the exiles of Israel."[30]

8. The return of prophecy.[31]

The absence of the supernatural during the messianic era Maimonides proves from the Bar Kokhva story:

Do not think that the messiah king has to perform miracles or create things anew or resurrect the dead and the like. This is not so. For Rabbi Akiba was one of the greatest scholars of the Mishnah, and he was an assistant of Ben Koziba the king [Bar Kokhvah] and said of him that he was the messiah king, and he and most of the scholars of his generation thought so, until he [bar Kokhvah] was killed by sin. When he died they understood that he was not. The Rabbis never asked him for a sign or a miracle.[32]

Bar Kokhva was a human leader without any supernatural powers, and all the sages of the Mishnah thought of him as a possible messiah king when he was ably battling the Romans for three years. When he lost to the Romans they understand their mistake. However, from this story we can learn that the messiah king does not require any supernatural powers. Basically, he has to bring to realization the goals of biblical messianism as mentioned above. If he does, he is the messiah king; if he doesn't, he is not. It seems like a clear-cut measuring stick. Maimonides believes that the messiah king will bring world peace. (This by itself may seem to many as supra-natural). Many nations will make peace with him and join him in his attempt to stabilize the nations in peace. "All nations will make peace with him and all countries will serve him out of respect for his great righteousness and the wonders which occur through him." However, wars will still be necessary, as there will always be dictators who are against world peace since it threatens their power. "All those who rise against him will be destroyed and delivered into his hands by God." These leaders will be brought to their knees by a world coalition of nations which the messiah king will head. Aside from the above goals of messianism the world will be run by the same laws of nature.

> In the days of the messiah there will still be rich and poor, strong and weak. However in those days it will be easy for men to make a living. A minimum of labor will produce great benefits. This is what the sages meant when they said: In the future the land of Israel will bring forth ready made rolls and fine woolen garments (Shabbat 30b). This is rather like what people say when someone finds something ready for use. They say, "So and so has found his bread already baked and his meal already cooked." ...The great benefits which will occur in those days include our release from oppression by other kingdoms, which prevents us from fulfilling the commandments — a widespread increase of wisdom, in accordance with the scriptural promise "For the earth shall be full of the knowledge of the Lord as the waters cover the sea" (Is. 11:19) — and the end of the wars, again in accordance with the scriptural statement: "Nation shall not lift up sword against nation neither shall they learn war anymore" (Micah 4:3). In those days [seeking moral] perfection will be widespread with the result that men will merit the life of the world to come.[33]

Nature will not change its course in the messianic era. However, a livelihood will be easier to come by. This could be the result of people caring for one another or even the idea that rain will be plentiful and the earth fertile. In the book of Genesis, Adam and later Cain were told that the earth has been cursed and that their livelihoods would be at the sweat of their brow due to their sins. The messianic era is a point where these sins have been atoned for and once again nature can work as it was supposed to, just as mankind can then function as it was supposed to; without hatred, wars or oppression. The ease in making a livelihood will free up time so that all human beings will be able to pursue a life of wisdom and good deeds.

> But the messiah will die and his son and his grandson will reign in his stead. The prophet has already predicted his death in the verse: "He shall not fail nor be crushed till he has set the right in the earth" (Is. 42:2). However, his reign will be a long one. All human life will

be longer, for when worries and troubles are removed men live longer. There is no reason for surprise that the messiah's reign will extend for thousands of years. As our sages have put it: "When good is gathered together it cannot be speedily dissipated."[34]

The messiah dies since he is human. Nature remains the same. However, when troubles are removed people live longer. This is a well-known motto of health. Tension and stress bring about cardiac disease, ulcers and untold ailments. There was a man in Columbia who was said to have died at 156 years of age. When asked of the secret of his longevity he said it was due to three things: black coffee in the morning, a good cigar and not worrying. I have doubts about the first two but not worrying is a proven factor in longevity (in addition to picking the right parents). In the book of Genesis the Bible speaks of those who lived for hundreds of years. The record was Methuselah who lived 970 years. Noah was 600 years old when the flood broke out. Ages decreased when God said that mankind should not live more than 120 years due to their sins. After Moses, few lived longer than about 120 years. However, we were originally created to live longer, as we can see from Genesis. In the ancient Chinese classic of internal medicine, *The Yellow Emperor*, the opening words are: "Why did our ancestors live such long lives and we live only 100 years?" Prof. Nathan Aviezer writes that with the discovery of the aging gene by scientists, we can now understanding what happened in the Genesis story. Originally human beings lived up to 1000 years. God decided that mankind should live fewer years, so He implanted an aging gene into the human gene pool. It took some generations until all were affected by this gene, and then no one lived longer than 120 years. There is no way of knowing if this theory is true, but it is interesting. Since Maimonides probably had no idea of this theory I assume that he assumed that longevity would increase in the messianic era through better living conditions, better human cooperation and less stress.

WHAT IS THE MESSIANIC ERA FOR MAIMONIES?

In the *Guide*, Maimonides claims that even though the world was created at a certain point in time, there is no reason to think that it will ever end.[35] If we add this to the equation we can now realize the deeper meaning of Maimonides' messianic era. For Maimonides, the messianic era is not the end of the world. It is not an apocalyptic time. True, there will be some wars to end war against the few countries who will not appreciate the new world order being established. However, this is not the end of the world in any sense. For Maimonides there is no reason to think that the world cannot exist forever. (He was not aware of the evidence that the sun will become a giant red star burning up the earth in about 5 billion years, and will evaporate its oceans in only about a billion years.[36]) Now, envision an infinite line:

0	X	∞
Creation	Messianic Era	Infinity

Every point on an infinite line is as far away from the end as the beginning is. This means that whenever the messianic era starts, it is as far from infinity as the beginning of time. In other words, the messianic era is not the end of the world but rather the beginning of the world. It is the beginning of a normal world. We live in an abnormal world. I remember as a child being taken with my school to the police station in Washington, DC. They had clocks there marking how many murders and thefts take place in the U.S. Every 10 minutes there is a murder, every five minutes a rape and every 2 minutes a theft. This is only in one country! A day does not go by on our globe where there isn't a war in some country. Do you call that a normal world? There are streets where you cannot walk at night, and parks and neighbourhoods where you cannot walk even during the day. Is that a normal world? When we see children fighting in kindergarten we stop them, excusing their behaviour since they are children and therefore do not know better. But when we see countries killing each other—that is politics; is this a normal world? If an alien were to find a link to our TV programs and watch the news or any of our programs for a few days they would probably be afraid to visit here. It's too dangerous and violent. Yet we are used to such violence and therefore are complacent until it reaches us. So you see, what Maimonides is describing is not the end of time, but the beginning of a normal world in which there is respect for life and property, individual rights and the pursuit of personal fulfillment. It is we who are living in pre-history. Maimonides' description of the messianic-era, therefore, is not impossible. Maybe it seems improbable, especially concerning world peace, but this is what a normal world should really look like. How will this happen? Maimonides hints to this.

"As our sages have put it: When good is gathered together it cannot be speedily dissipated." We are used to the idea that our democracies are run by mediocre politicians who are there for self-interest, fame, and power, but since there are a few hundred leading the country and they all eye each other and want to be re-elected, they also do their jobs in some minimal way, and the country runs. It was Winston Churchill who said, "Democracy is the worst form of government, except for all those other forms that have been tried from time to time." Democracy is not perfect, but it's the only form of government which seems to work in preventing dictators from destroying our rights as individuals. In countries where the idea of democracy has become entrenched it is difficult for politicians to change the structure, for the people will feel that their freedom is being taken away and will go to extreme lengths to protect these rights. Therefore true democracies are able to survive by the will of the people even if they tend to be a weaker form of government than dictatorships in which the main goal of the leadership is to keep its own power and control, and the population is expendable. Now imagine if the politicians in these democracies were actually all righteous and put the people's needs before their own personal interest and positions. If this actually were to happen, the people would love the idea and never again vote for a second-rate politician. That's what Maimonides means when he says that the good, when gathered, is not speedily dissipated. It will be the people who will make sure it continues.

In the television series "Star Trek: The Next Generation," there was an episode in which the Enterprise comes across an old space ship from the twentieth century. Aboard the ship are capsules filled with bodies frozen in liquid nitrogen, as is done in California to some individuals, like Walt Disney, in the hope that one day science will come up with the cure to all diseases, mortality included. Sure enough, the doctor brings these people back to life with the advanced medicine of the twenty-fourth century. There are three people in the capsules: a businessman, a housewife and a musical drifter. The businessman wants to get back to Earth as fast as possible to see if his shares of stocks have skyrocketed in the past 300 years. The ship's psychologist tells him that he has to understand that the world has changed since the twentieth century. People are no longer trying to subdue their brethren and wealth is spread more evenly. The businessman replies, "So what then is the challenge?" The challenge of the new world order is the real goal of Mankind: to pursue human traits and values, not to judge others by what they have but rather by what they are. To paraphrase a famous statement by Martin Luther King, Jr.: "When a man will be judged not by the color of his skin [or the money he has in the bank or the power and job he holds] but by the content of his character."

Maimonides concludes this discourse and says:

> We do not long and hope for the days of the messiah because of an increase of productivity and wealth which may occur then, or that we should ride on horses and drink wine to the accompaniment of song as some confused people think. The prophets and the saints looked forward to the days of the messiah and yearned for them because in them the righteous will be gathered together in fellowship and because goodness and wisdom will prevail. They desired it also because of the righteousness and the abundant justice of the Messiah king, because of the salutary influence of his unprecedented wisdom and because of his nearness to God. They also anticipate the performance of all the commandments of the Torah of Moses our teacher with neither inertia on the one hand nor compulsion on the other.[37]

Maimonides opens his summary with an anti-Marxist and anti-epicurean statement and then goes on to describe the era of the messiah as one of wisdom, goodness, and fellowship. He adds an important point, that in this era people will do good not out of compulsion nor out of inertia. These latter traits are symptomatic of a fundamentalist society which forces religion on the masses and frowns upon intellectual independent thinking and scholarship. That will not be the messianic era. The messianic era will be one of wisdom, goodness and fellowship, without curtailing individual freedom.

THE RESURRECTION OF THE DEAD

Maimonides writes little about this concept. That could be why the Rabbis of Provence attacked him and claimed that he did not believe in it. Maimonides in response wrote a treatise called "The Treatise of the Resurrection of the Dead" to defend his position and reiterate his belief in the concept. In his introduction to Helek he writes, "The resurrection of the dead is one of the cardinal principles established by Moses our teacher. A person who does not believe in this principle has no religion." It seems peculiar that after such a statement the Rabbis of Provence could have accused him of not believing in this principle. The answer, it appears, is that Maimonides had a different take on the resurrection of the dead than they did and this bothered them. However, they did not want to say that they disagreed with his opinion, since the people could understand this as a legitimate difference of opinion. Rather, the Rabbis of Provence, with their kabbalistic traditions, were not interested in Maimonides presenting a different interpretation of a concept they felt they had received in a tradition. Therefore they preferred to say that he did not believe in it. What was Maimonides' interpretation?

> Resurrection is only for the righteous. This is the meaning of the statement in Bereishit Rabbah (13) which declares: The creative power of rain is for both the righteous and the wicked, but the resurrection of the dead is only for the righteous. How, after all, could the wicked come back to life, since they are already dead even in their lifetimes? Our sages taught: "The wicked are called dead even while they are still alive; the righteous, however, are called alive even when they are dead" (Brakhot 18b). All men must die and their bodies decompose.[38]

The idea that the resurrection is for the righteous has a strong textual basis in rabbinic writings even though it is open for interpretation. Does a man who has done a few wicked things in his life lose out on the resurrection? If the resurrection is only temporary, what is the point in the first place? To figure out Maimonides' take on the resurrection we need to flesh it out from the few places where he discusses it and draw logical conclusions from the context. In his treatise, Maimonides bemoans the fact that people spend all their time pondering the concept of the resurrection of the dead ,which is an important concept but is a temporary state in the messianic period, whereas the real reward of the afterlife, the World to Come, no one seems to care about:

> We have found people discussing only issues pertaining to the resurrection of the dead: Will [the dead] arise naked or with garments, and other questions like these; whereas the World to Come—is totally forgotten. In addition, we have already explained there that

the resurrection of the dead is a principle of the Torah of Moses, of blessed memory, but it is not the ultimate goal. It [The ultimate goal] is the World to Come. This therefore clears up a great misconception, as if the Torah has no reward or punishment except in this world, and as if it does not mention the reward and punishment of the World to Come."[39]

Maimonides goes on to emphasize that the World to Come is devoid of any body or physical element. Therefore, even those who merit the resurrection, which entails the soul entering the body again, will eventually die and their souls will reach the afterlife of the World to Come.[40] He also argues with those who claim that he explains the resurrection metaphorically. The resurrection, he argues, is what it is; the idea of the soul returning to the body. Even if it seems irrational, since the body naturally decomposes like all natural things; it is a miracle promised by scripture: "The resurrection of the dead is one of the miracles and this is clear. It is obvious that one has but to believe in it, as it was brought down in the true statement [in the book of Daniel]. It is supra-natural and therefore cannot be proven by reason."[41] For Maimonides, the resurrection is a miracle that challenges human logic because normally, bodies decompose and are done with. However, the idea of the afterlife and the eternity of the intellectual soul he sees as a reasonable deduction; after all, if the body is a product of nature whereas the intellectual soul is created in God's image, doesn't it seem reasonable that this Divine gift, i.e. the soul, would remain after the body decomposes? Maimonides, as we explained earlier, tends to minimalize the miraculous and tries to explain things logically whenever he can,[42] unless he feels compelled to do otherwise. In the case of the resurrection, where the verse in Daniel openly mentions it as do the sages in the Mishnah, it must be accepted it even if it defies reason. However, miracles too have a pedagogical task. They teach us that God is above nature and therefore can create nature. After all, the very idea of creation ex nihilo defies reason as well, attesting to the possibility of the miraculous if God deems it so. However, since the resurrection is a miracle, it can only be temporary.[43]

Maimonides does not accept the idea of reincarnation of the soul into a new body, since there is no Talmudic basis for such an idea. However, his understanding of the resurrection of the dead seems close to this idea, since the dead are resurrected and then live a full life and die again. It is to be noted that the kabbalistic idea of reincarnation is part of the process of Divine punishment for those who do not merit the afterlife directly, whereas the resurrection of the dead, for Maimonides, is a form of reward for the righteous. So what is the point? For Maimonides, the idea of the resurrection of the dead is a statement of Divine justice. After all, if a person wanted to live a good life but died young from famine or war or sickness, or if a person lived a full life but it was full of hardships which left them little time to pursue wisdom and the good deeds they wanted to do for their friends, family and mankind; and assuming that one merits a place in the World to Come based on their deeds in this world, it seems unfair that one has more time due to the circumstances of their life which were easier, whereas another had less time since the circumstances of their life were more difficult. Therefore, God gives the righteous a second chance; a new life to live, after the messianic era has begun, in a world which now has overcome wars, famine and sickness and allows individuals to pursue the moral life and actualize themselves as human beings. The righteous who lived prior to the messianic era are given an opportunity to live out their lives again, this time in full, and therefore merit a better place in the World to Come. However, the final goal is the afterlife, the World to Come, which is devoid of any bodily elements.

Understanding the
Afterlife and Messianism:
A Kabbalistic Approach

THE AFTERLIFE IN KABBALISTIC THINKING

Despite the popularity of Maimonides, it appears that his ideas on eschatology did not permeate the minds of the average Jew. Possibly, the popularity of the Hassidic movement, which overtook Eastern European Jewry like wildfire in the late eighteenth and early nineteenth century and stressed the kabbalistic sources of the Zohar, brought about this change in mind-set. In Sephardic Jewish culture, the kabbalistic traditions in general and the Zoharic traditions in particular have held a wide influence since the sixteenth century. The very first terms explained by Maimonides, Gan Eden and Gehinom, are described quite differently in Zoharic tradition.

Rabbi A. I. Kook, the kabbalist and legalist who was the first chief Rabbi in Palestine until his passing in 1935, called death the ultimate lie.

Death is a perfidious concept. Its impurity lies in its falsehood. What people refer to as death is just an empowering of life, but the fall into existential pettiness that is brought about by the heart of man envisions this increased vitality in a dark and worry-some way, calling it death.....The fear of death is a collective illness of mankind, due to sin. Sin created the fear...all humans toil to save themselves from death, but this goal cannot be reached without increasing the inner light of the soul.[1]

The famous kabbalist Isaac Luriah of sixteenth-century Safed described dying as going from one world to another. The body descends and the spirit ascends. The Zohar sees this process as an ascent of the inner soul away from the body. The soul was locked into a physical form held together by the *Zelem*; however, the *Zelem* disappears thirty days before death as the soul begins to yearn for its source. "We have learned that the day a man leaves this world, on that day is a day of judgment when the sun cannot shine towards the moon, referring to the holy soul that is withheld thirty days before he exits the world and the *zelem* is withheld and is not noticeable."[2] As recorded by many of the NDE cases, the Zohar writes that one meets all of his deceased relatives at the moment of departure from this world.

We have learned that when the soul departs, all one's relatives and friends in the other world [lit. true world] come to greet him and show him his place in Eden and the place of punishment. If he is saintly he sees his place and ascends to it bathing in the bliss of the higher Eden. And if he is not saintly, the soul remains in this world until the body is buried in the ground. When buried it is held by prosecuting angels until meeting Dumah [the main guard of Gehinom] who shows him into Gehinom.[3]...Rabbi Judah said: All the seven days [of mourning] the soul goes from the house [of mourning] to the graveside and back to the house and mourns its body as it says: Surely its flesh shall hurt and its soul mourn [Job 14:22], and we have been taught that after the seven days, the body becomes what it becomes and the soul goes to its place and enters the cave of the makhpelah [the cave in Hebron where Abraham buried Sarah, used here as a metaphor].[4]

In the Zoharic tradition the process of death and judgment is quite involved. The process parallels the Jewish laws of mourning. In the laws of mourning the first day is the main day of mourning and is a Torah obligation. The rest of the seven days are rabbinic. The first day, called the "onen" period, lasts until the moment the body is interred in the ground and covered. From the Halakhic perspective, the mourner is exempt at this time from all positive commandments in order to prepare the burial. From the perspective of the deceased, they are in a period referred to as *Hibut HaKever*. The first aspect of this is the sudden confusion that the person goes through realizing they are now without a body. Our whole lives we associate ourselves with our bodies and all of a sudden we still exist but the body does not. Therefore, the soul hovers around the body until it is interred. In Jewish tradition it is customary to ask for forgiveness from the deceased until the body is interred since there is the kabbalistic belief that the departed is watching. Then the soul meets its deceased relatives and friends who help it find its place.

> "We have learnt: At the moment that the soul departs, all the relatives and friends of that world greet the soul and show it its place of reward and punishment. If the soul has merit it is shown its place and resides there in the upper bliss of that world but if it does not have merit it remains in this world until the body is interred in the ground....then it is taken to Dumah [the guard of Gehinom] and taken to Gehinom."[5]

Until the end of the first seven days the soul of the departed ascends and descends daily to see how the family is dealing with the loss. This is the period of mourning called the *shivah*, i.e., the seven days. In this period, no bathing and haircutting is allowed to the family. They sit on the ground or on cushions and speak only of the deceased. This is the main period of mourning their loss.

> Rav Judah said: the first seven days [the soul] goes from the house to the cemetery and back to the house and mourns [the loss of] the body...it goes to watch all those who are mourning it. After those seven days the body remains as is and the soul departs to its abode through the cave.[6]

Then from seven until thirty days the soul periodically returns to this world, for this is a time of judgment and it needs to remember ever detail of its actions in this world.[7] This is the third period of mourning for the family called *sheloshim* in which shaving or cutting the hair is not allowed. After this, the soul ascends to its place and the fourth period of the mourning process begins, lasting until the end of one year. In this year the mourner refrains from joyous occasions, live music and even wedding receptions. The Kaddish prayer is recited as the departed is still in the period of judgment until the maximum of twelve months. Judgment is called Gehinom, which sometimes is translated as hell. However, it is more of a purgatory, for its punishment enables the soul of the deceased to receive a pardon for its sins and continue on its journey. The Kaddish is recited only for eleven months so as not to imply that the departed was so wicked as to need all twelve months of Gehinom.

The process is slightly more complicated then I just described. In the Zoharic tradition the soul after death has at least three options after the initial *Hibut HaKever*, (lit. the shock of the grave):

1. If it was righteous it continues on to Gehinom. (No, that was not a typo.) Even the righteous need Gehinom. After all, Kohelet said "There is no righteous one in the land who will do good without sinning." All go through Gehinom: the wicked, the righteous, and the plain people. However the righteous go for less time since they have fewer sins. For the righteous, Gehinom is a sufficient purging of sin.

2. However, if it is calculated that Gehinom will not suffice, reincarnation (*gilgul*) is necessary. In this line of thinking, reincarnation is a form of punishment since it is seen as bad to have to return to this world for unfinished business. An important collection of kabbalistic traditions concerning the afterlife can be found in R. Elijah De Vidas' book *Reisheit Hokhma*. In it, he tries to explain the idea of kabbalistic reincarnation (*gilgul*) and why it is a form of punishment.

> In the issue of why the soul should need *gilgul* after it was purified in *gehinom*, my teacher [R. Moses Cordovero] explained that *gilgul* is needed for two reasons: one, if one lacks a mitzvah [an unfulfilled positive commandment] and therefore must make it up [since the human body has 248 limbs paralleling all the 248 positive mitzvot of the Judaism] therefore it needs *gilgul*. Secondly, one cannot fix and purify what *gehinom* could not, for there are sins that *gehinom* cannot fix and therefore they must be redone. This can be compared to one who has disease throughout his body. There are some diseases that the doctor can heal without cutting off the limb and some he cannot. He cuts off part of the body until the rest heals. Sometimes he must cut off a whole limb to save the body. This person is now missing a limb. In the same way the Holy One Blessed Be He does not want a person to lose, as it were, a whole limb in the purification of *gehinom* and remain so in Eden, so he returns him to this world to fix it and if he is still missing it, he can repent in this world before death and fix what he did wrong in the previous life.[8]

Here *gilgul* is an additional way of fixing one's past when the punishment of Gehinom is not enough. For the individual this punishment of *gilgul* brings great anguish, as R. De Vidas explains:

> It [*gilgul*] is bitter for the soul. More than the judgment of *gehinom*. My teacher [R. Moses Cordovero] wrote: that this can be compared to one who prepared for a business trip for two or three years. He was sure he would profit from it. However, upon arrival he was told: All your toil was in vain; for your product is worthless here....The meaning is clear. After a man knows that most souls in this generation are reincarnated and therefore he comes now to fix something he did not do before, if he should leave this world without doing that, all his labor here will have been in vain and he will have to return a third and fourth time until he fixes it.[9]

The kabbalistic idea of *gilgul* is first mentioned in the book of Bahir made public in 1176. The authorship is anonymous and the exact date of authorship is unknown. Kabbalists from the twelfth to the sixteenth century discussed how many times one can go through *gilgul*. The opinions seemed to extend up to four times. However, not all was clear. After De Vidas, Isaac Luriah clarified many ideas on *gilgul* in his *Shaar Hagigulim*. Ramhal claimed that *Gilgul* could be not only for an entire soul but even for parts of a soul. After all, there are five levels to the soul and each level has levels as well, so that it is possible for only a few levels to reincarnate to be rectified.[10] This novel understanding of *gilgul* (reincarnation) differentiates it entirely from other Eastern or Middle-Eastern concepts of reincarnation.

3. A soul who is not righteous enough to go directly to Gehinom, and it is not clear yet as to whether *gilgul* will suffice, is temporarily held in a no-man's-land which the Zohar refers to as the "*Kaf Hakela.*"

This latter concept is based on a verse from I Samuel in which Abigail tells King David, "May the soul of my master be bound up in eternal life with your God and the soul of thy enemy be cast in the sling shot (*Kaf Hakela*)" (I Sam. 25:29). The Zohar explains this slingshot as a temporary no-man's-land after death but before the soul reaches its heavenly abode. The existence in *Kaf Hakela* is a form of punishment since the soul has no body. However, it still remembers physical pleasure and has not yet experienced spiritual pleasure. In kabbalistic legends there are stories of dibbuks and other souls caught in the agony of this in-between existence, who try to enter a human body in order to gain the merit of a good deed to push their way up the spiritual ladder and break out of *Kaf Hakela*. Subsequently there are stories of rabbinic exorcists who come to remove them. There are cultures in which reincarnation is considered self-evident. The Druze in Israel and Syria have a strong tradition of reincarnation, and periodically they will discover a child who relates to them who he or she was in a previous life, naming the people they were married to and their families. In Druze culture the families create a bond with the children even if they are not biologically related to them. In Indian culture this is true as well. In 1998, I taught a group of diplomats' wives in Herzliah Pituah, Israel. The topic was Jewish Mysticism and the topics triggered discussion. One woman, who had been stationed in India for a number of years, related how she had witnessed a young girl possessed by a male soul. These things are regular occurrences in Indian society, much as reincarnation is for the Druze (and the Indians). Are these occurrences that happen only in these societies due to their belief in them or do they happen in the West as well, but are diagnosed with fancy psychological names? Is one man's dibbuk (possession by another soul) another man's multiple personality disorder?

In 1991, I met a young Israeli soldier who told me how at her base in the Negev desert her friends would hold a nightly séance. One girl was the medium and the others followed the cup on the Ouija board with their finger tips. She said how surprised she was when it seemed as if the cup was moving by itself. They 'contacted' the soul of a young man who died in an accident at the age of 27. He told them how it is a grave sin to speak with the dead. Then they asked him about his life. She asked me how they were able to contact such a soul. I told her that in the Zoharic tradition there are souls that are caught between this world and the next, often due to lack of merit, and they are the ones in close proximity to us.

In 1995, I met a young man who while working on another army base in the desert also spoke of witnessing séances. (It seems a strange pass-time, but they both claimed it was addictive). He spoke of how his friend had lost his father and wanted to contact him. Using the Ouija board they did this. They succeeded in "contacting" the boys' father, who told him that it was a grave sin to contact the dead. He subsequently asked the boy to say the kaddish prayer on his behalf. The son, a little shocked, did just that. The next week, the soldier related, "we again held a séance but could not contact the boy's father." They reached another soul and asked if he knew where the boy's father was. The soul told them that the boy's father's soul had already ascended. The whole story shook this fellow up so much that he took upon himself a religious lifestyle.

The issue of reincarnation is post-Talmudic. As I mentioned earlier, it is first recorded in Jewish sources in the mystical book of the Bahir, which appeared in 1176 CE. It is a book which possibly was based on earlier sources. The rationalists, like Maimonides, had an aversion to such ideas, but the kabbalists embraced it. They saw it as a function of Divine justice. After all, if one was a good person and wanted to live the good life but was killed by famine, wars or sickness, where is Divine justice? The reincarnation concept or *gilgul* fulfills this function.

Modern psychotherapy has brushed on this concept of gilgul in the field of hypnotherapy. There has been a new type of therapy called regression hypnotherapy where a person is asked to regress to past lives in order to heal a longstanding inner wound. One psychotherapist who brought this to the forefront was Brian Weiss in his first book, *Many Lives Many Masters*. In a sequel he writes:

> "Prior to my experiences with Catherine, I had never heard of past-life regression therapy. This was not taught when I was at Yale medical school...I can still remember the first time I had instructed Catherine to travel backward in time, hoping to discover childhood traumas that had been repressed, or forgotten, and that I felt were causing her current symptoms of anxiety and depression. Usually in [hypno] therapy, when forgotten traumas are remembered with their accompanying emotions, a process called catharsis, patients begin to improve. Catherine's symptoms remained severe, however, and I assumed that we had to uncover even more repressed childhood memories.... Carefully I took Catherine back to the age of two, but she recalled no significant memories. I instructed her firmly and clearly: 'Go back to the time from which your symptoms arise.' I was totally shocked by her response... Her name was Aronda, a young woman who had lived nearly four thousand years ago. She died suddenly in a tidal wave, which devastated her village.... Catherine had been gasping and having difficulty breathing during this tragic memory. Suddenly

her body relaxed completely, and her breathing became deep and even....She was resting. That lifetime had ended...Incredibly her lifelong fear of gagging, or choking, virtually disappeared after this session. I knew that imagination or fantasy could not cure such deeply imbedded chronic symptoms. Cathartic memory could. Week after week, Catherine remembered more past lives. Her symptoms disappeared. She was cured, without the use of medicines. Together we had discovered the healing power of regression therapy."

Weiss describes his skepticism and an event that shocked him. As he had Catherine under hypnosis describing the end of a past lifetime and floating above her body, she began to speak:

"She then began to tell me very private details about the lives and deaths of my father and my infant son. They had both died years previously, far away from Miami. Catherine, a laboratory technician at Mount Sinai Medical Center, knew nothing at all about them...There was no place to look up this information. She was stunningly accurate...'Who,' I asked her, 'who is there?' Who tells you these things? 'The masters,' she whispered, 'The master Spirits tell me. They tell me I have lived eighty six times in physical state.' Catherine later described the Masters as highly evolved souls not presently in body who could speak to me through her... The knowledge the Masters transmitted, seemed beyond Catherine's capabilities."[11]

In kabbalistic thinking, the soul after death and after the original shock of death and bereavement over the decaying body, is at a crossroad. The possibilities mentioned above, *gilgul, kaf hakelah*, or Gehinom will bring the eventual path to Gan Eden. The Zohar, in addition to the purging of Gehinom, relates another concept called the river of dinnur, which literally means the river of fire. R. De Vidas attempts to explain this as well:

Concerning the issue of the purification of the soul in the river of *dinnur*, my teacher [R. Moses Cordovero] taught the reason why the soul should, after the purifying through *gehinom*, again purify itself in the *dinnur* river. He said that there are two types of purification. One is in *gehinom* and it is for sins due to the evil inclination and transgressing the mitzvot and the second is purification for not sanctifying oneself in daily life.... Like gluttony and all things. These are not real blemishes for there was no transgression done, but it is a form of lust for this world which is full of enticements from the skin of the serpent... and this *gehinom* does not purify.[12]

The concept of the *dinnur* river is not atonement for sin but rather a way of ridding oneself of the materialism of the body. You might say that for the righteous, who emphasized the soul and the spirit, there is little trouble adapting to a spiritual realm, but for many of us, who saw physical experience as the central aspect of our lives, the pain of the realization that this is gone and now meaningless is quite a difficult experience to cope with.

Ramchal describes levels within Gan Eden. There is the higher Gan Eden and the lower one. In his essays he writes: "There exists a higher and lower Gan Eden. In the lower sit the souls in an appearance similar to the body and partake in spiritual delights... and in the higher sit the souls in their original form and partake in higher spiritual delights."[13]

He goes on to speak of levels in Gehinom as well, which I will not relate. These are expanded by R. De Vidas as well.

The kabbalistic idea of Messianism and resurrection of the dead are interrelated. I will present here the ideas as developed in the writings of Ramchal and the Vilna Gaon, who were the most detailed in their discussions of these concepts.

THE MESSIANIC ERA

Since the time of the Ari (Isaac Luria Ashkenazi, sixteenth-century kabbalist in Safed), messianism has been understood as a process and not as a one-time event. This stands in opposition to a tendency that has developed which sees messianism as related to a dynamic figure who is the hero of the story, a sort of Neo from the Matrix who comes to save the world. People love heroes, especially super heroes. They captivate the imagination of our youth, but they aren't real. People are just people. It's when we find within ourselves the power to change, that we all become super-human. Ronit Meroz pointed out years ago that in all the writings of the Ari, writings full of messianic yearning, not once is there a discussion on the persona of the messiah. This doesn't mean that there will not be such a leader; however, his leadership is secondary to the story. He is a tool to help realize the messianic period—no more. The Rabbis of old made many comparisons between the exodus story from Egypt (the first redemption) and the final redemption from exile. No doubt, the hero or messiah of the exodus story was Moses. However, in our Passover haggadah, a compilation from Mishnaic times retelling the exodus story and recited at the Passover seder, Moses is entirely left out and is mentioned only in passing in a verse brought for other reasons. This is in accordance with the midrashic statement mentioned in the Passover Haggadah that God took us out of Egypt, and not any messenger or angel.[14] That is not to say that there will not be a messianic leader. There will be, but the emphasis is on the process and the change brought to the world and the Jewish people. Therefore, I have argued elsewhere that it is really more fitting to call this period the period of redemption and not the messianic period, since the very term messianism,[15] developed from the research of Sabbatianism, assumes the central role of the messiah in the process and creates a preconceived notion based on a false premise.

For Ramchal, the six thousand years of history are taken seriously. That means that the period of redemption, at least in its natural form, the beginning of redemption, must occur before the end of the sixth millennium.[16] There are those who would argue that this has already happened with the rise of the modern State of Israel.[17] The later period, of Messiah Ben David, is a lengthy period according to Ramhal. Ramhal does not go into the details of the goals of this period as does the Vilna Gaon; however, he describes the various periods of time as affecting the relationship between body and soul. Ramhal, influenced by the mystical work *Brit Menuhah*, claims that the world is actually built on a temporal system of ten thousand years. The first seven represent the natural world, as with the *sefirot*, and the last three the hidden world. For Ramhal, then, the messianic era must begin before the end of the seventh millennium. However, the later stage of redemption is drawn out into long stages. Each stage represents the world moving from physicality to spirituality. The first stage, that of the era of the messiah from the house of David,[18] already necessitates a change in the human psyche. In our world, evil and good in the heart are equal, creating a constant struggle. Therefore, world peace is impossible. However, in the messianic period of Ben David, good will finally triumph over evil in Man's heart and therefore peace will be possible. In the seventh millennium as well as in the eighth through the tenth, human beings will develop spiritually. If in the messianic period good prevailed over evil in the heart, a psychological transformation from the seventh millennium will begin a gradual process in which human beings will evolve such that the soul will start gaining control over the body. Today, the body is dominant. After all, if I don't eat for a day I find it hard to survive, but if I do not pray for a month, it doesn't bother me. However, at some point in the distant future, the soul will slowly gain control over the body. This will happen until the soul becomes dominant. The more dominant the soul, the less physical the body will be. For Ramhal, it was the sin of the Tree of Knowledge which resulted in Adam and Eve receiving physical bodies that cannot deal with spiritual energy. However, in Eden, they had "lighter" bodies that radiated light. These original bodies did not need to die and return to the earth. The eventual result of the process of the soul dominating the body will be that the body will be only minimally physical and will live in harmony with the soul so that the separation of the body from the soul, i.e. death, will not be necessary any more. When one dies, the soul returns to Gan Eden, which is the creation on the sixth day before the sin. Each soul reaches a personal redemption in this manner. However, the collective redemption which Ramhal refers to as "olam Ha-Tehiyah" (the world of resurrection or renaissance) is the time in which the body and physicality will be so slight and so permeated by the spirit that the body will not need to die, as we mentioned before. At that point, mankind will open their eyes and realize that all the souls in Eden are actually right here, just in another dimension of reality which at that point will be recognizable, as the spirit dominates the physical. That point is called the resurrection since all the souls of Eden which were here all the time will be with us in our consciousness and in our new reality. This is the World to Come (Olam Habah) for Ramhal. It is the collective goal.

Ramhal's ideas on Messianism seem quite mystical and even a bit fantastic. Maimonides offered a rational approach which I called "not impossible" even if by today's politics world peace seems a bit improbable. However, Ramhal introduces ideas that seem to be hard to swallow; the body becoming more spiritual and less physical until we merge with a higher spiritual reality. This was true up until 150 years ago. However, with the modern ideas of evolutionary development, Ramhal's teachings all of a sudden seem more comprehensible. After all, if evolution is an ongoing process in the natural world, who says that it is over? If simple cells and primates evolved into human beings, who says that human beings will not evolve further? In New Age writings, it has been suggested that the next stage in human evolution will be telepathy. Ramhal is basically an evolutionist who does not describe how the world was created but rather in which way it is developing. Mankind will evolve into a higher state of existence and bring the world along with it. It is therefore not surprising that R. Isaac Kook, who was influenced by Ramhal's kabbalistic ideas, wrote at the beginning of the twentieth century:

> The doctrine of evolution, which is progressively conquering the world today, is in tune with the secrets of the kabbalah more than any other philosophic doctrine. The [idea of] evolution, which takes an ascending course, offers an element of optimism. [After all], how can one be in despair when one sees all [of creation] developing and ascending. When we analyze the basis of evolutionary ascent, we find in it a Divine aspect in unique clarity. In which actual infinity brings about that which was infinite in potential."[19]

CHAPTER 11

Belief in God: Is it a Mitzvah? An Unusual Problem Among the Legalists[1]

It is well known that Judaism is a religion which places great importance on action. According to the tradition there are 613 commandments to be found within the five books of the Pentateuch. This tradition is mentioned already in a third century Talmudic source:

> Rabbi Simla'i commented: Six hundred and thirteen *mitzvot* were said to Moses. Three hundred and sixty five negative [commands] like the days of the solar year and two hundred and forty eight positive [commands] like the limbs of the human body. Rav Hamnuna said: What is the [biblical] text [associated with this tradition]? "The Torah was commanded to us by Moses" (Deut. 23:4). *Torah* [תורה] in numerical value equals 611 [these commands we received from Moses, However] "I am the Lord Your God" and "You shall not have other gods besides me" we heard directly from God [Heb. *Mipi ha-gevura*].[2]

As it often happens in the Talmud, the third-century source from the Palestinian Rabbi Simla'i is related with a comment from the fourth-century Babylonian figure Rav Hamnuna. The basic tradition states that there are 613 commandments that break up into 248 positive commands of what to do and 365 negative commands of what not to do. The 248 positive commands parallel the limbs of the human body. The Mishnah actually enumerates the 248 limbs of the male body. The Talmud adds that the female body has 252.[3] The negative commands parallel the days of the solar year.[4] Rav Hamnuna draws on a verse in Deuteronomy as a textual basis for this tradition: "The Torah was given by Moses" (Deut. 33:4). The word Torah (תורה) in Hebrew has the numerical value of 611. Rav Hamnuna says that 611 commands we received from Moses, but two we heard directly from God. They are the first two statements of the Decalogue.[5] As can be seen from the biblical text, the first two statements of the Decalogue are in first person.[6] The rest are in third person[7] or just in the imperative. This is explained by the text in Deuteronomy. Moses describes there how the people feared to hear God's voice and actually ran away from Mount Sinai, asking Moses to be the mediator between them and God.[8] It appears that this happened between the uttering of the second and third statement of the Decalogue. Therefore Rav Hamnuna states that the first two statements of the Decalogue we received from God, but all the other *mitzvot* we received through Moses' mediation.[9]

The question now arises that if there are 613 *mitzvot*, 248 positive and 265 negative, which are they? After all, if one were to look into the Pentateuch and count each time it says to do something are not to do something, one would arrive at more than one thousand commands. So which commands are within the 613 and which not? What are the criteria? If it says in four places in the Torah to don tefillin, are they four different commands or just one; if it says in the Torah to keep the commandments and the precepts,[10] is this a separate command or just a general statement?

There were a few attempts at enumerating the *mitzvot*. The first serious attempt was an anonymous work entitled *Halakhot Gedolot* (Great Laws) written in the Geonic period in Babylonia around the ninth century.[11] This work enumerates the exact 248 positive and 365 negative commandments. The second serious attempt was that of Maimonides in his *Sefer haMitzvot* (Book of the Commandments) written in the twelfth century. Maimonides includes an introduction wherein he explains his criteria for what qualifies as a command and what does not.

The third attempt was the *Sefer Mitzvot Gadol* (The Great Book of the Commandments) by Rabbi Moses of Coucy in thirteenth-century Franco-Germany.[12] A few other attempts were made as well. Each of the works differs slightly from the others in its enumeration. Even though there are few repercussions concerning practical Halakha, the arguments are significant from a theoretical point of view of what is in or out. There are works, like that of Nachmanides in the thirteenth century, who did not write a separate book but wrote a commentary on Maimonides' *Sefer haMitzvot* called "The *Mitzvot* that the Rabbi of Blessed Memory Forgot." This work contains the areas where he differs with Maimonides. The title is a diplomatic way of saying that in his opinion Maimonides was wrong, since one cannot add a *mitzvah* without subtracting elsewhere.

One of the more interesting debates among the enumerators of the *mitzvot* is one concerning the question of whether there is a *mitzvah* to believe in God or not.

Maimonides begins his *Sefer ha-Mitzvot* saying:

> Mitzvah one: This is the command that we were commanded to **believe** [Hebrew- *ha'amanat*] [Arabic — Mu'átakada] in God which is to **believe** that there is a first cause which activated all other beings as it says: I am the Lord thy God (Ex.) and in the Talmud at the end of [the tractate of] Makkot they said: 613 mitzvot were given to Moses at Sinai as it says : "the Torah was commanded to us by Moses," meaning the numerical value of the word Torah [611], and they asked: "Torah comes out to 611?" Therefore they answered: "I am the Lord thy God and Thou Shalt not have any Gods beside me, we heard directly from God." From this we see that I am the Lord thy God is one of the 613 commandments meaning to believe in God as we explained.

Maimonides seems to claim that there is a positive command to believe in God. This he derives from the tradition mentioned above in the name of Rav Hamnuna that "I am the Lord your God" and "Thou Shalt not have any God beside Me" are two mitzvot that the people heard directly from God. Which are they? According to Maimonides the first is the positive command to believe in God and the second is the negative command not to believe in paganism. This seems quite a logical explanation. However, R. Hasdai Crescas, writing in fourteenth-century Spain, argued in the introduction to his book *Or Hashem* that Maimonides' argument that there is a command to believe in God is illogical.

Since the root of all the Divine Torah is the belief in the existence of God, may He be blessed, as is evident, for the Torah is full of commands from the commander and it could not be considered Divine without its author and commander being God. Therefore it is a mistake to enumerate belief in God as one of the commandments. For a command does not stand on its own and it cannot be fathomed without a commander. Therefore, if we say that there is a [particular] command to believe in God [the commander] we are saying that belief in God [the commander] comes prior to [the particular command] to believe in God. And if you should argue that this prerequisite belief itself is a [particular] mitzvah, it would require a further belief in God as a prerequisite, ad infinitum, which of course is absurd.[13]

To paraphrase, Crescas argues that it is illogical to say that there is a command to believe in the commander himself. After all, if I already believe in the commander then it is superfluous, and if I don't, then it will not help in any event. In his own words, he argues that since any scriptural command I fulfill is based on the fact that I already believe in God that would mean that if I am to fulfill the command to believe in God it would be on the assumption that I already do, which is absurd. It should be stated here, that Crescas is not arguing that belief in God is not central to Judaism. On the contrary, he is saying that it is the basis upon which all the commandments rest and therefore cannot be a particular command as one of the 613. Crescas bases himself on Nachmanides' explanation of the verses, so we will now explore his position. Nachmanides (d. 1270) seems to be of the same opinion as Crescas. He claims that there is no mitzvah of belief derived from the verse "I am the lord your God who took you out of Egypt." He writes: "This cannot be one of the commandments for it is the basis from which all the rest are derived as I have explained."[14] The problem with this position, however, is how does one explain the statement by Rav Hamnuna whereby there are two *mitzvot* contained in the two first statements of the Decalogue? Nachmanides continues:

In my opinion, what they [in the Talmud] said in answering the query that Torah is only 611 in numerical value, is that "I am the Lord thy God" and "Thou shalt not have any Gods beside me" we heard from God directly, and that there are two mitzvot therein which are: [1] not to make idols, including making and possessing, and [2] not to worship idols we learn from "do not bow down to them."

Nachmanides claims that there is no *mitzvah* derived from the first statement of the Decalogue, but the second statement, which begins "Thou shalt not have any gods beside me" contains two negative commands: not to worship idols and not to make them. Therefore we can explain that Rav Hamnuna's statement concerning two *mitzvot* contained within the first two statements of the Decalogue is referring to the second statement alone and not to the first and second as Maimonides thought. Crescas actually brings Nachmanides' explanation as an answer to this problem. Another approach can be found in the *Sefer Mitzvot Gadol*, a twelfth-century corpus written by R. Moses of Coucy, one of the Tosafists from Franco-Germany. R. Moses seems to anticipate Crescas' position and writes that the first statement of the Decalogue does hold within it a Divine commandment; however, he states that rather than belief in God the command contained within is to believe in Divine Providence: "Mitzvah One: [is] The mitzvah through which we were commanded to believe that the One who gave us the Torah at Mount Sinai through Moses our teacher is our Lord God who took us out of Egypt, as it says: I am the Lord Thy God who took you out of Egypt."[15] This position stresses that the verse does not just say "I am the Lord thy God" but adds: "Who took you out of Egypt." This implies, according to *Sefer Mitzvot Gadol*, that the idea is not just to believe in God's existence but to believe that he is concerned with human affairs and can even intervene if necessary. This is the belief in Divine Providence. The *mitzvah* to believe in Divine Providence rather than just believe in God circumvents the logical problem of Crescas, saying that belief in God might be a given and a prerequisite for the commandments, but there is a particular command mentioned here to believe in Divine Providence.

To summarize the positions until now, the two *mitzvot* derived from the two opening statements of the Decalogue according to Rav Hamnuna seem to be as follows:

Commentator	I am the Lord thy God	Thou shalt not have gods beside Me
Maimonides	Belief in God	Prohibition against idolatry
Nachmanides	———————————	1. Prohibition against making idols 2. Prohibition against worshipping idols
R. Moses of Coucy	Belief in Divine Providence	Prohibition against idolatry

It appears that Maimonides was well aware that his position, attributing the status of a *mitzvah* to the belief in God, was problematic. In his *Eight Chapters*, his philosophic introduction to the Ethics of the Fathers, he discusses the faculties of the soul and asks through which faculty one performs a *mitzvah* or a transgression. He writes: "As regards the rational faculty uncertainty prevails [lit. *mevukha*] but I maintain that observance and transgression may also originate in this faculty, in so far as one believes a true or a false [theological] doctrine, though no action which may be designated as an observance or a transgression results therefrom"[16] The idea that a passive transgression cannot be punished by a biblical court is unique to the Jewish perspective. Not only can transgressions of the mind such as "Thou shalt not covet" (Ex. 20:14) not be punished by a human court according to Talmudic law, but no passive transgressions can be punished by a human court.[17] This idea is quite different from those of the other Western religions, whose adherents fought bloody battles against those who dared to hold dissenting theological opinions.

Getting back to our subject, even if there is no action attributed to theological views, why does Maimonides think that they should have a lesser status concerning their being a *mitzvah* or transgression? After all, according to Maimonides, there are six daily theological *mitzvot* which have to do with the thought process. One of them, not to believe in paganism, can be derived from the second statement of the Decalogue and seems unanimous, so then what is the "uncertainty" to which Maimonides refers forcing him to "take sides" on this issue? It seems to me that when Maimonides refers to uncertainty concerning theological commandments he is not referring to negative commandments. After all, it is accepted across the board that if one believes in idolatry this is a transgression of the mind. However, the dispute involves whether there is a positive commandment fulfilled by the correct theological views. Maimonides says yes, and derives it from the first statement of the Decalogue whereas others might disagree, as was mentioned above.

What remains at this point is to ask the obvious question. What would have Maimonides answered to Crescas? Did he not think of the logical problem arising from enumerating a command to believe in the commander? Secondly, for Maimonides to consider belief in God a *mitzvah* seems to contradict his own criteria set down in his introduction to the *Sefer ha-Mitzvot*. There he establishes the fourth criteria as follows: "One should not enumerate commands that relate to all of the *mitzvot* [of the

Torah]."[18] Even though Maimonides uses the example of "you shall keep all the commandments and precepts," it has been assumed that he refers to all encompassing commands. Therefore, it is puzzling that he should enumerate something so basic and encompassing as the belief in God. To resolve this seeming contradiction and simultaneously answer our query of what Maimonides would have answered Crescas, we need to return to the sources and re-read the texts.

Maimonides wrote his magnum opus on Jewish law, the Mishneh Torah, in Hebrew, but his *Guide to the Perplexed* (from now on, the *Guide*), *Sefer ha-Mitzvot*, the *Eight Chapters* and his medical works he wrote in Arabic. This means that if we are reading a text from *Sefer ha-Mitzvot* in Hebrew we are reading a translation by Samuel ibn Tibbon, Maimonides' faithful translator. However, as a scholar and a philosopher himself, ibn Tibbon preferred to translate ideas rather than adopt a literal form of translating.[19] Therefore we must always check the original text before drawing conclusions. In addition, if one comes across seeming paradoxes, it is important to look for parallels in Maimonides' writings for cross references. Maimonides devotes the first volume of his legal work, the Mishneh Torah, The Book of Knowledge, to the issues of faith. As a legal text it is quite orderly and precise. In his Laws Concerning the Foundations of the Torah, Maimonides writes:

1. The Foundation of all foundations is to **know** that there is a first being that has brought everything else into existence. All that exists from heaven to earth and what is in between has been brought into existence from His true existence. If one were to think of His non-existence, there could not be anything in existence at all. However if one were to consider that He alone exists and that all other beings do not, that would not negate His being. For all beings need Him, but He, blessed be He, does not need them...
6. **Knowing** this is a positive commandment as it says: "I am the Lord thy God [who took you out of Egypt]" and anyone thinking that there is another god beside Him transgresses a negative command, as it says: "Thou shalt not have any gods beside Me" and has denied the basic principle; for this is the foundation upon which everything rests. [20]

Maimonides, writing in Hebrew, addresses the same issue as above. However, there is one difference. Here in Mishneh Torah he does not describe the commandment derived from the first statement of the

Decalogue as "**Belief** in God" but rather as "**Knowledge** of God." Is there a difference? If so, then why did he use the word belief in *Sefer ha-Mitzvot*? To understand this we need to understand what is contained within the word "belief" for Maimonides. In the *Guide* he writes:

> When reading my present treatise, bear in mind that by "faith" we do not understand merely that which is uttered with the lips, but also **that which is apprehended by the soul, the conviction** that the object [of belief] is exactly as it is apprehended. If, as regards real or supposed truths, you content yourself with giving utterance to them in words, without apprehending them or believing in them, especially if you do not seek real truth, you have a very easy task as, in fact, you will find many ignorant people professing articles of faith without connecting any idea with them.[21]

For Maimonides, real belief is not just to pay lip service to the opinions and beliefs of one's family or community, but to reach a level of personal conviction. This transformation of blind faith into a rational faith happens through the study of philosophy, metaphysics and the natural world until one is convinced of one's faith in a rational way. Maimonides reiterates this idea that rational faith is the highest form of faith at the end of the *Guide*:

> I will begin the subject of this chapter with a simile. A king is in his palace, and all his subjects are partly in the country, and partly abroad. Of the former, some have their backs turned towards the king's palace, and their faces in another direction; and some are desirous and zealous to go to the palace, seeking "to inquire in his temple," and to minister before him, but have not yet seen even the face of the wall of the house. Of those that desire to go to the palace, some reach it, and go round about in search of the entrance gate; others have passed through the gate, and walk about in the ante-chamber; and others have succeeded in entering into the inner part of the palace, and being in the same room with the king in the royal palace. But even the latter do not immediately on entering the palace see the king, or speak to him; for, after having entered the inner part of the palace, another effort is required before they can stand before the king—at a distance, or close by—hear his words, or speak to him. I will now explain the simile which I have made. The people who are abroad are all those that have no religion, neither one based on

speculation nor one received by tradition...Those who are in the country, but have their backs turned towards the king's palace, are those who possess religion, belief, and thought, but happen to hold false doctrines, which they either adopted in consequence of great mistakes made in their own speculations, or received from others who misled them. Because of these doctrines they recede more and more from the royal palace the more they seem to proceed...Those who desire to arrive at the palace, and to enter it, but have never yet seen it, are the mass of religious people; the multitude that observe the divine commandments, but are ignorant. Those who arrive at the palace, but go round about it, are those who devote themselves exclusively to the study of the practical law; they believe traditionally in true principles of faith, and learn the practical worship of God, but are not trained in philosophical treatment of the principles of the Law, and do not endeavour to establish the truth of their faith by proof. Those who undertake to investigate the principles of religion have come into the ante-chamber; and there is no doubt that these can also be divided into different grades. **But those who have succeeded in finding a proof for everything that can be proved, who have a true knowledge of God, so far as a true knowledge can be attained, and are near the truth, wherever an approach to the truth is possible, they have reached the goal, and are in the palace in which the king lives.**[22]

Faith must utilize knowledge to its maximum ability, according to Maimonides. The attempt to transform one's blind faith into a more rational faith is what Maimonides refers to as "knowing God" in his Mishneh Torah. Based on this understanding we can now answer the query of what Maimonides would have answered Crescas. It appears that when Maimonides stated in his *Sefer ha-Mitzvot* that there is a *mitzvah* to believe in God he was actually referring to "knowing God," as he clearly writes in his MishnehTorah. For Maimonides, simple belief in God requires no special effort. He was living in a generation where everyone believed in God, whether as Jews, Christians or Muslims. However, one is not to remain with this simple faith, but to transform it into a rational faith through questioning and study. This is what is meant by the *mitzvah* to "know" God. It is a specific mitzvah to study nature, religious philosophy, and metaphysics in order to transform one's belief into something more rationally mature. Therefore, being a specific *mitzvah*, there is no logical problem and no contradiction to Maimonides' criteria.[23]

If the above is correct, then why did Maimonides write in his *Sefer ha-Mitzvot* that there is a *mitzvah* to believe in God and not "to know God" as he did in his Mishneh Torah? R. Joseph Kafih has already shown in his translation of the *Sefer ha-Mitzvot* that the word Maimonides used, "*Mu'ataqada*," can be understood as "being firmly persuaded of such a thing"[24] rather than "faith." He therefore differs with ibn Tibbon's use of the Hebrew word "Ha'amanat" which means belief, substituting the word "Yediat," meaning "knowledge of."[25] Crescas, living in Christian Spain, did not speak Arabic and probably read ibn Tibbon's translation which brought him to question Maimonides' notion that there is a *mitzvah* to believe in God.

THE IMAGE OF ABRAHAM AS THE PROTOTYPE OF THE MAN OF FAITH

As I mentioned in a previous article, the biblical image of Abraham, for Jewish thinkers throughout the ages, becomes a prototype of the man of faith who finds God in a pagan world.[26] Therefore, the way each thinker describes Abraham will express how they see the man of faith. For Maimonides, Abraham is the prototype of the man of rational faith whose belief becomes one of personal knowledge:

Once Abraham was weaned, he, as a child, began contemplating and thinking day and night, and wondered how a sphere could follow a fixed path without being directed. If so, who directed it? Surely it would be impossible for it to rotate on its own! Abraham did not have a mentor, but was immersed amongst the foolish idolaters of Ur Casdim, where everyone, including his mother and father, served idols, as did he. In his heart, however, he continued to contemplate, until he realized the way of truth and understood the ways of righteousness from nature, and knew that there is a God who directs the spheres, created the world, and besides whom there is none other. He also knew that the whole world was erring, and knew that what caused the mistake was that they [had] worshipped the stars and figures for so long that the truth had vanished. Abraham was forty years old when he recognized his Creator. Once he achieved this, he began to reason with the inhabitants of Ur Casdim and to argue with them, saying that by serving idols they were not following the way of truth.[27]

In the *Guide*, Maimonides adds that Abraham used philosophic arguments to convince others of these theological truths.

> Thus Abraham taught, and showed by philosophical arguments that there is one God, that He has created everything that exists beside Him, and that neither the constellations nor anything in the air ought to be worshipped; he trained his fellow-men in this belief, and won their attention by pleasant words as well as by acts of kindness.[28]

Interestingly enough, Maimonides' claims that not only Abraham but all the forerunners of the Jewish people acted in this way. "Also Isaac, Jacob, Levi, Kohath, and Amram influenced their fellow-men in the same way."[29] Maimonides, thereby, takes his concept of rational faith and applies it not only to Jewish law by incorporating it into the 613 commandments but also describes the early forefathers as all going in such a path. Crescas, in contrast to Maimonides, sees belief as based on revelation. At the most one can have a rational inclination towards it but can never reach metaphysical truth without revelation. Concerning Abraham he brings a midrash which describes Abraham as one who questioned the origin of the universe:

> Rabbi Isaac said: this can be compared to one who passed from place to place and saw a palace all lit up. He said: Can it be that this palace is without an owner [lit. leader]? He said to him: I am the owner. So too since Abraham was saying: Can there be the world without a creator [lit. leader]? The Holy One Blessed Be He appeared to him saying: I am the owner of the world.[30]

Based on this midrash Crescas argues:

> What the Sages of Blessed Memory said in the midrash: This is compared to one who was passing from place to place and saw a palace all lit up. He said: Can it be that this palace is without an owner [lit. leader]? The Holy One blessed Be He appeared to him saying I am the owner of the world, etc. This means that even though he [Abraham] had an inclination towards the truth, he did not overcome his doubts until God sent his light of prophecy.[31]

We see clearly that Crescas sees faith as contingent on revelation. Therefore, this fits in well with his position that there can be no *mitzvah* to believe in God in the way in which Maimonides explained.

FURTHER PHILOSOPHIC IMPLICATIONS

The debate among the enumerators of the *mitzvot* seems to be one devoid of practical implications. After all, even if a command is not one of the 613 and even if it be of rabbinic origin it is still obligatory practice from a traditional perspective. However, in this specific case we have an example of an argument originating from each thinker's world view. Crescas, like Judah Halevi before him, saw faith as based wholly on revelation. Reason is at most a contributing player but for sure does not have a central role.[32] Faith, therefore, brings Man to a level that knowledge cannot reach. For Maimonides, the epitome of faith is knowledge. Even if human knowledge is limited, whatever we can utilize to prove our faith and make it rational transforms faith into a higher state of mind.[33] This type of rationalist theology characterizes most pre-Kantian medieval philosophical thinking. Here knowledge is seen as the highest form of faith. This was facilitated by a neo-Aristotelian metaphysical system which drew an orderly world in which Man and God had their respective places to occupy.[34] God was not only the creator of human souls but also an important player in the day to day understanding of how the physical universe runs.[35] Post-Newtonian physics leaves God without a role in the universe, and post-Kantian thinking puts even the knowledge of God's existence beyond the scope of human reason.[36] Is there then still room for Maimonides' *mitzvah* to "know" God through rational inquiry? Is this a *mitzvah* that can be fulfilled by modern man? In a simple sense, we can say that the fulfillment of this particular mitzvah according to Maimonides would be accomplished by delving into matters of faith and clarifying issues. Therefore, the very study of Jewish philosophy would suffice to fulfill this mitzvah according to Maimonides, regardless of the actual outcome. However, philosophically we might still ask whether one can actually achieve rational faith in a world that sees metaphysical issues as being outside the boundaries of human reason. The affirmative answer to such a question would be contingent on redefining what we mean by personal conviction as well as investigating what we mean by rational faith. This we discuss later.

CHAPTER 12

Belief in God:
The Classical Approach
in the Middle Ages,
Halevi's Critique,
and the Problems with
the Logical Proofs

In the Middle Ages, it was assumed that faith could and should be proven rationally. As I mentioned above, Maimonides saw the epitome of faith as knowledge of God. This knowledge was to be proven through various logical proofs, as a possible interpretation of the midrashic saying: "If one should say I toiled but did not find, do not believe [them]. I have toiled, but did not find, do not believe [them]; I have toiled and I have found, believe [them]." The assumption made in the middle-ages was that toiling meant the way of rational proofs. Many of the proofs brought in these works of yester-year were based on Aristotelian physics and therefore are not valid today. One such example is Maimonides' claim in the *Guide* 2:27, that even if one were to prove that the world was eternal, we could still prove the existence of God for, after all, who moves the heavenly spheres? This idea is based on Ptolemaic astronomy as well as Aristotelian physics. For

Aristotle, every movement in nature needs a cause. If the rock moved, it was due to the wind that moved it or some person. Without the notion of inertia, as proposed by Newton, each object moved needs a reason to keep moving as well. By way of illustration, if an arrow leaves a bow, the bow was the immediate cause of its movement. Since the arrow has now effectively left the bow and with no concept of inertia, the next question is why it continues to fly. Aristotle answered this by claiming that no vacuum is possible in nature. Since the arrow created a vacuum where it used to be, the air rushes in to fill the empty spot and effectively pushes the arrow forwards. As the arrow again moves forward, the air again fills the new void created, again pushing the arrow further. The next question of course is: why does the arrow fall? Aristotle answers this by introducing another notion, which is that all the four elements are attracted to their source. Earth and water have a downward source (which can be demonstrated by the fact that they fall down) and air and fire have their source above (which can be demonstrated by the fact that they rise up). The arrow, therefore, being mostly of earthy element, strives to reach its downward source, forcing it gradually downwards creating the arc type movement we witness. That was Aristotelian Physics 101. Based on this theory of nature, it is hard to understand why the planets continue to move. Even if God originally created the world and pushed the planets, why do they continue to move? There were two possible answers to this question, which I will call the religious and the secular answers. The religious answer was that God moves the spheres constantly. The secular answer was that the spheres have a soul (anima) and therefore they can move themselves just like mankind and animals. Maimonides did not think that the planets had a soul and therefore it was obvious to him that if the planets were moving eternally, then God had to move them. Therefore, even if one did not believe in creation, they would need God to move the spheres. This is a proof not valid in today's thinking.

In his *Critique of Pure Reason*, Immanuel Kant claims that of all the proofs for the existence of God argued in the middle-ages, three of them can still be seen as valid. They are: the cosmological proof, the ontological proof, and the physio-theological proof.[1] He commences with the ontological argument for the existence of God, which I will diplomatically skip since I see it as being based on the false premise that existence is a predicate; something which Alfarabi pointed out ages ago. Kant purposely begins with this argument since he sees it symbolically as the hidden premise of the other two. This I will discuss later.

THE COSMOLOGICAL ARGUMENT

This argument has no known author but was used in antiquity. It is based on a simple logical deduction, which is probably why it weathered the logical attacks of the ages. Simple is always best. The more complicated something is the more things can go wrong. (For example, just think of the Citroen car, which has to rise vertically before travelling horizontally.)

The cosmological argument goes something like this:

1. We evidence causality in nature. All effects have causes.
2. If this is true than we can ask what was the cause of the previous cause leading us to seek a first cause.
3. If this first cause was in nature then it too must have had a cause.
4. Therefore the first cause must have been beyond the laws of nature.
5. This first cause is God

The strength of the cosmological argument is the fact that it is based on the idea of causality, which is fundamental to our understanding of nature. All of scientific thinking is based on the assumption of cause and effect in nature. That does not mean that there were not attempts to undermine this argument.

The first attempt to undermine this argument can be inferred from the writings of Descartes. Descartes in his second meditation asks the question of what is real in the world. After all, if we perceive the world through the five windows of bodies, which are our five senses, and we cannot affirm for certain if our senses are objective since all which is perceived is done through the senses, therefore we have no certainty that anything out there really exists for sure. For example, if I ask my neighbor a question, I need to perceive his or her answer with my eyes and ears. However, what is to say that these five senses are not preprogrammed to give me the feeling that there are people, animals and plants in this world. Maybe the world is a figment of my sensorial imagination. A sort of virtual "Matrix" world. After all, if I drink a little too much alcohol I will see two policemen instead of one. Drugs will slow my sense of time and space, so how do I know that I perceive correctly when I am sober? Descartes doesn't argue that the world does not exist; he just doubts that one can ever be certain of its existence. The only thing one can be certain of is that which is not dependent on my senses, i.e. my thoughts. Therefore Descartes concluded that if I think, I am. "Cogito ergo sum."[2] Getting back to the cosmological argument, how can I argue that there is causality in nature if I am not certain that anything has real existence outside my own thoughts? Therefore, Leibnitz (and Descartes) rewrote the cosmological argument. This is how Kant quotes Leibnitz' formulation of the argument:

1. If something exists, an absolutely necessary being must likewise exist.
2. Now I at least exist, since I can think.
3. Consequently, there exists an absolutely necessary being (which brought me into existence).[3]
4. This being is God.

This new structure of the same argument from causality circumvents the problem of whether the world exists or not. However, that new version does not solve all the problems.

THE ATTACK ON CAUSALITY

In the nineteenth century the Scottish philosopher David Hume questioned the very notion of causality in nature. His thinking created many a wave in the intellectual ocean of his times. Kant said about Hume that the latter had awakened him from his intellectual slumber. Hume's argument, which in a sense was argued prior to him by the Kalam of the tenth century, goes something like this:

I see a boy with his arm raised in the air in front of his body. I see a ball flying in the air. I see a ball land. Based on the calculations of Newtonian physics I can actually demonstrate that the ball left the boy's hand at a specific moment which I can then calculate by the velocity of the ball and its angle of flight. This, of course, is based on the assumption that the world works according to causality. However, theoretically I can argue the point differently. Consider an animated film. In an animated movie, Bugs Bunny appears to be moving even though we all know that the film is made up of many frames. In one, Bugs Bunny's hand is down, in the next it is up, and therefore it appears to the eye that he actually moved, but it was just two frames set side by side in a sequence. Maybe that is how the world works. Life is many frames of being. In the first frame, the boy has a ball in hand, in the second, there is a ball in the air, but just as in the animated film, there is no causal connection between the frames.[4] Hume cannot prove his thesis but his goal is just to postulate an alternative to causality. After all, if one can offer an alternative explanation to natural events that means that causality is not certain. If it is not certain then we cannot base a proof upon it.

This argument seems strong; however, experience seems to render it a bit weak. You see, if David Hume is correct, then all of science is a farce. In actuality, it means that if I board an airplane assuming it can fly based on the theories of aerodynamics, I am basically taking my life in my hands by relying on this unconfirmed thesis since causality cannot be proven, and neither can any scientific theory for that matter. However, people seem to place their lives in the hands of these scientific theories daily, which means that they don't buy Hume's argument. This I call a dichotomy between human philosophical skepticism and human experience. The latter usually wins.

The most serious argument against the cosmological argument was Kant's. To understand Kant's argument we must review the argument. David Hume aside, Kant seems to accept the notion of cause and effect. If I exist, then this necessitates a cause that brought me into existence as does anything else. Aristotle postulated that the universe was eternal based on the idea of cause and effect. After all, if every effect has a cause, then even the first cause must have a cause.[5] In return Maimonides argued that it is absurd to argue that there are infinite causes since it is tantamount to arguing that there is no cause at all, which is absurd.[6] Therefore he postulates that the first cause must be beyond the laws of nature. This is the gist of the argument. However, Kant points out, in a nutshell, that even if there is logic to this argument[7] there are some presumptuous aspects as well. It is true, says Kant, that causality in nature points to a first cause, but if we seek this cause outside of nature we then have nothing to stand on. We do not even know if causality exists outside of nature. Therefore, even if the argument appears to be sound, we do not know what we are looking for. We cannot assume that this first cause is the God of the Bible, entailing an infinite unified being with a pathos and idea of reward and punishment. This is a presumptuous assumption beyond the scope of human understanding.[8] One might say that Kant seems less worried about the cosmological argument speaking of a first cause than the attempt to posit what this first cause might be, which is beyond the scope of human understanding and therefore becomes a statement of faith more than a logical proof. This would mean that if we return to the second model of the cosmological argument, Kant is willing to admit steps one through three to a certain extent, but step four is a mere statement of faith.[9]

THE PHYSIO-THEOLOGICAL ARGUMENT

Kant considered this the most convincing of the three arguments for the existence of God.[10] It goes something like this:

1. We observe in the world manifest signs of purposeful arrangement and calculated reciprocity.
2. Since these things in nature did not arrange themselves according to these principles,
3. Therefore there exists a sublime and wise cause which is all powerful which produced these beings and arranged them accordingly.
4. The unity of this cause can be inferred by the unity of the reciprocal relations existing between the parts of the world.
5. This unified being is God.[11]

To illustrate this argument, let's assume that Neil Armstrong, the first man to set foot on the moon, while taking his small step for man and large step for mankind, would have looked down and seen a can of Coca-Cola. What would have been his immediate reaction? If your answer is: "It's amazing how nature created a Coca-Cola can even on the moon to mimic what we have on earth" then you do not share the view of the above argument. However, if your answer was that he was thinking, "Oh my God, the Russians were here before us," then you have understood the physio-theological argument. A Coca-Cola can is just a piece of tin with a simple drawing on it. However, we would never assume it was caused randomly by nature but that its design indicated an intellectual inventor, i.e. Man must have created it. In the same vein, a watch indicates a watchmaker and a painting a painter. If I were to argue that my watch was not made by a watchmaker, but that there were pieces of loose metal that were blown together by the wind at random, I would probably find myself hauled away in a strait jacket on the way to the funny farm. It seems illogical. Well, then, the world is also filled with purposeful arrangement: we breathe in oxygen which is released from the plants and trees, and we breathe out CO_2 which they take in; the earth turns at a specific velocity which if sped up would cause the oceans to flood the land; the earth is at a specific distance from the sun, enabling life; the whole ecological system of the planet is perfectly designed to support life; within our bodies there are multiple intelligent systems; we take a bite of bread and then our digestive tract takes care of the rest; our body has a complicated system which fights the bacteria in our bodies at every moment. Without this complicated immune system we could not function. The brain is probably the most sophisticated system. It is so complicated that it makes the most complex computer look like child's play, since it's a computer that programs itself. These systems are so complicated that we barely understand how they work. Can we say that all this is random? This is the gist of the physio-theological argument. In modern times there are those who say, "Well okay, but this is all a result of evolution." However, the counter-argument is that this is just pushing the question back in time. After all, who designed the evolutionary process, which in itself is a complicated system? In the nineteenth century it was argued that all is random. The argument went like this: if you give a monkey a typewriter and endless time, he eventually will write Shakespeare. Even though statistically this sounds right, the flaws in the argument are multiple. For one, where did you get the monkey and who made the typewriter? Secondly, ever since the theory of the big bang was developed we have known that the universe was created at a certain point in time. This means there was not endless time for a random act.

The physio-theological argument is a strong one. Many scientists in the middle-ages, like Newton and Mendel, studied the physical world to discover the Divine intelligence therein.

Kant argues that the physio-theological argument can at most demonstrate the existence of an "architect of the world whose efforts are limited by the capabilities of the material with which he works, but not of a creator of the world, to whom all things are subject."[12] Kant therefore, claims that no cosmo-theological argument can ever prove the existence of a supreme Divine being but rather only indicate the notion of a prima-causa or an intelligent architect. Kant personally thought that the only route to trying to prove a Supreme Being and Commander of mankind was through understanding the essence of human morality rather than theology.[13] He felt that the notion of a Supreme Being cannot be proven or disproven since it is beyond the capability of human reason.[14] The limitation of theology was voiced already in the eleventh century by

R. Judah Halevi in his Kuzari. Concerning speculative metaphysics he wrote: "A religion based on logic, which is used to run the State, might be based on contemplation, but many doubts arise therein...this sort of religion is built on tenets only some of which can be proven by the philosophers, others can be proven in a limited way, and the rest can neither be demonstrated in any fashion nor proven in any way".[15]

Even though Kant did not claim that these proofs for the existence of God were defunct, by demonstrating their limitation and claiming that they could never actually prove a personal God or a Supreme Being and creator he sidelined the whole field of metaphysics. Since the end of the eighteenth century philosophy has taken a turn and divorced itself from the timeless issues of metaphysics. Instead, it has dealt with language, epistemology and other notions of the human experience. The problem is that by doing so it rendered itself irrelevant to modern man. After all, what human beings really want to know is why they are here, why they die, if there is a soul, if there is a God, and what happens after death. If philosophy cannot answer these questions, they look in other directions. This is an important point and one of the reasons that mysticism has re-emerged in our times. I will discuss this in a later chapter. In the meantime, we have to ask whether rational faith is possible after Kant. If I cannot prove my belief in God, can I even say that I am "convinced of my faith" and refer to a faith of reason or is it just a blind leap or an emotional feeling?

CHAPTER 13

Belief in God: A Modern Approach

In order to understand the answer to the above question it is necessary to split this chapter into two. First we must address the question of whether or not a spiritual path is at all legitimate in the twenty-first century. Second we have to investigate the question of whether one can actually speak of being convinced rationally of their faith and beliefs in modern times.

PART ONE:
IS A SPIRITUAL PERSPECTIVE LEGITIMATE
IN MODERN TIMES?

As I mentioned in a previous chapter, in Newtonian physics the world of nature seemed like clockwork. Everything moved by predestined laws, to such a degree that Newton himself wondered what job was left for

God to do in such a precise world. After all, if God didn't need to move the spheres, according to the newly-discovered concept of inertia, what role did He have in the physical world after creation? Newton, however, discovered that the planets did not follow a correct pattern according to the laws of gravitation and therefore he found a role for God. This flaw in the astronomical laws were actually not due to a flaw in his calculations but rather to the absence of the existence of Pluto, Uranus and Neptune in the astronomical science of the day, since these cannot be seen without the proper magnification. Therefore Newton found a role for God in his theory of blind natural laws. In post-Newtonian thinking the question arose that if all of the universe is governed by predetermined laws, why then should mankind have free will. Or is it just an illusion? The answer given was that Man has a soul which gives him the power of free will, rendering him different from all other animals. Man was therefore the exception to the rule. The universe was seen as being a material mass run like clockwork by unbending rules. It is not surprising therefore that the next question was whether Man was just another material part of the puzzle and maybe the soul was just a convenient myth to solve the problem. Materialism was the name of the day in the nineteenth century. With the move of philosophy into realism, departing from metaphysics, it was science that now controlled the heart and mind of Man. The scientific revolution, which started in the mid-nineteenth century, just served to strengthen this feeling of the omnipotence of the human mind and the endless possibilities ahead. The pace of change was so radical that from 1850 to 1930 Western society went through so many changes as to become almost unrecognizable. In the field of technological discoveries the railway system and the newspaper brought knowledge to all and made distances traversable. The discovery of electricity, and the inventions of the gramophone, the telephone, radio, and television, had a profound effect on communication and the dispersion of information. The car, the bus, and the airplane made the world just that much smaller. In the field of medicine, the discoveries of insulin, x-rays, antibiotics, and various vaccines made infant life expectancy as well as that of the average adult higher. It seemed just a matter of time until all disease would be conquered, and maybe even mortality itself. In the early part of the twentieth century, a center was founded in California where one could freeze their loved one's body in liquid nitrogen in the hope that one day science would cure their sickness or possibly mortality itself. The belief that the West had brought something superior to the world was woven so deep into the social fabric of society that the masses excused the selfish political agendas of Western Imperialism in the claim of bringing an advanced culture to primitive societies. Most of the inhabited world was dealt out between England and France like some type of Star Trek: Voyager landing on primitive planets, enlightening the locals with their advanced technology and know-how. This scientific approach to the world created a weltanschauung that depicted a material world run by blind laws. Beliefs were seen as superstition, religion was seen as run by power-hungry clergy who used it to manipulate the masses, mysticism as primitive, and spirituality as old wives' tales. Science was on the way up and metaphysics was the science of yesteryear.

However, in the beginning of the twentieth century things started to change. By the late nineteenth century scientists were beginning to understand that the real world is quite different than what appears to the naked eye. Let me illustrate. There was once a television program called "Northern Exposure." In it, Dr. Fleisher explains to his girlfriend how the human body is covered with microscopic bacteria and parasites that cannot be seen by the human eye, necessitating washing the hands before eating. (Thank you, Louis Pasteur). The girlfriend is so shocked by this revelation that she cannot even approach him since she imagines his body covered with microscopic organisms. (Who ever said what you don't know can't hurt you?) The late nineteenth and early twentieth centuries taught us that we live in a world where much is hidden and only some things are revealed. Those things hidden from the human eye enable us to go on with our lives without worrying too much. Every time you drink a glass of water you are digesting thousands of bacteria. When you devour that steak, you are taking in thousands of the little guys with it. These bacteria multiply so fast that if you leave your steak for more than about 6 hours without heating it, they will ruin the meat and make you very ill. Our bodies are constantly fighting foreign invaders. The immune system is an army of soldiers in a constant battle. If they are weakened, you fall into bed with exhaustion. The world reveals to us just what we need to live and no more. We know that there are colors that exist that we cannot see. Some can be seen through the aid of instruments like infra-red or ultra-violet. Others cannot be seen even though they exist. There are sounds we cannot hear, but dogs can, hence the dog whistle. Sometimes a supersonic plane flies above, and we hear nothing but the dog barks. Elephants can hear very low sounds that are not audible to the human ear and call their mates over miles of flatland with sounds undetected by human ears. Can you imagine what types of symphonies or works of art we could produce if we could expand the human sensorial perception? What would our world look like then? We are told that the human being is 70% water. However it is not a notion we can live with daily. We learn to live in denial. But science does not stop there. It teaches us that the very matter of the world, the "stuff" of the material realm, is not really what we think. The early twentieth century was witness to a major leap in the understanding of matter, of the "stuff", so to speak, of the physical world. With the development of nuclear physics and the discoveries of Max Plank, Ernest Rutherford, Niels Bohr and Albert Einstein, the world at hand was starting to look different. It wasn't the same old material of Isaac Newton's universe. It appeared that the world was basically a conglomerate of electromagnetic fields and various forms of energy, and the material "stuff" or mass of matter played an insignificant role in this equation. In other words, it seemed that the material world was not as material as it appeared to be. Let me illustrate. If I hit the table, according to Newtonian physics my hand is one material working on another by force. The stronger force will survive; either I break the table or my hand will be sore. In twentieth-century science I was told that my hand produces a force such that in order to stay whole the table actually has to push back at me. On the molecular level, the table is not at all static. Its molecules are in constant motion. Then I am told that if I observe further I will find that these molecules are made up of atoms that are also in constant motion. This needs further illustration. I remember as a kid reading the *World Book Encyclopedia*, which gave the following example: If one could take the simplest atom, the hydrogen atom, which has only one electron orbiting its nucleus, and theoretically enlarge the nucleus of the hydrogen atom to the size of a pin head, the distance between this nucleus and the electron orbiting it would be several kilometers. This means that most of the atom is really electromagnetic field. The actual material mass of the atom is contained in the nucleus, since the electrons have a negligible weight. The article continued by saying that in theory, if we could take all the atoms of planet earth and squash the electrons into their nuclei, thereby getting rid of the "space" taken up by the electromagnetic fields, all we would have left would be one cubic meter. That would be the sum total of the "matter" of planet earth. The question now arises: according to this, what exactly do we mean when we say we are living in a material world? With all respects to Madonna, are we really material people in a material world? We seem to live in a world which is predominantly energy dominated by electromagnetic fields and nuclear energy; maybe also the energy of life. What type of material is this? According to Einstein's law of the conservation of matter, all matter can be transformed into energy and vice versa. Is energy the material of the world? If so, what type of world is it?

Not only had nuclear physics introduced a new perspective on the material world, but it has also raised many unanswerable questions, and the more one looks, the more the questions outnumber the answers. The earlier questions seemed quite science-oriented, like: "Is light a wave, a particle, or both?" However, by the second half of the twentieth century reputable scientists were asking questions like: "Do electrons have free will?" and, "Are there simultaneous universes?" These are questions which seem more suitable for a class in Eastern mysticism or possibly a Star Wars sequel rather than the marble halls of the academic world.[1] Niels Bohr is quoted as saying, "Anyone who is not shocked by quantom theory has not understood it."[2] It is little wonder then that an American physicist by the name of Gary Zukav wrote a popular book in the early seventies on the philosophic relationship between modern science and Buddhist thinking,[3] and Paul Davies wrote his book on God and the New Physics from a liberal Christian standpoint. I am not trying to prove that the world is spiritual. This is a nebulous word in need of definition. All I am saying is that the modern perspective of the world is much less material then the Newtonian model and therefore a spiritual explanation is no more far-fetched then a material one. As one physicist put it:

> "the traditional arguments for the existence of God...are for better or for worse, being resurrected from the dustbins of theological life through the dialogue wiith modern physics. In the twentieth century one is pressed to find a single theologian of note...who has employed any of the three traditional arguments for the existence of god. Ironically , one need not look so hard among twentieth century physicists. Edmund Whittaker, Siegfried Muller-Markus, Freeman Dyson, Charles Misner and Frank Tipler have all openly employed at least one of the traditional proofs in order to argue the existence of a supreme being."[4]

In other words, in this new light that we need to understand that a spiritual approach to the world is at least as valid as a material one.

PART TWO:
CAN ONE SPEAK OF RATIONAL FAITH
IN A POST-KANTIAN WORLD?

In the Western tradition of thought mankind was defined as a homo-sapiens, a thinking being. However, human reason itself was defined in a very narrow way. Greek philosophy under Aristotle saw its goal as making statements about the world that could be proven or disproven through human logic. This of course was a major innovation, as I explained in an earlier chapter. However, it was also a limited view of human reason. Is human reason comprised only of logic? Definitions of human logic developed over the centuries. Aristotle spoke only of deductive logic through syllogisms. In the Middle Ages they developed theories of inductive logic. But logic is just one mode of how the mind reasons.[5] The advantage of a logical argument is that it is a closed model of thought that has a premise and reaches an unequivocal conclusion as does mathematics. However, the downside of such thinking is its application to the real world. Mathematics is a pure science which exists within itself, detached from the real world. After all, 2 chairs and 2 chairs equal 4 chairs in mathematics but in the real world there are no four chairs that look identical under a microscope. This means that we superimpose mathematics on our reality to help us with certain needs. However, its ability to help, as a pure science, is limited. Logic like math is a pure science which can exist within its own. If $a=b$ and $b=c$ then $a=c$ with or without a world. The problem with using logic in a real world is the definitions needed to enter the model. In recent years a book was written, entitled *Fuzzy Logic*. The book basically asked the question of what to do with categories undetermined by regular human categories. At what point do grains of sand become a pile of sand? How can I count four piles of sand if I can break them down into indefinable piles? How much water is a pool of water? The life definitions seem to be anything but scientific.

When speaking of proving something, or reasonable truths, a logical or mathematical proof is just one form. There are at least six forms of rational proofs or truths.

1. A mathematical or closed proof.

By closed I mean that there is a statement with an unequivocal conclusion. Math and logic are similar in this sense.

1 and 1 $=2$ or $a=b$, $b=c$, therefore $a=c$

In both cases the answer is a closed logical formula with a single conclusion. This is one form in which human reason proves a statement, and in the world of philosophy there is a bias towards it, but is by no means the only type of proof.

2. Axiomatic statements.

Euclidean geometry is based on axioms. These axioms are unproven truths upon which this science lies. For instance: two parallel lines will never meet, or, the shortest route between two points is a straight line. There is no way of measuring two infinite parallel lines but we know they will never meet. An axiom is not "an agreed upon basis" but rather a known truth which cannot be proven but is obviously correct. This brings us to a similar concept outside the world of geometry.

3. A Priori statements or truths.

Emanuel Kant coined this term for truths that one knows without the ability to prove it. These types of truths are quite common on the realm of ethics. For instance, the statements "Human life is sacred" and "one should not murder" and "stealing is wrong" are universally accepted and rational ideas which are impossible to prove. To say that we have no right to take another life is rational but no proof is possible. In fact, any proof falls short of the original idea, making a mockery of it. If one should say: "Well, I shouldn't murder because maybe they can murder me," that would mean that if one was invincible then it would be permissible. If I say that I cannot steal because they might steal from me, this sort of morality of thieves doesn't work if they cannot steal from me. Therefore, such an a priori statement is rational and understood universally but cannot be proven by regular logic.

4. Holistic or Simple systems.

This is where the reader is thinking, "Okay, here starts the new-age stuff." Actually this type of thinking has been used in scientific models for ages. When Copernicus, Galileo, and Bruno came along and argued that the sun and not the earth was at the center of the solar system they did not have a space ship that could take them out of the solar system to see it from afar. (In fact, neither do we.) So how did they know that the sun is at the center? After all, movement is a relative concept and needs a point of reference. For instance, if I am traveling in a subway and I see another train pass me by there are three possibilities: either my train is moving and the other is stationary, or the other is moving in the opposite direction and I am stationary, or both trains are moving in opposite directions. Only a point of reference, like the ground, can enable me to conclude what is really correct. Since there is no point of reference in the solar system, it is possible to argue that the earth is at the center of the system. This is exactly what a navigator does on a ship in the ocean. They assume that they are in the center and navigate by the stars. However, if I assume that the earth is at the center of the system, the other planets will move in unusual asymmetrical movements. In Ptolemaic astronomy this was referred to as epicycles. Sometimes the planets will seem to stay in one place or even go backwards (retrograde), but the system is workable. However, if I assume that sun is at the center, I can calculate smoother courses of paths for the planets which will move in constant ellipses around the sun in only one direction and at a constant speed. Since this model seems more reasonable and simpler an explanation in the larger picture of things, we assume it to be true. In the realm of physics a similar thing happened. I discussed earlier the Aristotelian theory of physics. This theory explained the physical world and was accepted as true for a thousand years. How then did the scientific community come to believe the superiority of the Newtonian system? Even though on planet earth the Aristotelian model had a complete explanation for the law of nature, Newton's theory of gravity was universal and explained not only what happens on earth but also the relationships of the planets between themselves and the sun. This theory, being more encompassing and a simpler explanation of the whole picture, was then decidedly truer than Aristotle's. When Einstein came along, again his theory added something that Newton had not thought about. Einstein explained that Newtonian physics appeared correct at slow velocities; however, when one came closer to the speed of light, new elements had to be introduced into the equations. Therefore Einstein's physics was more encompassing, since it also took into account higher velocities and was therefore considered closer to the truth. This type of thinking is what we use when in our own lives we try to understand if a new idea is true or not.

5. Assimilation and experience.

This category is connected to the previous one since we assimilate new ideas into our general concepts of life. If they harmonize we accept them. If they don't we don't, unless we are given hard evidence which forces us to accommodate the new information. This is how Piaget explained this concept. However, our own past life experience is a major reference point for all of our understanding of the ideas we hear or new phenomena we encounter. Therefore I put assimilation and experience together. To illustrate: if I attend a psychology class for the first time and I am not sure psychology is a real science or not, I will test the ideas. Let's say the professor says that according to psychologists people enter elevators and immediately move to the side in order not to attract attention or be the center of focus. If I then enter an elevator and see this happening it will strengthen my belief in his statements, past and future. If next day he says that research has found that people tend to get tired at around four o'clock p.m. and at four o'clock I look around the class and see the students yawning, again it will strengthen my belief in this system of knowledge. In addition, if the general ideas of this system also agree with my own understanding of the world, I will assimilate it into my life perspectives as well.

6. Intuition.

Kant thought that intuition was an intellectual faculty and not an emotional one. The intuitive sense might actually work on both levels. I would like, however, to focus on the intellectual level. We use our intuitions all the time. In fact we probably use category 5 and 6 much more than the first three in dealing with real life issues. After all, when we pick a spouse it is hardly based on hard logic. At the most, logic assists our decisions. In a recently published book, *Gut Feelings*, new research has been done on how heavily human beings depend on their intuitions and their "gut feelings." These premonitions are actually ways our brains help us take scholarly guesses at what the outcome of an event will be. Scientists have used this for centuries; they call it a 'hypothesis.' What is a hypothesis? It is a scholarly guess which has not been proven. Well, if has not been proven, then is it true? If it is proven, then ipso facto we know it was right. If it is proven incorrect then we understand that it was wrong. So what is it? Not every hypothesis will be considered. A layman's hypothesis in physics will not be studied. It will take time and money that no one will invest. Only the expert who has spent time in the research of physics, with the proper credentials, will see his or her premonitions studied. These are scholarly intuitions based on past study. It is the mind leaping forward, hopefully not beyond its limit. A student sits in an algebra exam. He studied hard and feels he knows the material. He reads the problems. He can't figure out the answer. All week he has worked on these problems but it just isn't coming to him. All of a sudden, in an intellectual flash of lightening, the idea comes to him. He tries it, it works. The problem is solved. Where did the idea come from? What process led up to it? What state was the idea in before being applied to the actual problem? In 2009, I taught my introductory course on Jewish philosophy to a group of students taking an evening course in Logistics who were not familiar with logical thinking and argumentation. I drew a diagram of Maimonides' description of Aristotle's rule of the golden mean on the blackboard (See above diagram 2a, p. 64). I asked the class which side was the more difficult attribute to bring to the mean (above p. 64) and intuitively, all the students could tell me the side which was easier to bring to the mean. However, when I asked them what the logical rule was that brought them to this conclusion, they were unable to explain this to me. Each mind had reached the right conclusion but was incapable of explaining logically how it had achieved this result. However, after I explained to them the logical principle behind their conclusion they all agreed with me.

"A close friend of mine (call him Harry) once found himself with two girlfriends, both of whom he loved, desired and admired. Two, however, were one too many. Confused by contradicting emotions and unable to make up his mind, he recalled what Ben Franklin had once advised a nephew in a similar situation. April 8, 1779: 'If you doubt, set down all the reasons, pro and con, in opposite columns on a sheet of paper and when you have considered them for two or three days, perform an operation...observe what reasons or motives in each column are equal in weight...'

"Harry was greatly relieved that a logical formula existed to solve his conflict. So he took his time, wrote down all the important reasons he could think of, weighed them carefully, and went through the calculation. When he saw the result, something unexpected happened. An inner voice told him that it wasn't right. And for the first time, Harry realized that his heart had already decided—against the calculation and in favor of the other girl. The calculus helped to find the solution, but not because of its logic. It brought an unconscious decision to his awareness, based on reasons obscure to him. Thankful for the sudden solution but puzzled by the process, Harry asked himself how it was possible to make unconscious choices in contradiction to one's deliberate reasoning. He was not the first to learn that reasoning can conflict with what we call intuition."[6]

This chapter is shorter than what is needed to fully explore this topic, but it is just the beginning of an understanding. In most of our life situations we tend to use our intuition, premonitions, holistic thinking and a priori beliefs much more than we use standard logical thinking. The complexity of life issues forces us to act in such a way. In the martial arts, after one has learned the moves well, one is encouraged to reach a "no-mind" state in which one does not use analytical thought. Just let the mind flow with the knowledge learned and the application will come. In daily life, logical thinking is used. However, in our major life issues, such as choosing a spouse, picking an ideology, forming an opinion on politics or social matters, or picking a religious belief, we tend to rely more on our intuitions. As Gigerenzer writes: "Rigid logical norms overlook that intelligence has to operate in an uncertain world, not in the artificial certainty of a logical system and needs to go beyond the information given."[7] We are assisted by logic, but the intuitive faculties are the ones that will decide the matter. We have rational systems working full time to comprehend the world we live in. These systems were formed well before we developed fully logical thinking, because as a child we needed to learn language skills and cope with life early on. William Wundt, the father of experimental psychology, wrote:

> At first it was thought that the surest way would be to take as a foundation for the psychological analysis of the thought processes the laws of logical thinking, as they had been laid down from the time of Aristotle by the science of logic. These norms only apply to a small part of the thought processes. Any attempt to explain, out of these norms, thought in the psychological sense of the word can only lead to an entanglement of the real facts in a net of logical reflections. We can in fact say of such attempts, that measured by the results they have been absolutely fruitless. They have disregarded the psychological processes themselves."[8]

As Gigerenzer adds:

> Generations of students in the social sciences have been exposed to entertaining lectures that point out how dumb everyone else is, constantly wandering off the path of logic and getting lost on the fog of intuition. Yet logical forms are blind to content and culture, ignoring evolved capacities and environmental structure. Often what looks like a reasoning error from a purely logical perspective turns

out to be a highly intelligent social judgment in the real world. Good intuitions must go beyond the information given, and therefore, beyond logic.[9]

Therefore, if we ask the question of whether modern man can be convinced of his belief, the answer will be in the affirmative, as long as we recognize that rational thought is more inclusive than just logical formulas.

*Changes in the
Perception of
Monotheism Over
the Ages[1]*

Monotheism is an idea, attributed to Jewish origins even though there exists no equivalent term in the Hebrew language.[2] So despite the fact that this statement is a truism and Jews have believed de facto in one God since the times of Abraham, theology per se has never been a Jewish vocation and therefore it is only through the Western philosophic influence of the Middle Ages that Jewish thinkers have systematically delved into the fine points of their monotheistic belief. That does not mean that changes have not taken place that need to be understood. The movement from a pagan perception of reality to a purely monotheistic one is a gradual process which is not without growing pains. Maimonides describes Abraham's struggle with his faith as a process that reached its maturation by the age of forty.[3] The midrash describes Abraham as a militant monotheist who destroyed his father's idols in order to prove the point that they are powerless.[4]

The prophet Isaiah mocked the idol-worshippers as simpletons who bowed to human-made instruments: "The idol? A wood-maker shaped it, and a smith overlaid it with gold forging links of silver. As a gift he chooses the mulberry, a wood that does not rot, then seeks a skilful woodworker to make a firm idol that will not topple" (Isa. 40:19-20). He then described how the same sticks and stones they used for heating and cooking were used for idol worship: "The makers of idols all work to no purpose and the things they treasure can do no good...who can fashion a God or cast a statue that can do no good?...The craftsman in iron, with his tools, works it over charcoal and fashions it by hammering...He chooses plain trees and oaks....half of it he burns in a fire; on that part he roasts meat, he eats the roast and is sated, he also warms himself and cries "Ah, I am warm! I can feel the heat!" Of the rest he makes a God — his own carving" (Isa. 44:12-17). This use of humor or mockery can be found as early as the book of Samuel. When the Philistines took the Ark of the Covenant, a sort of showdown is described between Dagon, the god of the Philistines, and the ark. "Early the next day the Ashdodites found Dagon lying face down on the ground in front of the ark of the Lord. They picked Dagon up and put him back in his place but early the next morning Dagon was again lying prone on the ground in front of the ark of the Lord. The head and both hands of Dagon were cut off, lying on the threshold; only Dagon remained intact" (I Sam. 5:3-5). In a similar fashion, Elijah mocked the priests of the Baal: "When the noon came Elijah mocked them saying: Shout louder! After all he is God. But he may be in conversation, he may be detained or he may be on a journey, or perhaps he is asleep and will wake up" (I Kings 18:27). Based on this and other passages the Talmud declared: "All jesting is forbidden except for that which concerns idolatry."[5] Despite this, the question is whether the prophets saw idolatry in such black-and-white terms or just used this as a pedagogical approach. It's hard to fathom that generations of humans would have followed a religion that believed in sticks and stones as gods. What we are told in other accounts is that Paganism was a religious belief that saw the idol or icon as a symbol or a means to reach a transcendent power within nature. The priest or shaman would be the facilitator to harness this power for the benefit of the worshipper. Since these icons were central symbols acting as conduits for the powers, they became a focal point of the pagan worship. The Bible calls the pagan gods "Elim," meaning powers. God is sometimes referred to as "El," meaning the power; sometimes as "eloha" including the letter "heh" from the tetragrammaton and sometimes as "Elohim," meaning the one single force behind multiplicity.[6] R. Judah Halevi explains that the pagans worshipped the powers within nature either since they could not fathom a single united force that transcended these powers or because they thought that praying to such a transcendent force was a useless endeavor.[7] The belief in one God was therefore a novelty which entered into a world that had a conceptual bias against it. In light of this, it is always interesting to see the encounters between monotheists and pagans in ancient times. A biblical recording of such an encounter can be found when Abraham won the battle over the four kings. After freeing Lot from captivity, Abraham was greeted by Melchizedek the priest of Salem.[8] "And King Melchizedek of Salem brought out bread and wine; he was a priest of God most high [el elyon]. He blessed him saying; blessed be Abram of God most high [el elyon] who has delivered your foes into your hand... But Abraham said to the King of Sodom: I swear to the Lord God most high, [YHVH el elyon] creator of heaven and earth"(Gen. 15:18-22). Abraham gave Melchizedek a brief lesson in monotheistic theology. Whereas Melchizedek believed in the Babylonian gods El and Elyon,[9] who were highly regarded as the apex of the polytheistic pantheon, Abraham believed only in YHVH, that is, the one God who dwells above and beyond the powers of the natural or even supra-natural world.[10] A second biblical account of a meeting between a monotheist and a pagan is the story of Joseph interpreting Pharaoh's dream. Pharaoh saw Joseph as one who possesses esoteric powers of dream interpretation: "I have had a dream but no one can interpret it. Now I heard it is said of you that for you to hear a dream is to tell its meaning." Joseph answered Pharaoh, saying: "Not I! God will see to Pharaoh's welfare" (Gen. 41:15-16). Joseph mentioned God's name five times in his discourse with Pharaoh until Pharaoh said: "Could we find another like him, a man in whom is the spirit of God?" (Gen. 41:38). The Midrash saw Joseph as an ardent monotheistic activist who actually forced the Egyptians to circumcise their male children.[11] Interestingly enough Josephus saw this as a historical fact. If this is true, we can see the discussion between Joseph and Pharaoh as a sort of theological debate. Joseph is pushing the one God theory to win Pharaoh over to his point of view.[12] The Jews in Egypt spent hundreds of years in such a society and must have been swayed by these notions, making the shift to pure monotheism a difficult one.

FROM PAGANISM TO MONOTHEISM

What were the main problems? For the ancient pagan mind, there were two incomprehensible aspects to monotheism. The first was the exclusivity of the one God, excluding any form of divinity aside from the one God. The polytheistic mind could comprehend the idea of an all-powerful sovereign god, a Zeus among a larger pantheon, but not an exclusive one. The idea of God being "one without an enumeration [of a second]"[13] was incomprehensible to them. I assume that the claim that no other Gods existed besides the one God might have been seen as a sign of intolerance in those days. The second was the claim that God is devoid not only of physicality, but has no picture or physical representation in any way, shape or form. Even the Hebrews in Egypt who had a tradition that the God of Abraham, Isaac and Jacob was different than the Egyptian belief,[14] and probably understood the exclusivity of God; which was reinforced in the exodus story,[15] had difficulty understanding how such a God could be worshipped without some type of representation. According to R. Judah Halevi,[16] this is the reason they sought the medium of a golden calf when Moses was delayed on Mount Sinai. They saw Moses as the medium through which the God of Israel was to be worshipped[17] and panicked when he seemed to disappear. Therefore, we have to understand the phrase, "These are your Gods O Israel who took you out of Egypt"[18] not as a naïve belief that the golden calf was the corpus of God, but an attempt to create a new medium to reach the God of Israel. They could not comprehend the idea of worship without a medium. R. Halevi compares this to the modern inability to fathom religion without prayer and houses of worship.[19] One just has to look eastward, to see how Buddhist temples were erected in India to pray to the Buddha, to realize how difficult it was for the average Buddhist to deal with his or her non-deistic religion. This then is the first stage of movement from a pagan way of thinking to monotheism. The Hebrews understood that God was one and exclusive, but did not as yet comprehend that He has no physical representation, not even through a medium.[20] To reinforce this point Moses broke the tablets, the first medium that God created for the people, to drive home the point that there is no absolute sanctity to any medium between God and the people. This is the same Moses who said to God: "If your countenance will not go with us, do not take us out of here."[21] Moses did not want any angel or intermediary at all. One might say that as a tribute to Moses' efforts in teaching the direct worship of

God, our sages deliberately left his name out of the Passover Haggadah to stress that Moses, who was an intermediary, could not be made central to even the exodus story itself, for it was God who delivered us from Egypt. Moses then teaches the Hebrews the first lesson in Monotheistic theology, that no representation in any form, even as an intermediary, is possible.

FROM MONOTHEISTIC BELIEF
TO INTELLECTUAL MONOTHEISM

Moses' lesson was internalized, but there still was a certain tolerance to the mental imagery that one might conjure in one's mind concerning the one God. This was more difficult to fight since the Bible itself implemented such imagery. Didn't Moses speak of the hand,[22] eyes[23] and feet[24] of God? Didn't Isaiah call the heavens God's chair and the earth His foot stool?[25] Therefore, the fight for intellectual monotheism was a much more difficult one, with the goal being to eradicate the corporeal imagery which necessitated neutralizing the anthropomorphic language of the Bible. This is exactly what Maimonides did in his *Guide for the Perplexed*, the whole first part of which was written for just this purpose. Maimonides led a merciless battle against anthropomorphism, reinterpreting every such statement in the Bible and condemning a well-known piece of literature of his day, namely the *Shiur Komah*. His fiery sword of battle did not spare even certain midrashic passages in *Pirkei De Rabbi Eliezer*[26] and *Midrash Rabbah*.[27] Maimonides went as far as claiming that one who considers God to possess a body is a sinner and should repent for this on Yom Kippur.[28] This latter statement seemed radical even to Maimonidean sympathizers like R. Joseph Albo, who considered such a person mistaken but not a sinner.[29] The relentless attack on anthropomorphism brought certain rabbinic figures, specifically of kabbalistic bent, to express their concerns about Maimonides' position.[30] The kabbalists had long used the corporeal terms for God in the Bible as keys to an exegetic code and were not happy to see what they perceived as Maimonides' "changing the rules" of exegesis.[31] Later kabbalists even criticized Maimonides for over-rationalizing Judaism, being too partial to Aristotelian philosophy.[32] For Maimonides, the goal was to purge Judaism of what he considered to be pagan materialist beliefs.[33] However, while Maimonides attempted to create a purist intellectual form of belief, in doing so he created a cosmic theocentric system in which God was formless, immaterial and infinite, but transcended the human abode. He was, so to speak, up there, and we were down here, reflecting the verse: "For God is in heaven and you are on earth; therefore should your words be few" (Eccl. 5:1). God's connection to mankind was through his Divine Providence over human beings.[34] This perception was based on the common neo-Aristotelian world view which saw the Deity as the highest strata of the order of heavenly intelligences, each more removed from the mundane sub-lunar world than the others. Due to this world view, it was difficult to perceive the God-man relationship in any other way. Interestingly enough, in the Hassidic post-Aristotelian world, R. Shneur Zalman of Liadi actually condemned an unnamed kabbalist who held the "faulty" opinion that God watches over the world from a distance.[35] What seemed obvious to the medieval thinker was again challenged in early modernity, this time however not by the rationalists but rather by the mystics.

FROM INTELLECTUAL MONOTHEISM TO THE KABBALISTIC "EIN SOF"

Since post Kantian philosophy kept its distance from classical metaphysics, the need for a new monotheistic perception would have to come from elsewhere. Already in the thirteenth century, the appearance of the Zohar created new theological perceptions: "There is no place devoid of Him," it claimed.[36] God not only transcends all, "sovev kol almin," but also permeates all of existence, "memaleh kol almin."[37] This concept of permeating existence is different than the philosophic idea of Divine immanence. God's immanence can be perceived as the way a human being relates to the Divine presence. Even the Talmudic idea of the *Shekhina*, the Divine presence, further developed in the Middle Ages, never meant to say that God's presence is found equally in all of existence.[38] The *Shekhina*, referred to by Maimonides as "the created light" of God, represented Divine Providence or some form of presence in the world but not God's essence.

> Whenever he [Onkolos the proselyte, in his translation of the Bible] encounters one of the terms indicative of one of the kinds of motion, he makes motion to mean the manifestation and appearance of a created light, I mean the *shekhina (indwelling)* or the action of providence.[39]

This understanding is based on the approach of Saadiah Gaon, who explained the shekhina as "the created glory,"[40] and is close to R. Judah Halevi's perception of this concept.[41] Isaac Luriah, the sixteenth-century kabbalist who saw his writings as an interpretation of the Zohar, saw this issue of the Divine presence in a created world as the central new mode of thinking of post-Zoharic kabbalah. The doctrine of the *zimzum* was aimed at explaining not only how the infinite God could create a finite world, but how such a world was possible in light of the knowledge that God's existence permeates all of reality. How can there be room for the existence of such a world?[42] R. Hayyim Vital spelled this out from a kabbalistic vantage point: "Since the infinite one [*ein sof*] is equally infinite with no up or down, back or front, which all designate limitation in the infinite light, God forbid, and since the infinite light permeates all the *sefirot*...as is mentioned in the Zohar...and since all the *sefirot* are close to the infinite light and receive from it, how can there be any difference between them?"[43] The answer found in the doctrine of the *zimzum* created as many questions as it raised. Was the act of the *zimzum* a metaphor and if so, what did it mean? Did this act happen only from our human perspective or did it happen from an objective point of view? These theological questions, which the Ari himself preferred to avoid,[44] created new insights into pure monotheism. I see here an additional three stages. The first is that of the Zohar, which brought God's presence (and not just his providence) down from the heavens to permeate all of existence, as mentioned above. The second stage is the writings of the Ari, in which there is an attempt to pinpoint how exactly the infinite existence of God could create a finite universe and then proceed and permeate it without jeopardizing its independent existence. The third stage is to be found in the writings of the Hassidic and mithnagdic kabbalists who took the Ari's thinking a step further. The Hassidim argued that the only way to preserve a purist monotheistic idea of God is to claim that creationism never really happened from God's point of view. This sort of acosmic[45] approach to reality, placing reality into the subjective human arena, should be seen as an attempt to free monotheism from inconsistencies. There is only God. Man and God are in a Divine relationship within the Divine existence; a reality whose truth is perceived by God alone:

> If the eye could perceive the vitality and spirit within each creature, [given to it] through the Divine spirit, no material or physical element would be seen, for its existence is null and void in face of the vital

and spiritual [source] without which it could not exist; [just as it did not exist] before the six days of creation.[46]

There are Hassidic thinkers who explain the whole act of creation as a subjective act perceived by humans alone as holding a separate reality.[47] The attempt to doubt the validity of the material world was an attempt to attain a purist understanding of monotheism based on the Zoharic idiom that there is nothing but Godliness, "Leit Atar panui minei."[48] Interestingly enough, the mithnagdim, who opposed this point of Hassidic theology, do not seem to differ too greatly.[49] The Vilna Gaon argued that God cannot be referred to even by the term *Ein Sof*, which would be a human appellation putting His existence into an artificial category: "Know that the infinite [*Ein Sof*] cannot be contemplated at all, neither can we speak of it as having a necessary existence...and even the [term] *Ein Sof* cannot be used to describe it."[50] Rabbi Kook, a student of the mithnagdic kabbalistic school, continued this line of thought, criticizing the whole field of theology as being a derivative of Pagan thinking, creating artificial categories to contain the human concept of the Divine:

> It is true, and has always been known and neither did we need Kant to reveal this secret to us, that all human apprehensions are subjective and relative; this is the [idea behind the kabbalistic concept of] the "*malkhut*" which is devoid of self...no intellectual or metaphysical form can be attributed [to God], and we know that this is of necessity but all [existence] comes from Him.[Despite this] we do not speak or ponder the source of sources...[the theology of] Monotheism was invented by strangers and translated [concepts of faith] into foreign terms [lit. "translated into Aramaic"] which are anything but exact. It is a sort of perceived infinity, which is of course an oxymoron and is meaningless.[51]

In one of his bolder statements Rabbi Kook goes as far as arguing that one's very belief in God is a compromised perception of His infinite existence, for it is impossible for Man to conceive of God without compromising the very idea of God in its purist state. "In comparison to the absolute Divine truth, there is essentially no difference between the [human] perception of belief and atheism; both are far from the truth, for all active human perception falls short of the Divine truth."[52]

The mystical monotheistic perception, commencing with the Zohar, continuing with the Ari, and brought to fruition in the Hassidic and Mithnagdic writings, brought Jewish monotheism to its purist state in which no intellectual concepts were considered capable of any legitimate theological descriptions. If Maimonides in his day formed an intellectual monotheistic theology of the negative attributes of God,[53] the post-Zoharic monotheism of the *hassidim* and *mithnagdim* could not tolerate even the idea of categories. Monotheism was now at a point where rational theology was not possible. It is therefore not surprising to see how the kabbalistic theology of the Ari, based on revelation instead of reason, replaced all the intellectual theological forms of the middle-ages.

CHAPTER 15   *Why Mysticism
is So Popular Today*[1]

In 2004, the mass media informed the public all about Madonna's trip to the Kabbalah Conference in Tel Aviv, sponsored by the questionable Center for the Research of Kabbalah. This was after Roseanne Barr and Michael Jackson had studied *hassidut* with R. Shmuley Boteach. But kabbalah's popularity in the West has not begun just today. It is a trendy fashion that has taken the place of the cults and eastern religions. It is a sort of non-conventional and non-establishment movement seen by the religious establishment as genuine. In the e-mail site "Idra", where academics in the field of kabbalah can get feedback from their colleagues, the question was posed if the pop kabbalah can be seen as a legitimate new school of thought.[2] What is this new craze? Is it really new or just a more conventional version of what we have seen since the seventies in the eastern cults and afterwards the eastern religions? Is it a coming of age or a regression to an infantile simplicity of faith? Is it a turning of the back to reason or an attempt to reach new depths?

The answer to these questions is a bit complex in my opinion and we have to differentiate between different cultures: the West and Israel, for example. In dealing with the West, particularly with North America, I feel we have to examine a few aspects. First, whether this trend entails some type of reaction or growth or perhaps both; second, where this is leading us; and third, where this can lead in a positive sense. I would like to start out by explaining the new-found legitimacy of mysticism in Western culture before discussing any particular phenomenon. As a rule, the world of ideas is slow to influence society, so we need to see the historical events that have led up this point.

The French revolution was an attempt to break with established religion and had long lasting effects on the West. The Goddess of reason, crowned by the exponents of this tidal wave that swept Europe politically and culturally, created the groundwork for the age of reason so firmly established in the nineteenth century. Free education for the masses was a necessary byproduct. The enlightenment of the early nineteenth century is a direct product of this desire for reason. As I mentioned earlier, the scientific revolution, which started in the mid-nineteenth century, strengthened this feeling of the omnipotence of the human mind and the endless possibilities ahead. In the field of technological discoveries the railway system and the newspaper brought knowledge to all and made distances attainable. The discovery of electricity, the gramophone, the telephone, radio and television had a profound affect on communication and the dispersion of information. The car, bus, and airplane made the world just that much smaller. In the field of medicine, the discoveries of insulin, x-rays, antibiotics, and various vaccines made infant life expectancy higher as well as that of the average adult. It seemed just a matter of time until all disease would be conquered and maybe even mortality itselfAnd yet things have now changed once again. So what changed? Where did the promise of the omnipotence of reason go sour?

I believe that the answer to this question can be found in three regions, in the fields of philosophy and physics and in the political and social events that have shaped our present situation. The first two have to do with the theoretical conceptions that influenced the upper echelons of society and the third is of a socio-political nature.

1. The nineteenth century was one of a deep-seated belief in the supremacy of reason, as I mentioned above. However, already by the mid-nineteenth century there were uncertainties in the field of

philosophy. Already in the end of the eighteenth century Kant had separated metaphysics from philosophy, the argument being that there is no philosophic certainty in metaphysical matters.[3] Despite the fact that Kant meant to purify philosophy from speculation and religious belief, this de facto robbed philosophy of a major task in the human condition and actually paved the way towards its irrelevance in life. For, in the mind of the average thinking person, if philosophy cannot answer the basic existential questions of why I am here, what happens after, why should I be a moral person and is there a God, then why do I really need it? Philosophy then underwent a major change: on the one hand, its focus became language, human symbols and the mind, echoing developments in psychology. Simultaneously, there developed an existentialist trend that was there to pose questions and describe life more than to answer questions. Finally skepticism became the name of the day, closing the lid on any further discussion of truths.[4] These trends have made philosophy, with the possible exception of France, the arena of an elite group, detached from the day to day concerns of mankind.

2. The second development was in the arena of the sciences, specifically in the area of physics. As I mentoned earlier, the early twentieth century was witness to a major leap in the understanding of matter, of the "stuff," so to speak, of the physical world. With the development of nuclear physics and the discoveries of Max plank, Rutherford, Neils Bohr and Albert Einstein, the world at hand was starting to look different. It wasn't the same old material of Isaac Newton's universe. It appeared that the world was basically a conglomerate of electromagnetic fields and various forms of energy, and the material stuff or mass of matter played an insignificant role in this equation. In other words, it seemed that the material world was not as material as it appeared to be. There were also unanswerable questions, like whether light was a wave, a particle, or both, and the more one looked, the more the questions outnumbered the answers. As one historian wrote:

In the bewildering universe of quantum mechanics, three dimensional space and unidimensional time had become relative aspects of a four dimensional space-time continuum. Atoms were not the solid, indestructible building blocks of nature but were found to be largely empty. Time passed at different rates for observers travelling at different speeds: it could go backward or even stop entirely. Euclid's geometrical laws no longer provided the universal and necessary structure of nature. The planets did not move in their orbits because they were drawn to the sun by gravitational force operating at a distance but because the space in which they moved was actually curved. Subatomic phenomena were particularly baffling because they could be observed as both waves and particles of energy. "All my attempts to adapt the theoretical foundation of physics to this knowledge failed me," Einstein recalled. "It was if the ground had been pulled out from under me, with no firm foundation to be seen anywhere upon which one could have built." If these discoveries were bewildering to scientists, they seemed utterly impenetrable to the layman.[5]

By the second half of the twentieth century, reputed scientists were asking questions like: "Do electrons have free will? Are there simultaneous universes?" — questions which seemed more suitable for a class in Eastern mysticism rather than the academic world. The books by Gary Zukav and Paul Davies mentioned earlier were an inevitable outcome of the new thinking about the universe.

These two developments in the world of the academia, in the realm of philosophy and physics, which influenced at first only the elite upper echelons of society, eventually seeped down to the average intelligent person, who seeing that philosophy had no answers and science was starting to sound like mysticism, started to wonder whether the mystics were as primitive as previously thought.[6] However, all this is just a partial picture. In my opinion, ideas can set the stage for change but the catalyst is usually socio-political.

3. Science and technology, until the First World War, was both the greatest pride and joy of human reason as well as a great beneficiary of an improved quality of life. The world of medicine had prolonged human life, technology had shortened distances and passed us limitless information about the world, and new inventions were improving the day to day quality of life. The First World War reminded us that to every Dr. Jekyll there is a Mr. Hyde. The advances in technology allowed for the production of weapons of mass destruction, killings millions of French and German soldiers in a war that went nowhere. The newly developed artillery was the nightmare of the battlefield, and various forms of gas were used to brutally mutilate the enemy. The discovery of antibiotics helped sweeten the bitter herb of this rude awakening,

but this did not last. The swift onslaught of the Second World War, even more advanced in its technological brutality with its eventual tragic finale of atom bombs launched on Hiroshima and Nagasaki, sent a bitter message home that the new science had created a real monster. The Second World War proved both the supreme power of scientific technology as well as the threatening implications of the misuse of that power. The subconscious social impact of the atomic bomb attacks on Japan, and a war that used modern technology to claim millions of lives, cannot be underestimated. The Cold War, with the constant fear of a world atomic tragedy, served to reaffirm this fear and this new truth. The question became: "How can one put the monster back into the bag?" Even if faith in science remained unscathed for the first decade and a half after the war and the scientific community emerged from the war with an enhanced prestige,[7] these events planted the seed for the disillusionment with science which put it on the defensive in the late 1960's and the 1970's.[8] If the technological boom of the nineteenth century into the twentieth led to a belief in the omnipotence of science,[9] by the seventies, attacks on science gained legitimacy, and the popular reaction to it was now a mixture of enthusiastic support and profound mistrust.[10] The fear of science, which according to Ben David begot the doubting of science in the early seventies, in my opinion was a reaction to this bitter truth of the Second World War. The new generation, born just after the war, was the first to rebel, on campuses, against anything conventional, religion, government, police, morality and the establishment in general. This produced the sexual revolution of the hippies, and the anti-government riots in North America, France and England. It was a generation looking for new truths to replace the old ones before they caused more damage. It is of interest that the most popular and longest-running TV program in the U.S. after the Second World War was Tarzan of the Apes. This fascination with the primitive world was part of the attempt to seek answers elsewhere. The new thinking was that perhaps the East is not as primitive as was previously thought. They might be devoid of science but maybe they know something about life that we do not.[11] This naïve turn to the East was exploited by cheap eastern charlatans in the era of the cults in the seventies, but eventually came of age, with a newfound interest in Eastern religions as well as an interest in mysticism in both academic and lay circles. Eventually, a further coming of age brought about a partial dissipation of the fear of the established religions (in

North America), but the preferred area of interest was the modes of thought sidelined by the formal religions: Sufism in Islam, healing and meditation in Christianity, and kabbalah in Judaism. These newly found ancient traditions were more palatable than the more established modes of religious thought and were dealing with the new quest which was more spiritual than religious per se. It also addressed questions that philosophy had long abandoned and seemed to supply new creative answers to the queries of modern science. This is not to say that the present trend does not have its share of charlatans and charmers, but we cannot dismiss it as being a fad with no basis either.

Taking the issue a bit closer to home, we may wonder what it is in kabbalah that attracts the masses. This question too hasn't a black and white answer. There are three types of kabbalah. The first, which is found in Christian mysticism as well, is what Eliade describes as a longing for a lost paradise.[12] It is a desire for a first-hand experience of the Divine. This is experiential or prophetic kabbalah.[13] While this type of literature can be found already in the Heikhalot literature from the second to the fifth centuries,[14] it was eventually sidelined by the central schools of kabbalistic thinking and developed more by unconventional kabbalists like Abraham Abulafia of thirteenth-century Castillia and his students. Abulafia's writings go into great detail regarding his techniques and personal spiritual experiences.[15] His writings show the influence of eastern spiritual techniques as well as his own additions.[16]

The second brand of kabbalah, sidelined by Ashkenazic and most Sephardic and Yemenite kabbalists, is what we call practical or magical kabbalah. This area, developed in early Ashkenazic writings of the eleventh century and in works like *Razial Hamalakh*, describes techniques and amulets that affect this world. The use of such amulets is prominent among Iraqi as well as some Moroccan kabbalists.

The third area, theoretical kabbalah, deals with the world of ideas. It presents the world view of kabbalah in the realm of psychology, the human soul, metaphysics and eschatology. This is the bulk of kabbalistic writings and historically it has been the main area of study. The only exception is the use of incantations and Divine names (Yihudim) to enhance the prayers, which were studied by mainstream kabbalists of all communities. The New Age trends of kabbalah tend to use ecstatic kabbalah heavily as it is closest to the eastern traditions. Often they adopt ideas from Jewish kabbalah to fit into patterns of post-modern thought by mixing them with New Age concepts. Recently, Boaz Huss of Ben Gurion

University wrote an article discussing the New-Age Kabbalah Centre of Phillip Berg, Madonna's mentor. He says:

> R. Philip Berg presented (first, in English, later in Hebrew and other languages) the principles of Ashlag's Kabbalah in a simplified and comprehensible manner, suited for Western, urban (not necessarily Jewish) readership. From his first publications, during the 70's, Berg downplayed the socialist elements of Ashlag's Kabbalah, and integrated various elements from contemporary Western culture and New Age spirituality in his version of Kabbalah, connecting the revelation of the Kabbalah with the arrival of the new age of Aquarius. Since the 90's some of these elements, as well as some kabbalistic practices which did not play a central role in Ashlag's Kabbalah (such as scanning the Zohar, and, the meditative use of the 72 Names of God), overshadow the Ashlagian elements in the doctrines and practices of the Kabbalah Centre.[17]

Huss discusses Madonna's use of the 72-letter name of God, a name central to Bergian kabbalah, in a recent video release, and adds:

> The traditions of the 72 names of God do not play an important part in most contemporary Jewish cultural forms (including mystical and kabbalistic ones), and most contemporary Jews probably are not aware of this tradition, or of the meaning of the letters LAV. Yet, these Names do feature extensively in the practices of one contemporary kabbalistic group—the group that Madonna is affiliated with—the Kabbalah Centre, headed by R. Philip Berg."[18]

One might counter this argument by asking, if kabbalah is a living tradition then who is to say what is mainstream or not? If the 72 letters of the name of God is an authentic tradition, what does it matter if it is mainstream among kabbalists today or not? After all, after the passing of the Ari there were kabbalists who placed a ban on the study of all kabbalistic works not ascribed to the Ari through his student Hayyim Vital, and despite this there were schools of Lithuanian kabbalists who disregarded this ban.[19] Huss argues that what defines this new school of kabbalah is its extensive use of New Age and postmodern ideas in which the kabbalistic element is used to serve these goals and not vice versa.[20] Another apparent feature of what Huss calls "Post modern Kabbalah" is the interest in the practical elements more than the narrative.[21] I recall watching an Israeli talk show in November 2004 in which the viewers were introduced to two individuals said to be the most important kabbalists of the day. The first gave an exhibit of the power of energy concentrated in his hands, a technique used by many New Age demonstrators of the power of Chi and then proceeded to link three rings through this energy, a trick that would not have shamed David Copperfield. The second demonstrated the art of fortune telling using the age-old technique of Goralot literature, making it seem a technique half way between tarot cards and the Chinese I-Ching tradition. Without trying to shortchange the tradition of Goralot literature, which was quite popular in Jewish communities in Iran and Iraq in the past few hundred years, one cannot overlook this populist understanding of kabbalah as a form of knowledge for practical benefit devoid of grand narratives. Possibly this mimics a larger trend in contemporary education to prefer the useful over the true.[22] There is a dimension in this postmodern mysticism which can be described as a form of post-capitalist narcissism that seeks instantaneous self benefit without the cost of years of study and ethical self improvement.[23] Jameson goes to the extreme in describing the postmodern cultural atmosphere as: "A new kind of flatness or depthlessness, a new kind of superficiality in the most literal sense."[24] In spite of the kernel of truth in his statement, in the context of understanding the new interest in mysticism I do not think that we are talking of an insignificant phenomenon. The in-depth study of theoretical kabbalah will probably always remain the lot of a select few in each generation. On the other hand, the popular interest of the masses, however superficial it might seem, shows a social change where the accepted norms and social dictates are seen as insufficient, and a real desire for new answers in the arena of philosophy and psychology of man are being actively pursued. Putting aside the belief in receiving blessings from saints and obtaining amulets, a rather dubious practice found among Israeli non-practicing traditionalists, or the attempt to gain instant Truth or health, found around the West, there is a new wind blowing which is trying to give alternative modes of thinking a fair chance. Possibly there are also other reactions entailed in the new mysticism to postmodern society. Mysticism tends to see the world not just as anthropocentric, but as holding the individual in the center. My soul becomes the center of the physical and spiritual world. This is a possible reaction to modernism, in which an individual is just a small pawn in the realm of society. This is the paradox of modernity. Writing in the mid-twentieth century, Fromm describes the maturation of society, a state in which individuals gain their independence and individuality.[25] Therefore, states Fromm, the identity of the individual has been a major problem of philosophy since Descartes.[26] Fromm claims that society has accustomed itself to the individual but that the individual is afraid to claim this status out of fear and insecurity.

> Modern man…clings to the notion of individuality; he wants to be "different," and he has no greater recommendation of anything than that "it is different." We are informed of the individual name of the railroad clerk we buy our tickets from; handbags, playing cards, and portable radios are personalized, by having the initial of the owner put on them. All this indicates the hunger for difference and yet these are almost the last vestiges of individuality that are left.[27]

Fromm argues that individuality means freedom but it also entails the insecurity of being on your own. Since it is hard to be free to act if you don't really know what you want, modern man prefers to conform to anonymous authorities, taking away his newly found freedom and leaving himself miserable.[28] To sum it up, Fromm writes: "modern man…has been freed from traditional authorities and has become an individual, but at the same time he has become isolated, powerless, and an instrument to purposes outside of himself."[29] His suggestion is that freedom entails understanding one's potential and how to use it. Jameson, writing at the end of the twentieth century, sees postmodernism as the disappearance of the individual into a mindless monad in society.[30] The new mystical trend seems to take both ends of the cord at once. It is the paradox of postmodern man, who is insignificant as an individual in a large metropolitan society[31] but succumbs to advertisements and fashion gurus which tell him to address and develop his personal individuality. Hassidism puts the individual soul at the center but sees it as ultimately merging with a greater reality. All of the spiritual realm can be reached through the human soul.[32] The Hassidic master R. Shneur Zalman of Liadi writes: "If only the eye had permission to see…no physicality of creation or any matter would be observed for it is all null and devoid of reality from the perspective of its spiritual life force…like before the six days of creation…for in truth there is really nothing but He."[33] Here we have a belief which is the epitome of individuality, whereby all existence depends on human action, and in a deeper sense, one can observe here the acosmic idea that there is no existence except for my own soul. However, continues, R. Shneur Zalman, I am not left alone; my soul is closely linked to the Divine, and is "a part of Divinity from above."[34] If Fromm is correct in his description of the predicament of modern man, then mysticism in the form of *hassidut* and kabbalah, somewhat detached from institutionalized religion, slightly nonconformist, but not really rebellious, is understandably attractive. If we add to this the aspect of postmodernism which takes the realm of history from an objective tale of what happened toward representing our ideas and stereotypes of what took place,[35] then this movement away from realism is a direct movement towards mysticism of the kind we just described.

Where does this leave us? Where is it all going? Is it a passing trend, and if so, what may take its place? In the academic world, there has been a growing interest in the research of kabbalah. Gershon Scholem legitimized the research of kabbalah in the academic world. The new mystical trend and the renewed student interest in these ideas have forced the universities to expand their courses in kabbalistic literature. From my own experience I see how the departments of Jewish philosophy both at Hebrew University and Bar-Ilan have developed more of a mystical bent than they had fifteen years ago. However, to limit this discussion to the arena of academia would be a mistake. I think that no less an important question than the influence on academia is how this trend is influencing institutionalized religion. It is forcing the latter to deal with what used to be "the embarrassing questions"; to talk again of God and the soul, the spiritual quest and human self-fulfillment. In this sense, this wave of mystical adoration from groupies, yuppies, and just run-of-the-mill people is a positive challenge to religious leaders and guides. To see young people interested in a spiritual quest is quite refreshing. This desire should be met by religious leadership with serious and profound discussion of all basic beliefs and morals. Discussion should be encouraged without the embarrassment of exposing one's own inadequacies. To learn is to question, not to supply the answers. The basis of a real quest is humility and not omniscient arrogance. Humility is a prerequisite for true wisdom and a facilitator of its acquirement. This is a Talmudic principle as true then as it is today.[36] The academic world does have a role to play here, especially in exposing fraud, but this is a grass-roots trend that needs to be addressed in the synagogues and community centers as a catalyst towards a revival in Jewish learning. For in the end, what is more mystical than the belief in God and what is more meditative than genuine prayer, and what is more rewarding than the good deed?

CHAPTER 16

Attitudes Towards Modern Cosmogony and Evolution Among Rabbinic Thinkers in the Nineteenth and Early Twentieth Centuries: The Resurgence of the Doctrine of the Sabbatical Years

INTRODUCTION

Evolution Versus the Creation Story

Science and religion deal with very different topics. Science asks how things work and religion speaks of why things are there. These are two very different fields of interest. Let's take for example the area of biology. Biology is the science which studies life. However, should you ask why there is life in the first place, the scientist will answer that this is not a scientific question but rather a philosophic or religious question. Since these are really two different fields the question that follows is, how can there be any contradictions between science and religion? The question in the case of Judaism is even stronger, since it does not hold any dogmas concerning the natural world. The answer is that the Bible, the central religious document, makes statements about the natural world. As soon as this happens the scientist can say that since the Bible has entered his arena, he can now ask if these statements about the natural world are correct. The contradiction begins if we first assume that the Bible describes how God physically created the world, and this is an assumption not accepted unanimously by Jewish rabbinic scholars as I have demonstrated in an earlier essay.[1] The Jewish tradition sees the creation story in Genesis 1-2 as one of two major secrets of the Bible. If the story is only meant to be understood literally, what secret is there? Judaism contains oral traditions to understand the written texts and it is these that we turn to in order to understand such major texts. Just to point out a simple item, we measure the length of a day by the rotation of the earth on its axis vis a vis the sun. This takes about 24 hours. However, in the book of Genesis the sun, moon and stars were created on day four, but the Bible says, "and it was evening and it was morning day one....day two, etc." Without a sun, who is to say that these days were 24 hours? Perhaps they were just concepts or possibly undetermined periods of time. The Genesis story is more complex than it seems. In the nineteenth century, the French revolution was raging and Europe was trying to break away from the shackles of the church. Until this time, scientists of the Newtonian persuasion saw the Divine origin of the universe as the only plausible interpretation of cosmogony. Darwin's theory of evolution was seen as an opportunity to present a secular alternative to the Genesis narrative. "After Darwin it was possible to deny God's existence without flying in the face of the most authoritative scientific evidence."[2] As the nineteenth-century French physicist Pierre Laplace was quoted as saying, upon being asked what role God plays in his theories, that he has no need for such hypotheses. The battle between church and evolution, which could have been resolved fairly easily under a different social climate, was perceived as a battle of world views.[3] After the court battle of 1925 between John Scopes of Dayton, Tennessee, and William Jennings Bryan, on whether or not the theory of evolution could be taught in US classroomst, it became "impossible to discuss the issue rationally, because evolution was no longer merely a scientific hypothesis but a symbol."[4] However, the twentieth century created a new scenario which actually offered much more promise of reconciliation than the spontaneous concepts of the nineteenth century. In 1954, George Gamow, a Russian Jew who had immigrated to America, wrote an essay describing how according to Einstein's theories, the world was going from a state of order to disorder (second law of thermodynamics) and originally started at a single point of condensed matter which begot the world through nuclear reactions. This essay was originally ridiculed by the scientific community and jokingly nicknamed the Big Bang theory. In 1972, Wilson and Penzias won the Nobel Prize when they proved a key point of this theory. Ever since, the Big Bang theory has been accepted by the scientific community. This was a major rapprochement between science and the creation story. Since then scientists believe the world began at a certain point in time. Considering that the Bible is not a physics book, it would now seem that as long as science talks of a form of creationism, without mentioning if by God or by any other force, the religionists could now easily adopt this new idea and harmonize it with the creation story. After all, the Bible says that God created the world, what does it matter how he did it? But since this issue has many facets to it, I would like to present here my article on rabbinic attitudes to evolution as a paradigm for how Jewish thinkers have dealt with this issue in the past.

ATTITUDES TOWARDS MODERN COSMOGONY AND EVOLUTION AMONG RABBINIC THINKERS IN THE 19TH AND EARLY 20TH CENTURY

The Resurgence of the Doctrine of the Sabbatical Years

In this essay, I will present some of the early rabbinic responses to the conflict between Jewish tradition and the scientific views of cosmogony from the nineteenth century until the mid-twentieth century.[5] The thinkers chosen were R. Israel Lipschutz, R. Eliyahu Benamozegh, R. Samson Raphael Hirsch, R. Shem Tov Gefen, and R. Abraham Isaac Kook.[6] All these thinkers were Orthodox rabbis, from a traditionalist environment; most of them served in important rabbinic posts and were not interested in compromising tradition for the sake of political correctness. Having said this, one can now appreciate the two factors common to these thinkers. First and foremost is their genuine attempt to meet the issues head on in the pursuit of a viable synthesis with tradition. This was the way of pre-modern Jewish thinkers from as early as Philo and through R. Saadia Gaon and Maimonides, all of whom looked for inroads and bridges between Jewish tradition and the scientific thinking of their day, whether it was neo-Platonic or Aristotelian.[7]

Modern theories of cosmogony, especially the theory of evolution, posed a challenge to traditionalists. The rabbis of the eighteenth and early nineteenth centuries who did not see scientific research as a threat to religion looked for syntheses to solve any problem that might arise. Some of these thinkers predated the battles between the Church and Evolutionism and were therefore unaware of, or simply ignored, what I call the political element of the issue, and dealt only with the heart of the matter. This political element played a dominant role in the debate in the late twentieth century. By then the literalists had become an almost dominating voice. But before that happened, there was a creative and profound attempt to relate modern ideas to ancient sources, in this case to relate modern theories of cosmogony to biblical or midrashic sources.

A second factor common to these thinkers is their use of the Midrashic tradition of "the worlds that God created and destroyed," in order to harmonize between tradition and science. This idea was developed and discussed extensively in kabbalistic literature between the twelfth and sixteenth centuries, yet whereas the Midrash centered on the book of Genesis, the kabbalists discussed allegorical interpretations of the Sabbatical years discussed in the book of Leviticus. This motif disappeared after the sixteenth century until its resurgence in the late nineteenth in the discussion of tradition and modern cosmogony. Since this idea, referred to as the "Doctrine of the Sabbatical Worlds," or the "secret Doctrine of the Sabbatical Years" became the groundwork for discussion, I think it is crucial to examine it at the beginning of this essay.

The Doctrine of the Sabbatical Worlds: The Source of a Tradition

The book of Genesis commences by stating that God created the world, an idea which has become a fundamental belief of Judaism.[8] However, the idea that this world comes to an end or some form of transition from its present state is not obvious from biblical texts, which describe only the future ingathering of the exiles or the renaissance of Jewish life in Israel after a period of exile. The idea that the world has not just a beginning but also an end wherein all life will be destroyed can be found in the apocryphal *Vision of Ezra*.[9] In the *Book of Enoch*,[10] this "end" is at the end of seven thousand years, mimicking the seven days of creation. This idea was restructured in the Talmud, differentiating between the six millennia and the seventh millennium: "Rabbi Katina said: six thousand years does the world exist and one [thousand it lies] destroyed."[11] The Talmud then goes on to compare this idea of Rav Katina with the commandment of the Sabbatical year in which the six years of working the land come to an end.

A baraita supports [the opinion] of Rav Katina: just as the Sabbatical year falls once every seventh year so too the world is put to rest one thousand out of every seven thousand years, as it says "none but the Lord shall be exalted on that day" [Is. 2:11] and it says "a psalm, a song; for the Sabbath day." [Ps. 92:1] "A day which is entirely Sabbath," and it says [as well] "for in your sight a thousand years are like yesterday that has passed [Ps. 90:4]."

According to this Talmudic teaching of Rav Katina, the six millennia of creation parallel the six years wherein one toils the land and the seventh millennia parallels the sabbatical year of rest. What happens at this point of rest is not clear. It is also unclear from here whether this is a one-time occurrence or a cycle. This query is addressed in the midrash.

The Midrash in Genesis Rabbah Chapter 7 begins by quoting Genesis 1:5.

R. Judah B. Simon said: "Let there be evening" [yehi erev] is not written here, but "and there was evening" [va-yehi erev]. From this you can infer that a time-order existed before this. R. Abbahu said: this teaches that [God] created worlds and destroyed them until He created this one. He said: This one pleases me and the others do not please me. R. Phinhas said: R. Abbahu's [scriptural] basis [for his teaching in the previous midrash] is: "and God saw all that he had made and found it very good" [Gen. 1:31], [meaning], this [world] pleases me but the other [worlds] do not please me.[12]

This midrash is found again in a slightly different version in Chapter 9:

"And God saw all that he had made and found it very good" [Gen. 1:31]. R. Tanhuma commenced [his exposition]: "He brings everything to pass precisely at its time" [Ecclesiastics 3:11]. R. Tanhuma said: "The world was created when it was due, and the world was not fit to be created earlier." R. Abbahu said: "Hence we learn that the Holy-one-Blessed-Be-He, created worlds and destroyed them, created worlds and destroyed them, until he created this one and [then] He said: 'This one pleases me and the others do not please me'."[13]

The second version of the midrash, which mentions twice that God built and destroyed worlds, is of special interest to the commentators.

After all, the midrash itself is quite vague. What were these earlier worlds, why are they in the plural and why is it important to know about them? The expansion of this concept in light of the Talmudic sources mentioned above began in the twelfth century in a mystical commentary whose object however is not the verse in Genesis, but Leviticus 25:1-14, the commandment of the sabbatical year, as was hinted to already in Rav Katina's teaching.

The Book of Leviticus states: "Six years you may sow your field and six years you may prune your vineyard and gather in the yield. But in the seventh the land shall have a Sabbath of complete rest, a Sabbath of the Lord (Lev. 25:3-4)."[14] These ostensibly matter-of-fact verses pertaining to the *mitzvah* of the Sabbatical year were understood as a portal to esoteric secrets by mystical thinkers from the twelfth to the sixteenth century. R. Abraham ibn Ezra (1089-1164) wrote: "And the reason [the verse says] 'a Sabbath for the Lord,' [is] like the Sabbath day. The secret of cosmic history [*yemei olam*] is hinted to in this place."[15] What is the cosmic historic secret to which this section on the Sabbatical year hints?

R. Moses B. Nahman (Nahmanides, 1194-1270) wrote concerning these verses:

Behold [these verses] here draw our attention to a great secret of the Torah, as Rabbi Abraham [ibn Ezra] has already hinted ... And curl your ear to hear that which I am allowed to tell you in the way I shall tell you, and if you will be deserving you shall understand. I have already written in the order of Genesis [16] that the six days of creation parallel [lit. are] the history of the world [*yemot olam*] and "the seventh day is a Sabbath of the Lord your God" [see Ex. 20:10], for it will be the Sabbath of [His] great name. [This is] just what we learned [elsewhere] about the seventh [day]: What did they [the Levites] say [in the temple], "A psalm a song for the Sabbath day: [a song] for the future which is all Sabbath and eternal rest" [Tamid 7:4]. Now the "days" hint at what was created in the Work of Creation, and the "years" hint to what will be in the works [lit. creation] of the entire history of the world ... And possibly this is what our Rabbis hinted at when they said: "Fifty gates of knowledge were created and all were given to Moses save one," because every sabbatical [year represents] the gate of one house. [Therefore] we see that he [Moses] was taught all of existence from beginning to end except for the holy Jubilee.[17]

Nahmanides expounds upon the secret mentioned by ibn Ezra. He cites a tradition whereby the Sabbatical year mentioned in Leviticus 25:1-13 parallels the Sabbath day that followed the six days of Creation. As he stated already in his commentary to Genesis, these six days of Creation hint at the history of the world — which according to Talmudic tradition is six thousand years long — and the seventh millennium parallels God's Sabbath. This is the first secret. However, Nahmanides adds that: "these years hint to all which will occur in creation throughout all the history of the world." This means that in addition to the idea that the Sabbatical year parallels the seventh millennium of history, there are also seven sabbatical years in a Jubilee which parallel "all the history of the world." What is the difference between our history and "all the history of the world"? This secret, referred to in kabbalistic research as the "Doctrine of the Sabbatical Worlds," assumes that our world is not the only one. There were worlds that preceded ours and there will be worlds that will come after ours. The notion that there were previous worlds was mentioned already in the midrash mentioned above.[18] The connection between the sabbatical years and world history was hinted at in the Talmud as well as by Abraham ibn Ezra.[19] However, the Doctrine of the Sabbatical Worlds was developed extensively in the writings of the kabbalists of Gerona, specifically R. Ezra and Nahmanides. According to Nahmanides, every world is destined, like our own, to exist for seven millennia. Not only does this doctrine parallel the idea of the sabbatical years and the jubilee, but each world with its seven years parallels the kabbalistic idea of the seven lower sefirot, from *hesed* to *malkhut*, which represent the natural world. There are seven worlds like this one and ultimately they all reach the grand jubilee that redeems them. This grand jubilee, in kabbalistic terms, parallels the sefirah of *binah*, called the fiftieth gate, the beginning of the hidden sefirot, representing the idea of redemption. This is what Nahmanides means when he says: "and possibly this is what our rabbis hinted at when they said fifty gates of intelligence were created," meaning there are forty-nine thousand years which comprise these seven worlds and then will follow the Grand Jubilee.

R. Isaac of Acre, a student of Nahmanides, who in his commentary to the Torah seeks to expound on all Nahmanides' kabbalistic interpretations, adds clarity to our understanding of the secret of the sabbatical worlds. He sees in the theory of the fifty thousand years of the world a single process that falls into seven successive worlds. He states:

You should know that as the Jubilee in one generation is fifty years, in a thousand generations you have fifty thousand years. This is what [King David said:] "the promise he gave for a thousand generations" [Ps. 105:8, and scripture says:] "who keeps his covenant faithfully to the thousandth generation" [Deut. 7:9]. And this is the order of the Sabbatical and Jubilee years about which it says "and each man shall return to his lot"; that all shall return to the Jubilee which is the foundation, and the believer shall keep silent. And the scholar said, all was from the first cause and all returns to the first cause,[20] and this secret now explains the meaning of the Sabbatical and Jubilee [years].[21]

According to R. Isaac of Acre, all seven worlds created and destroyed are part of a single process, therefore it is of particular interest how he interprets the phrase "and one [millennium] it is destroyed." This means that each world is laid waste in its seventh millennium. He clarifies this in the following comment:

"One [millennium] laid waste" — this means that there will be time, despite the absence of humans, fowl and animals, and their causes, which will stop their activity and their continuity and therefore will need and depend upon something to reinstate them and this is [what it says] "The Lord supports all who stumble" [Ps. 145]... And during that millennium [the world] awaits the time when it shall be remembered for renewal.[22]

According to R. Isaac the phrase "it will be laid waste," which refers to the seventh millennium, does not mean that the world will be destroyed; only that life upon it will stop. This interpretation can also be found in the writings of the Italian kabbalist R. Menahem Recanati (late thirteenth to early fourteenth centuries)[23] who writes:

"One [millennium] it will lie destroyed," this does not mean [that the world] will return to the chaos [of the beginning] as in the year of the Jubilee. Rather the meaning of destroyed [haruv], [is:] without man, animal and other living creatures. And all things composed of the four elements will return to their fundamental state.[24]

Recanati explains that it is only during the Grand Jubilee, and not at the end of every sabbatical, that all of creation returns to the primordial state of being. So what is gained after the end of each successive world?

There is a certain amount of progress reached when each world finishes its term and the next one starts: "And in every one of them [i.e. every world] there will be additional goodness and added blessing, more than there was before."[25] Recanati is one of the first to mention that there were kabbalists who were disturbed by the Doctrine of the Sabbatical Years, as he writes:

> However I have found that some of the kabbalists of our time who have delved into the secrets of Torah do not agree with what we have just written [the Doctrine of the Sabbatical Years], for they find it troubling that the messianic period for Israel should be so short, less than a thousand years. For reason dictates that the days of quietude [i.e. the messianic period] should be a thousand times longer than the time during which the nations oppressed us when we suffered to sanctify God's name, may He be blessed.[26]

Recanati says that what troubled the opponents of the Doctrine of the Sabbatical Years was a problem of logic—how could it be that the duration of the ultimate reward be less than that of the suffering which preceded it? He also raises an objection from scripture: if the world is to be destroyed in totality in the fiftieth millennium, the Grand Jubilee, then what is the meaning of the verse in Kohelet that "the earth stands forever," from which Maimonides learned that the universe had a beginning but no end?[27]

This last issue was addressed in the thirteenth century[28] by R. Bahya Ben Asher, a student of the Rashba. R. Bahya, commenting on the passage in Leviticus concerning the Sabbatical year, interprets its secret in the same way Nahmanides did, and quotes him directly with the addition of the verse in Ecclesiastes that "the earth shall stand forever":

> This hints at the Grand Jubilee which is the culmination of the history of the world [kol yemey ha-olam], [a world] which exists for forty-nine [millennia], because forty-nine in days and in years and in thousands [and the concept] of the gates of intelligence [binah] which were taught to Moses, are all one. They all hint to the length of the world's existence as it indicates in the beginning of the book of Kohelet: "and the earth remains the same forever" [Kohelet 1:4], where forever [le-olam] refers to the Grand Jubilee [which is also called olam].[29] This is the secret of the fifty gates of intelligence [binah] through which the world was created and all of them were revealed to Moses save

one....This means that he was taught of every millennium which parallels each gate of intelligence, and that he was told of all of existence from beginning to end except for the Holy Jubilee which is the fiftieth gate, the inner most [gate] of intelligence [binah].[30]

R. Bahya interprets the term "forever" [le-olam] in Ecclesiastes as referring to the period up to and including the Grand Jubilee, which is fifty millennia altogether. He also explains what will happen between each Sabbatical world, that is, after every seven millennia, though his explanation is different than Recanati's: "[the verse] 'and the land shall observe a Sabbath of the Lord' refers to the one [millennium] of destruction, which is [a time] of total Sabbath and eternal rest. This is the world to come [that will become manifest] after the resurrection."[31] According to this explanation, each world exists for seven millennia, and in the seventh it has its own respective messianic era, resurrection and World to Come. In this WorldtoCome, the spiritual dominates the material and the soul dominates the body; the material world is therefore considered destroyed because only the spiritual remains real. This interpretation is not so different from those of Recanati and R. Isaac of Acre, but it emphasizes the spiritual state of humanity rather than the state of the cosmos.

Another interesting explanation can be found in the writings of R. Judah Hayyat (1450-1510). Quoting Nahmanides and Recanati, he explains that one millennium of destruction is not a total destruction of the earth. He then proceeds to explain that according to those who criticize the Doctrine of the Sabbatical Years, the seventh millennium is necessary because of the Talmud's insistence that, "the son of David shall not come until all the souls have immerged from their abode [and become actualized]."[32] Therefore, all the souls must emerge before the seventh millennium, which is its state of rest. Consequently the seventh millennium is not a physical state, for only existing souls continue for its duration and go from one spiritual state to another.[33]

Recanati explained that each new world is better than the previous one. This idea is well developed in the book Maarekhet Ha-Elohut, a book written by an anonymous author in the fourteenth century and ascribed to Rabbeinu Peretz.[34] Why does each world exist for seven thousand years? "Because each world has a sevenfold cycle, that is, seven worlds that parallel the seven upper [heavens], for each sefira is called a world, and these are the 49 years [of the Jubilee] which are the 49 thousand [years of all seven worlds]."35 According to this explanation, each world corresponds to one of the *sefirot* from *hesed* to *malkhut*. So in which world are we now? The author of *Sefer haTemuna* claims that we are in the second world, corresponding to *gevura*; a world in which the attribute of stern judgment is dominant. 36 R. Isaac of Acre came to the same conclusion in his commentary to Sefer Yezira.37

One can already see how this theory could be used to explain paleontological findings by relating them to earlier worlds, but how does this help if the Doctrine of the Sabbatical Years can conceive of no more than 50,000 years altogether? For the answer, one need only look again into the writings of R. Isaac of Acre. In his still unpublished work *Ozar haHayyim*, he gives an unusual twist to the whole Doctrine of the Sabbatical Worlds:

> I have reason to write a great and Divine secret, which should really be hidden. Know that God's day is a thousand of our years, as it says: "For in your sight a thousand years are like yesterday that has passed" [Ps. 90:3]. Our [solar] year is 365 days and a quarter, therefore the [Divine] year above is 365,000 [and 250] years.38

R. Isaac relates this idea directly to the Doctrine of the Sabbatical Years. Since, according to Psalms, a thousand of our years is equal to one Divine year, he concludes:

> And now I shall say something that needs meditation. It is that 100 years for the Holy One Blessed Be He, are 36 times 150,000 of our years. And since we said that the year above is 365,000 and 250 years which is a quarter of a thousand years, calculate for a 100 years and for a 1000 years and you will not need any more thought. Therefore our eyes can see that the world shall exist for a very long time. This is contrary to those who say that it will exist only 49,000 years, which are seven sabbaticals.39

According to R. Isaac of Acre, the whole Doctrine of Sabbatical Years which gives each world 7,000 years is referring to Divine years. This means that in our terms, each world is 365,000 x 7000, or 2,555,000,000 years.

The Doctrine of the Sabbatical Worlds was discussed by scholars from the era of the Spanish expulsion (Don Isaac Abarbanel40 and R. Judah

Hayyat) and even later by kabbalists of sixteenth-century Safed. There it came to a full stop. R. Joseph Caro (1488-1575) mentions the doctrine in his *Maggid Meisharim*, where he re-interprets "one millennium laid waste" in a metaphorical sense, "that in that millennium [physical] activity and creativity will be weaker than in the previous millennia."[41] R. Moses Cordovero (Ramak, 1522-1570) mentions this doctrine in a positive light in his *Pardes Rimonim*,[42] but changes his mind in *Shiur Komah* attacking the view of the *Temuna* and *Sefer haKanah*.[43] In his *Eilima Rabbati*, he ascribes the doctrine to the later kabbalists and says that it is pointless to delve into it at all.[44] The noted kabbalistic authority R. Isaac Luriah of Safed (Ari, 1534-1572) rejected the entire doctrine, claiming that there were no worlds before us and there will be none after us. He claimed the whole doctrine was born out of a misunderstanding of the secret of the Sabbatical years, which referred to spiritual worlds that preceded the creation of our physical world.[45] It is perhaps owing to the Ari's influence that later kabbalists disregarded the Doctrine of the Sabbatical Worlds.[46]

Therefore it is of particular interest how this motif has been revived in the past 150 years as a possible answer to the challenge of the modern theories of cosmogony. I will now analyze the writings of five scholars, most of whom have revisited the Doctrine of the Sabbatical Worlds as an answer to the challenges of modern science: R. Israel Lipshutz of Danzig, R. Eliyahu Benamozegh, R. Samson Raphael Hirsch, R. Shem-Tov Gefen and R. Abraham Isaac Kook.

THE DOCTRINE OF THE SABBATICAL WORLDS:
ITS MODERN REEMPLOYMENT

R. Israel Lipshutz of Danzig

If the Doctrine of the Sabbatical Worlds was an eschatological theme of the middle ages, its reemployment had the special task of looking for inroads between the new theories of cosmology and the Jewish tradition. Rabbi Lipschutz is the first of a group of Jewish thinkers who see in this doctrine a Jewish way of addressing the new findings in geology and anthropology.

R. Israel Ben Gedaliah Lipshutz (1782-1860) was born in Germany and served as rabbi of Wronki (1821), Dessau and Colmar (1826-37), and Danzig (1837-60). He is best known for his commentary on the

Mishnah entitled *Tiferet Yisrael*, which is widely read and is found in the libraries of all greater Yeshivot to this day.[47] Most of the biographies on R. Lipschutz discuss his commentary and his halachic abilities and seem to leave out his interest in the sciences. This interest is intermittently exhibited in his commentary to the Mishnah.[48] In a short essay entitled "Or ha-Hayyim" (Light of Life), which was based on a sermon he gave on Passover 5602 (1842), Rabbi Lipshutz discusses the idea of the afterlife in Talmudic sources. In the third part of the essay he discusses the concept of resurrection, which he attempts to prove from both tradition and nature. If, he writes, one can prove that there were worlds that existed before our own, in which life was destroyed and then created anew, it would prove that a resurrection has already taken place, and could therefore happen again. To prove from the tradition the existence of these past worlds, he introduces the Doctrine of the Sabbatical Worlds.

> It states in Sanhedrin [97a]... "six thousand years [does the] world exist and one [it is] laid waste. And we have learned, just as the sabbatical [year] stops everything once every seven years, so too the world stops every seventh millennium."... This is the secret of what will be, but the secret of what was, we also can find in the precious writings of our sages, to get a glimpse through the eye of a needle. In Genesis Rabbah it says: "And it was evening and it was morning said Rabbi Abahu: 'This teaches that the order of time existed previously... teaching that the Holy One Blessed Be He built worlds and destroyed them'... And in order to give us a broader understanding of this, Rabbeinu Bachya revealed to us this Kabbalistic secret in Parshat Behar."[49]

He goes on to explain that according to R. Bahya each world is greater than the previous one, and he refers to Nahmanides and ibn Ezra. Rabbi Lipshutz then adds:

> The Lord's secrets are for those who revere Him, for they have received [the tradition] that we are in the fourth world, which in order of the seven days of creation, parallels the forth day in which God created the luminary bodies. Therefore, in this cycle, the light of Torah has arisen which is the sun that lights up the entire world. So even if the honour of the holy nation is at a low, the holy Torah stands as a luminous light on the horizon... for the whole world. However, if the Torah is the large luminary of the day, the small

luminary is human reason that rules in this world. It too arises in this cycle, and in the coming years it will reach heights previously unknown to the human mind. [50]

Now that R. Lipshutz brought a proof from tradition attesting to the existence of previous worlds, he proceeds to demonstrate that the scientific exploration of nature attests to the very same thing:

> And now my beloved brothers see on what a sound basis our holy Torah stands. For this secret [the Doctrine of the Sabbatical Worlds] handed to us from our ancestors, revealed to us hundreds of years ago, can be found in nature in our own times in the clearest manner. The restless spirit in man, the desire to discover all mysteries, has [brought him to] dig and search the belly of the earth like a mole, as well as the highest of mountains, the Pyrenees and Carpathians, and in the Cordillera mountains in [South] America, as well as the Himalayas, digging and searching until they found an awesome order of rocks [sela'im, — fossils?], one on top of another at a hair's distance, where one can only assume that a world revolution [velten revolutzian — catastrophe?] caused through His Divine hand, which sends fury through the land and causes it to tremble.[51]

He continues to describe at great length the paleontological discoveries of his day, in particular the fossils of creatures buried under four layers of earth. The lower layers contain creatures that are larger than those in the higher layers, but the higher layer possess "more refined [shlemut ha-yofi -developed?]." He then explains that according to scientists, the earth was crushed on its southwestern side, destroying all life upon it. The previous life was different than the present creatures.

> They found, in 1807 of their calendar, in Siberia, in the north of the earth under the permanent layer of ice, a mammoth elephant, three or four times the size of those of today. Its bones are now exhibited in the Museum in Petersburg. Since that country does not normally have elephants, this is also a proof that the earth was crushed...changing its climate from that which was hot enough to support elephant survival there.[52]

R. Lipshutz seems to be familiar with some of the discoveries of his day. Who are these scientists he mentions? R. Lipshutz himself indicates his source: "We find as well in the depths of the mountains, sea animals who have fossilized into stone and one scholar and natural researcher, whose name is Cufier, wrote that of the 78 species found in the depths of the earth only 48 exist presently."[53]

"Cufier" refers to Baron Georges Cuvier (1769-1832), who was considered the man who brought to life extinct animals of the past. He published three works on general zoology: *Tableau elementaire de l'histoire naturelle des animeaux* (1797), *Lecons d'anatomie comparee,* (1800) and *Le regne animal* (1817). His classification of animals influenced Lamarck despite the battle between them over the latter's materialism. He believed creation had taken place in stages and for many years disputed the accepted theory of the "Great Chain of Being," a theory which he later accepted. His work on fish entitled *Histoire des poissons* (1828) became the basis of modern ichthyology. [54]

R. Lipshutz uses this new knowledge to answer textual problems in Genesis: why does it say, "and the earth was without form [*tohu*] and void [*bohu*] (Gen. 1:2)." If the world had just been created, why should there be anything at all? "Here our holy Torah revealed to us a handbreadth of this secret we just mentioned. For the world is not here for the first time. Even the four elements were created in previous cycles and therefore were not mentioned as being created this time around."[55] The meaning, therefore, of the verse in Genesis is that the world had been laid waste due to its previous destruction.

R. Lipshutz, who feels he has found a total agreement between modern science and Jewish tradition, also offers us a new interpretation of an old Aggadic tradition. On the verse in Job, "How they were shriveled up before their time" (Job 22:16), the Talmud says in the name of R. Simeon the Saintly: "these are the 974 generations that were cut off before the creation of the world and were not created. The Holy One Blessed Be He, therefore, planted them in each generation, and they are the brazen ones of the generation."[56] Rashi explains that the Torah was supposed to be given after 1000 generations, as it says: "The promise he gave for a thousand generations" (Ps. 105:8). However, it was given after 26 generations instead. In order for this to happen, 974 generations had to be skipped. The simple understanding of the passage is that they were not created until later; R. Lipshutz, however, explains that they were created, namely in a previous world cycle, and therefore before the giving of the Torah. This he proves by way of the anthropological discoveries of his day.

In my humble opinion, those men who lived in prehistoric times, called Pre-adamites[57] in their [i.e. the scientists] language, are really the people of a world before Adam of our world. These are the 974 generations mentioned in [The Talmud] in Shabbat [88a] and Haggigah [13b] who were created before this world....Since their world was corrupt, they were cut off 26 generations before reaching 1000 generations....If we reckon that each generation is 70 years, this means that their world was destroyed after 6818 years from its creation. These 26 generations that were missing in their world were completed from Adam to Moses our Teacher...in which the world was prepared and refined well in order to receive the Torah.[58]

R. Lipshutz explains that of the four worlds that have existed, including our own, humans have populated only the last two. He proves this homiletically, explaining why the Torah starts with a large letter bet:

Notice the large "bet," that with which the Torah begins, and notice the four crowns [taggin] upon the bet. We have received from the Kabbalists that the four crowns hint to the fact that the world with all its hosts is here for the fourth time, and the large "bet" tells us that the greatest of creations, human intelligent life, is here for the second time.[59]

R. Lipshutz is unique in that he goes into details about the previous worlds and the scientific evidence for them. He is probably the first to claim that humankind inhabited only some of the worlds. Even though, according to his theory, each world is more developed than its predecessor, he does not mention the idea of evolution; yet he does consider seriously the paleontological and anthropological discoveries of his day, from fossils of prehistoric animals to prehistoric humans. R. Lipshutz sees these discoveries not as a threat to his religious belief but as providing conformation for it. Although R. Lipshutz does not address the idea of the evolution of species,[60] he does apply himself to many of the problems presented by the new scientific theories, which were prompted by the discovery of early forms of human life as well as animals that are now extinct, from mammoth elephants to dinosaurs. This extinct animal life was, he believed, the leftovers of a previous world, (one of the three past worlds), whose life was destroyed to enable a new world to form. The early forms of humans could belong to a world that did not reach a high enough level to merit the giving of the Torah. R. Lipshutz does not address the questions of the age of the world and of humankind, or the concept of evolution per se, which was under debate in the scientific community at that time.

R. Elijah Benamozegh

R. Elijah Ben Abraham Benamozegh (1822-1900) was an Italian Rabbi and philosopher. Born in Leghorn to wealthy Moroccan parents, he served as a rabbi in Leghorn and taught in its rabbinical school. He was influenced by kabbalah and philosophy, especially by the Italian philosophers Rosmini-Serbati and Gioberti, and attempted to show affinities between Judaism and contemporary philosophy. He was well-versed in many fields, including philology, archaeology and ancient history, and published numerous works in Hebrew, French and Italian on a variety of topics, including: notes on Targum Onkelos; a commentary to the Bible; an introduction to the oral law; and a treatise defending the authenticity of the Zohar.[61] R. Benamozegh is both deeply rooted in Orthodox Jewish tradition and fully acculturated in the land in which he lived. Unlike many of his counterparts in eastern Europe, he did not see secular studies as a threat to Jewish orthodoxy, as long as one does not lose sight of their order of priorities.[62] His surprisingly cosmopolitan approach, incorporating the ideas of non-Jewish philosophers and religionists in his discussions, is somewhat of an anomaly to Orthodox rabbinic thinkers of the nineteenth century. Therefore it should not be surprising that R. Benamozegh sees it necessary to address the challenging ideas of evolution so central to the modern thinking of his day. R. Benamozegh, as did R. Lipschutz, links the scientific discoveries in geology and anthropology concerning the age of the universe and humankind to the Doctrine of the Sabbatical Worlds. However, unlike R. Lipshutz's, his later writings address the issue of evolution as well.

In *Eim la-Miqra* (1862), his commentary on the Torah, R. Benamozegh considers the length of the days in the creation story, in light of scientific research. He understands these "days" metaphorically and claims that they might be many thousands of years long.

> Recently, researchers wanted to explain that those days [i.e. of Genesis] were not literal but were one thousand years or more. There is nothing new under the sun for I have seen that R. Abraham ibn Ezra wrote this (*Otzar Nehmad*, 215, 2), saying that each day was

a thousand years; and, who knows, maybe this was what our sages meant when they said: This means that there was an order of time beforehand [i.e. before creation]."[63]

The idea that each day of Genesis is one thousand years long may not be a literal interpretation of the text, but through it, one still sees the creation in terms of days. It replaces, so to speak, regular days with Divine days.[64] However, R. Benamozegh says that each day was "one thousand years *or more*" which is already a non-literal way to explain the six days of Genesis, and argues that this is what the midrash meant when it referred to the "order of time" that came before creation.[65] Just like R. Lipschutz, R. Benamozegh demonstrates that scientific discoveries prove the rabbinic viewpoint, which speaks of an earlier order of time as well as earlier worlds.

For us, due to the natural research of our times, we know that there actually was an order of time beforehand—and in researching the sages of the Divine Kabbalah, we find that the writings of our sages [in the midrash] are to be understood literally. Close to this we find their other statement saying: This teaches that that Holy-One-Blessed-Be-He was creating worlds and destroying them... The earlier scholars already interpreted this statement in a fine way that is close to the opinion of Leibnitz, for it is a fundamental ethical principle that this world was created by God through an act of will, therefore it is the best of all possible worlds... Therefore we can say that God did not actually create and destroy worlds, but that [the midrash] teaches us through a parable that this world is the best of all possible worlds... However, nowadays, we can even understand our Sages of blessed memory literally, and we do not need to sit in the shade of a parable, for it has been proven by natural scientists that before this creation of matter, plants and animals, that there was another order to the worlds, of very different matter, plants and animals. These worlds were literally destroyed and the remains of their destruction we can still witness today in the belly of the earth.... all in accordance with the statement of Rabbi Yehuda Bar Simon. [66]

R. Benamozegh uses the midrash that speaks of an earlier order of time combined with the midrash of the earlier worlds to show that the scientific discoveries of his day serve to reinforce our belief in the sayings of our sages, and lead us to three new principles:

1. We see that the sayings of our scholars are true in their literal sense; and this is not just the spirit of an ancient tradition speaking from their mouths, for our sages were not even aware of the natural discoveries of today. [2.] The second is that the words of the sages are identical with those of the sages of Kabbalah concerning the [Doctrine of the] Sabbatical [Worlds] as is known. 3. This is a sign and proof that the Torah should not be understood without the [oral] tradition for without it we would not be able to see the connection to the wisdom and natural discoveries of our days. It is incumbent upon us to say that the writings of our sages of blessed memory have root in earlier times, for in the fourth book of Ezra, found in the Apocrypha, it says that the world will return to a state of turmoil as was at the time of creation.[67]

R. Benamozegh shows the same enthusiasm as did R. Lipschutz. Both believe that the new paleontological discoveries prove the ancient midrashic tradition of earlier worlds that predated our own. R. Benamozegh goes so far as to see in these discoveries a proof for the Divinity of the Torah.

In conclusion, this belief in earlier worlds is an ancient one in our nation, and it stands as a proof for the divine nature of the Torah, which natural science now confirms... And I finish [this discussion] with the dear words of the scholar in the Kuzari who said [1:40]: If a believer in Torah had to admit to the existence of primordial matter of earlier worlds that predated us, this would not blemish our faith.[68]

Elsewhere Benamozegh uses the doctrine of earlier worlds as proof that Judaism believes in the doctrine of progress:

To be sure, the Great Year of the pagans bears an apparent resemblance to those seven-year cosmic cycles which the Kabbalah calls *shmitot*, or the fifty-year cycles called *Yobelim* (Jubilees). But there is an essential difference: In the pagan cycles, there is merely a repetition of what had come before, whereas in the Hebraic, the occurrence brings improvement.[69]

This idea of progress Benamozegh finds in the creation story as well and sees it as a precursor of the evolutionary theory:

In any event, the perception in Genesis of the creation of life as a progression from lower to higher forms has always attracted attention. It is a remarkable anticipation of what science would establish much later. Anaximander has sometimes been called the precursor of Darwinian theories, but in fact he has only a vague idea of progression...We have only to reread the first page of the Pentateuch to be convinced of the superiority of biblical conceptions to the theories of the Ionian philosopher.[70]

He later adds that the Doctrine of the Sabbatical Worlds is the best example of progressive improvement in creation.[71] So it appears that Benamozegh's enthusiasm was not just for the scientific discoveries of the prehistoric age, but also for the new theory of evolution which speaks of a developmental process. According to Benamozegh's understanding, if the evolution of the species describes a process whereby simple organisms developed into humankind, cannot humankind develop into something more spiritual? This he states in another work:

I believe, as Science teaches, that animal forms appeared on the earth and evolved into more perfect beings, either as Cuvier said, by revolutions and cataclysms, or by a slow evolutionary process, like the opinion of the modernist Lydell, or Darwin and others. More and more perfect species have developed, one after the other, over the course of millions of years on the face of the earth. The most perfect form is Man. But will nature stop here? This would indeed be strange. Present mankind, as Renan says, will evolve into another, more perfect human being. But Renan and the others stop here. They do not say that the "order" that reigns in the physical world has to reign in the moral one as well, and that there is no reason to believe that the "I," that force which created the actual human, does not have to create the future human as well. They do not say that the monads, the atoms, which are minuscule forces, are indestructible (as science teaches), for it is inevitable to believe that they will compose the future Man on a regenerated earth. All this is stated by Judaism, and is called the Resurrection. [72]

R. Benamozegh claims that the same creative force which formed present humankind will bring about a new Man, one who is more morally and spiritually aware, in a new world, which in Jewish belief is called the world of the Resurrection.[73] This optimistic view of the evolutionary theory is developed more in the writings of Rabbi Kook as I will demonstrate below.

R. Samson Raphael Hirsch

While R. Hirsch (1808-1888) is a slightly older contemporary of R. Benamozegh, I present his ideas only now, since R. Benamozegh shares R. Lipshutz's enthusiasm for the idea that the new scientific discoveries support ancient rabbinic traditions. R. Hirsch, on the other hand, makes use of the midrashic tradition of earlier worlds (albeit not in its kabbalistic form), but differs from both from R. Lipschutz and R. Benamozegh in his skepticism towards the new scientific theories.

R. Hirsch was born in Hamburg, the son of R. Raphael Frankfurter. R. Raphael was an opponent of the Reform congregation in Hamburg but a supporter of Hakham Bernays, who included secular studies in the curriculum of the Talmud Torah. R. Hirsch himself was quite influenced by R. Barnays and also by R. Jacob Ettlinger, whose yeshiva in Manheim he attended.[74] He then attended the University of Bonn, where he befriended Abraham Geiger (who would subsequently become his opponent). In 1830, he became the *Landrabbiner* of Oldenburg. There he published his *Nineteen Letters on Judaism* (under the pseudonym "Ben Uzziel") in 1836, and *Horeb* (1837). In 1841 he moved to Emden, where he served as rabbi of Aurich and Osnabrueck in Hanover, and afterwards he served as the rabbi of Moravia. Despite his battle against the Reform movement, Hirsch believed that revisions were necessary, not of the principles of Judaism but of externals. His insistence on Bible study, his method of teaching, and his donning a robe during services aroused opposition among the extreme Orthodox elements. Finally, in 1851 R. Hirsch moved to Frankfurt, where he found a group of like-minded friends. There he created a synagogue and a school that embodied his ideas of modern Orthodoxy.[75]

Much has been written on R. Hirsch as a central figure of European Jewry in the nineteenth century. Recently, L. Kaplan wrote an important article on his relationship to the sciences.[76] In this discussion, I will limit myself to R. Hirsch's thoughts on cosmogony and evolution. He explains in his essay, "The Educational Value of Judaism," that although Judaism believes that God created the universe, it has no dogmas about the specific order of creation or of the universe.

What Judaism does consider vitally important is the acceptance of
the premise that all the hosts of heaven move only in accordance
with the laws of the one, sole God. But whether we view these laws
from the Ptolemaic or Copernican[77] vantage point is a matter of total
indifference to the purely moral objectives of Judaism. Judaism never
made a credo of these or similar notions".[78]

R. Hirsch claims that even if Judaism holds no dogmas concerning
the natural world, one still should not rush to adopt the latest scientific
theories, which have yet to be substantiated. After all, scientific theories,
unlike absolute truths, are subject to change.[79] In addition, he expresses
some skepticism about modern science's ability to assess the age of the
earth.[80]

Having stated this skepticism concerning some of the scientific
theories of his day, R. Hirsch goes on to explain that they can coexist
peacefully with tradition. The first question he addresses is the age of the
universe, with which he deals by using some of the same arguments as
his predecessors:

Judaism is not frightened even by the hundreds of thousands
and millions of years which the geological theory of the earth's
development bandies about so freely. Judaism would have nothing
to fear from that theory even if it were based on something more
than mere hypothesis, on the still unproven presumption that the
forces we see at work in our world today are the same as those that
were in existence, with the same degree of potency, when the world
was first created. Our rabbis, the Sages of Judaism, discuss (Midrash
Rabbah 9:2, Tractate Haggigah 16a) the possibility that earlier worlds
were brought into existence and subsequently destroyed by the
Creator before He made our own earth in its present form and order.
However, the Rabbis never made the acceptance of this and similar
possibilities an article of faith binding on all Jews. They were willing
to live with any theory that did not reject the basic truth that "every
beginning is from God."[81]

R. Hirsch's basic notion is that the Torah wants to teach us that God
created the universe, and not how He did it. If one so desires, one can
find a rabbinic foothold for the new theories of the age of the universe in
the midrashic tradition of earlier worlds, but the truth is that the Rabbis

in general were interested more in the moral messages of the Torah than in speculating about what actually happened at the point of creation.[82] Therefore, it doesn't matter what theory is held, as long as one believes that God was the creator. R. Hirsch deals with the theory of evolution in a similar fashion:

> Even if the latest scientific notion that the genesis of all the multitude of organic forms on earth can be traced back to one single, most primitive, primeval form of life,.... Even if this notion were ever to gain complete acceptance by the scientific world,...Judaism in that case would call upon its adherents to give even greater reverence than ever before to the one, sole God, who, in his boundless creative wisdom and eternal omnipotence, needed to bring into existence no more than one single, amorphous nucleus and one single law of adaptation and heredity in order to bring forth, from what seemed chaos but was in fact a very definite order...[83]

Having argued that evolution is acceptable if attributed to a Divine origin, R. Hirsch then goes on to hypothesize that the idea of evolution might actually be hinted at in the Torah:

> This would be nothing else but the actualization of the law of le-mino,[84] the "law of species" with which God began his work of creation. This law of le-mino, upon which Judaism places such a great emphasis in order to impress upon its adherents that all of organic life is subject to Divine laws, can accommodate even this "theory of the origin of species." After all the principle of heredity set forth in this theory is only a paraphrase of the ancient Jewish law of le-mino, according to which, normally, each member of a species transmits its distinguishing traits to its descendents.[85]

While R. Hirsch mentioned the tradition of earlier worlds, he didn't try to use that tradition in any detail. His chief concern was to explain that Judaism can accommodate any theory as long as it does not conflict with the idea that God is the ultimate origin of the universe. Upon that premise, any theory is plausible, for the Torah comes to teach us an ethical teaching and not physics. R. Hirsch argues that the Rabbis were not concerned with theories of cosmogony, and therefore did not mention the theory of earlier worlds, nor any other theory, as a binding dogma.

By definition, therefore, no particular scientific theory of nature should be seen as a threat.

R. Shem Tov Gefen

While R. Shem Tov Ben Mordecai Gefen (1856-1933) does not discuss the Doctrine of the Sabbatical Worlds, he does follow his predecessors by seeking synthesis between science and tradition. However, his ideas come from an entirely different perspective. Rabbi Gefen was born in the Ukraine in 1856 and passed away in Tel-Aviv in 1933. Already in his youth he was well-read in Talmud (both Bavli and Yerushalmi), kabbalah, Jewish and general philosophy, and science. He was an original thinker, as well as an innovator in the Hebrew language. Rabbi A. I. Kook referred to him as a "man with perfect Torah and scientific knowledge."[86]

R. Gefen opens his essay "The Creation and Geology" with the statement that the order of creation, as determined by geologists on the basis of their findings, almost parallels the order of creation in the book of Genesis. The major difference is the time it took for these events to take place.[87] R. Gefen offers a creative approach to solve the conflict based on Kantian philosophy. Kant differentiates between our perception of something, the phenomenon, and the essence of what is perceived, the noumenon. Since I can imagine space without an object and time, without a thing, it appears that these coordinates are a priori concepts of my mind.[88] This does not mean that Space and time are illusions. They are real concepts of my mind but not necessarily of the object perceived.[89] This brings to mind the famous philosophic question concerning the senses: "If a tree falls in the forest and there was no one there to hear it, did it make any sound?" R. Gefen connects this idea to our discussion.

> Since the time of Kant we know well, in a way not to be doubted, that the forms of time and space do not exist in the essence of things, by themselves, but are forms used by the person perceiving these objects, just like color, heat, cold and the like, for all these forms have no existence but in the human psyche which perceives them.[90]

R. Gefen goes on to say that the only way to perceive the noumenon of an object would be through prophecy, which originates beyond the human mind.[91] How does this solve the problem? The geological findings are correct. The animal fossils and early human forms do suggest a progressive order in creation. The fact that the human is at the end of this progressive order is likewise compatible with the creation story in Genesis. However, since the human being comes last in this progressive order, any finding that suggests an order of things before humankind has no temporal meaning, for there cannot be a concept of time without human beings.

> From what we have said until now, the deep difference between two parts of geology, the "order of creation" and the "course of time," becomes clear. Through digging in the earth, which has been done lately in many areas, we can perceive the chain of creation and the making of life-forms, in a progression, from the lowest strata, where we find inorganic things, to strata above them, where we find vegetation, and to higher strata where we find animal life, until we reach the highest strata where we find early human life forms. However, the time factor cannot be perceived by any human being. The simple reason is that this whole process and chain of events took place before Man was on this earth, whose forms we find only in the highest strata of the digs.[92]

Therefore, even though geologists draw conclusions about the amount of time it should have taken for these events to happen, based on an analogy with events which they themselves have perceived, this analogy is based on an un-provable assumption. One would therefore have to assume that the events of creation happened without reference to time.[93] R. Gefen admits that this seems like a strange conclusion, but it is the "impeccable truth firmly seated on deep contemplation."[94] Of course, R. Gefen admits that by the same logic, it is also impossible to assess what the Torah meant when it spoke of the six "days" of creation. For if Man was created at the end of creation, then neither can the six days have any temporal meaning.[95] R. Gefen then mentions the Darwinian theory by name,[96] a theory with which he does not seem to be bothered. He only argues that the evolution of species could not have taken place in the framework of time, which is a human tool of perception.

Rabbi A. I Kook

Rabbi Kook (1865-1935) was a well known rabbinic figure from the twentieth century. Born in Griva, Latvia, he held rabbinic posts locally before settling in Palestine in 1904. He served as the chief rabbi of Jaffa and the settlements of the new *Yishuv*. Caught on a visit to Europe at the outbreak of World War I, he accepted a position in London for the duration of the war. Upon his return to Palestine he was appointed the chief rabbi of Jerusalem, and became the first chief rabbi of Palestine in 1921.[97] R. Kook was a deep and gifted scholar. His writings reach from Halakha to Mussar, Aggadah, Jewish philosophy and kabbalah. His strong point was the ability to give new perspectives on familiar sources in ways that were both original and at the same time loyal to their original context.[98] R. Kook is a great believer that holiness cannot exist without being rooted in the secular world.[99] This is true in both in the realm of knowledge and the realm of ethical conduct, where one cannot build up a spiritual environment without the proper natural understanding of right and wrong.[100] Therefore it is not surprising that in his speech at the inauguration ceremony of the Hebrew University, he stated that it is important to learn secular sciences in order to absorb the best of them into traditional Jewish life. This combination is not to compensate for a deficiency in Torah but to create a richer mode of understanding.[101] Despite the importance of secular knowledge, one must still take the right precautions since its source originates from outside of Judaism.[102] R. Kook, like R. Hirsch, tends to seek synthesis between the tradition and the positive challenges of modernity,[103] but different than him, he sees secular studies as did the disciples of the Vilna Gaon, as contributing to the understanding of Torah and Jewish life but inferior to it, like the relationship of a branch to the tree, its source.[104] I say this only as background-setting for our discussion of his relation to the theories of evolution so rampant in his day. He discusses modern cosmogony and the theory of the evolution of the species in a few places.

I will begin with a letter that R. Kook wrote to Dr. Moshe Seidle. At the time of the letter in 1905, Seidle was a young student of Bible and Semitic languages in Bern, Switzerland. He eventually founded the Efrata Religious Teachers College in Jerusalem. R. Kook opens his letter with the Doctrine of the Sabbatical Worlds as it is found in the midrash.

> As to the calculation of the number of years since the creation in relation to the calculation of today's geologists, it is generally accepted that there were many earlier epochs preceding our recorded epoch. This was common knowledge among all our kabbalists,[105] and is mentioned in Breshit Rabbah [5: 3 ,9], "He was building worlds and destroying them."[106]

R. Kook begins by following in the footsteps of R. Lipschutz, whose work *Tiferet Yisrael* was well known by that time. He understands the Doctrine of the Sabbatical Worlds as did R. Lipschutz, and before him Menahem Recanati—that each world lies lifeless at its end, but is not totally destroyed.

> Excavations may teach us that there were living creatures, including humans in [earlier] periods, but there is no proof that there was not in the interim a planetary cataclysm and a new formation [of life]. Rather there is just an unsubstantiated hypothesis [progressive evolution] that need not worry us.[107]

Up to this point, R. Kook is following R. Lipshutz's line of argument in its entirety. He even argues that evolution per se is just one possible explanation of the scientific findings, and that there may have been a series of completely new worlds (or epochs), followed by the regeneration or re-creation of life. However, R. Kook now brings up a few new ideas of his own. The first one occurs a propos his discussion on the Doctrine of the Sabbatical Worlds, and is intended to show, as R. Lipshutz suggested, that there might have been humans at the beginning of each world.

> Indeed in the Zohar on the portion of Leviticus, it is written that there were other types of humans in addition to Adam mentioned in the Torah. However, one must understand well the profound words [of the Zohar], which need a comprehensive explanation.[108]

Where does the Zohar say this and why does R. Kook suggest this idea only half-heartedly, adding that one needs to understand the words of the Zohar? It seems to me that the passage referred to is to be found near the beginning of Leviticus. The Zohar comments on the verse, "When any of you [lit. when a man (*adam*) of you] presents an offering to the Lord" (Lev. 1:2):[109] "R. Elazar said: This verse should have been written, 'A man who brings an offering,' why [does it say] 'of you'? This is to exclude Adam who offered an offering when God created the world. Therefore it is written, 'of you,' from this Adam, to exclude other Adams that are not of you."[110]

I have translated the passage according to how I think R. Kook understood it. However there is an alternative reading to the text: "This is to exclude Adam who offered an offering when God created the world.

[Therefore, it states] here 'of you,' from this man [who comes from you to offer a sacrifice], to exclude the other man [Adam] who was not from you [i.e. not born from humans but created by God]."[111] Since the idea of additional humans in addition to Adam is not conclusive from the text, R. Kook brought this as an auxiliary argument for the Doctrine of the Sabbatical Worlds, and not as an independent one. He now proceeds to suggest some of his own thoughts:

> But actually we do not need this [attempt to synthesize between modern scientific theories and tradition], since even if it were proven true that the order of creation was through the evolution of the species, this would not contradict our calculation of time. We count according to the literal text of the Torah's verses, which is much more meaningful than all the knowledge of prehistory, which has little relevance to us.[112]

The above statement appears to be a retreat into a fundamentalist argument that scripture is more important than science. However, a second look reveals that it is anything but that. R. Kook is not rejecting prehistoric findings because of scripture; he is simply saying that scripture overlooks prehistory, which it considers irrelevant for its own purposes. In other words, even if it is true that the world is older than the simple meaning of the Torah suggests, and that there were prehistoric humans before us, the Torah is only concerned with modern Man, the intelligent Homo Sapiens to whom God spoke and gave a moral code. We therefore do not have to resort to the Doctrine of Sabbatical Worlds in order to understand the new scientific discoveries. In another text, R. Kook states this clearly.

> To compare the creation story with the latest [scientific] studies is of importance. There is nothing to stop us from explaining the passage concerning the creation of heaven and earth to include worlds containing millions of years until reaching a man who realized that he is different from the animals and therefore came to the realization that he needs a unique type of family life with a woman who he would embrace more than his parents.[113]

There is, then, no reason why one cannot say that Adam was the end product of a developmental process, either in earlier epochs or in earlier worlds (as R. Lipschutz said) and that the Torah is interested only in the end product. To understand this idea better, one must realize what is entailed in the Jewish enumeration of years in a calendar that marks the year of writing as 5765. This chronology is based on the work *Seder Olam Rabbah* ascribed to the Tannaic scholar R. Jose Ben Halafta.[114] This work uses the biblical text to calculate the years from Adam until the Tannaic period. Its calculations were later expanded and updated, bringing us today to 5765. An interesting point that R. Kook fails to mention is that this calculation begins with Adam, that is, with the sixth day of creation. According to the Talmud, Rosh Hashanah is the commemoration of the creation of humankind and not the world per se.[115] This means that as of this writing, the world was created 5765 years and 5 days before the past Rosh Hashana. This of course assumes that the days in Genesis 1 consisted of 24 hours each, an idea challenged by some thinkers, but which I will not discuss here. Let it suffice to point out that since the sun was created on day four, it is difficult to understand the first three days of creation literally. Did all of evolution happen during the six days? R. Kook does not discuss this. He just says that the Torah is interested in Man as we know him. If, however, it is true that (as we have demonstrated) that the six days of creation might have been longer than 24 hours each, it would only strengthen his argument.

The next question with which R. Kook deals is whether the book of Genesis is giving us a literal account of creation.

The Torah certainly obscures the act of creation and speaks in allegories and parables. Indeed everyone knows that the stories of Genesis are part of the secrets of the Torah, for if all the narratives were taken literally, what secrets would there be?[116]

R. Kook is following Nahmanides,[117] who had difficulty understanding the question posed by Rashi in his commentary to Genesis 1:1, "Why does the Torah, if it is a law book, begin with the creation story and not with Exodus 12:1?" After all, Nahmanides writes, isn't the creation of the world a principle of faith, and therefore obviously necessary? His answer:

Since the Work of Creation is a deep secret and is not clear from scripture and cannot be known in its totality except through a Divine tradition from Moses and those who do know it must conceal their knowledge, therefore R. Isaac says that the Torah should not have started from Genesis.[118]

If the creation story is a secret of Torah, how can one take it literally, and claim, on this basis, that it negates a certain scientific theory? One could ask as well whether the Torah is in fact concerned with the scientific truths of the world, or just the moral ones. This non-literalist claim of Nahmanides, which was adopted by R. Kook, is a particularly strong one, because the Mishnah states that the real meaning of Genesis 1 is to be transmitted cryptically to the select few who are worthy of such secrets. This of course assumes that the simple meaning of the text is not the "real story."[119] In fact, Nahmanides himself does not see the six days of creation necessarily as a temporal concept at all. R. Kook's final argument concerns the idea of evolution of the species. If this is what happened, why did the Torah not mention it? R. Kooks answers:

> Just as we say "and then Solomon built [the temple for God]" [I Kings 6:1] rather than say that Solomon gave the order to the ministers and the ministers in turn to their subordinates and they to the architects and the architects to the craftsmen and laborers, for this is as obvious as it is secondary.[120]

Obviously it is the one who started the process and gave the order who is the builder. So too it is possible to understand Genesis 1:1 as saying that God gave the order and the world evolved through a process of evolution. Not that this is necessarily what happened, since evolution is just a theory, but it could have been what happened and this would not contradict the Torah which in any event does not disclose the manner of creation. R. Kook stresses the point that evolution is just a theory, and that he is simply demonstrating that it does not contradict the Torah:

> We do not have to accept theories as certainties, no matter how widely accepted, for they are like blossoms that fade. Very soon science will be developed further and all of today's new theories will be derided and scorned and the well-respected wisdom of our day will seem small-minded.[121]

He concludes: "At any rate there is no contradiction whatsoever between the Torah and any of the world's scientific knowledge."

To sum up, let us look at the major points of the argument. If we again turn to the three major questions—the age of the world, the age of humankind and the concept of evolution of the species—R. Kook addresses these as follows: as far as the age of the world and humankind is concerned, he adopts the argument used by R. Lipshutz and R. Benamozegh that there might have been previous worlds or epochs that were destroyed, and offers an additional proof from the Zohar. He then continues with the statement that the creation story cannot be understood literally if it is a part of the secrets of Torah. One therefore cannot claim, based on its literal interpretation, that a particular scientific theory is right or wrong. He then goes on to say that even if it were proven that there were prehistoric animals and men beforehand, this would not concern us, for we can say that the Torah is addressing modern man, and it therefore doesn't matter what came before. Finally, he argues that the fact that the Torah omits the evolution of the species does not necessarily mean that the world was not formed in this manner. Just as the Book of Kings attributes the building of the temple to Solomon despite the fact that he gave only the order, so too one can postulate that even if the text in Genesis makes no mention of a process of creation, a process would not contradict the statement that God created the world per se. Therefore, as long as evolution is ascribed to God, it does not conflict with the Torah. Finally, R. Kook reminds us that evolution is merely a theory, which in any case does not necessarily conflict with the Torah.

Until now I have presented R. Kook's ideas from letter 91, a letter wherein R. Kook tends to separate between science and religion even while attempting a synthesis.[122] However, in _Orot haKodesh_ one finds a different approach. If R. Kook sounded apologetic in his letter to Moshe Seidle, calling evolution a mere theory, in _Orot Hakodesh_ he displays an unprecedented enthusiasm towards it, seeing it as being close to kabbalistic thinking.

> The theory of evolution which at present is conquering the world is in harmony with the eternal secrets of the Kabbalah more than any other philosophic theory. Evolution, which talks of the ascent [of life], gives optimism to the world. After all, how can one despair if we see that everything develops and is elevated constantly? When one delves deeply into the basis of evolutionary ascent, one finds a clear and luminescent Divine element within it, whereby actual infinitude is bringing forth potential infinitude.[123]

Two questions arise at this point. 1. With which secrets of the kabbalah is the theory of evolution in harmony? 2. Why does R. Kook react so enthusiastically to evolution, given that, in his letters, he was no more than apologetic about it? R. Kook answers the first question elsewhere; there he discusses the changes which occurred in the modern period, in our concepts of society, the cosmos and evolution. In this context, he explains why the evolutionary concept makes sense from a kabbalistic perspective.

> The concept of evolution, which has gained popularity in all fields due to the new understanding of nature, has made a conceptual revolution. Not in the minds of those special few masters of knowledge and thought [i.e. the kabbalists] who have always seen the order of gradual emanation even in the spiritual realm from a hidden perspective. For it is not unusual for them to understand by analogy that this is the way of physical development in the tangible world. It should be so, for [the physical world] should be in harmony with the spiritual emanation of existence, which does not miss or skip a level. [124]

R. Kook explains that since, according to the kabbalists, the spiritual worlds that preceded our own were created through a series of gradual emanations, it therefore stands to reason that the physical world should work in the same pattern of gradual development. In this idea of applying the kabbalistic concept of emanation to worldly events R. Kook is following in the path of R. Moses Hayyim Luzzatto (Ramhal), who used it to formulate a developmental understanding of history.[125] In his *Daat Tevunot*, Ramhal develops a theory of historiosophy whereby the Divine element of unity *hanhagat hayihud* pushes all of creation to its telos.

> You have already heard how an end will be to all the darkness of good and bad [mixed together] during the six thousand years [of history]. For [God] had decreed from the beginning that end will come to this and his unity will be revealed and [only] the goodness of the world will remain forever. Therefore, every day that goes by, the world is that much closer to its perfection. Also, the Holy One Blessed Be He, according to his deep plan, does whatever necessary to bring the world to this perfection.[126]

Ramhal's concept is that since, logically speaking, the world will always be full of both good and evil and there will always be wicked and righteous people, the only way for the redemption to come is if God pushes a bit from behind the scenes to help the course of history towards its goal.[127] Ramhal describes a concept of moral or spiritual evolution, which focuses on the future, in contrast with the modern theory of evolution which focuses on the past; however, if one were to postulate that the past also developed from simple to complex and from animal to moral man, this should make us optimistic about the future. After all, who says that evolution stops with modern man? Maybe humanity is developing into more ethical and morally sensitive beings than before. So despite the fact that evolution is but a theory, if it is understood as part of a greater Divine scheme wherein God works behind the scenes to propel the world forward, it becomes an idea in close harmony with Ramhal's writings. R. Kook takes this idea a step further and transforms it into a philosophic concept close to that of Ramhal, with an additional imprint on nature itself. Here the discussion no longer has to do with the science, but with the concept of development and progress in history.[128] R. Kook was able to overlook the "threat" of scientific evolution and go straight to the heart of the issue as he sees it.

R. Kook also answers our second question, i.e. why he was so apologetic in his letter to Moshe Seidle. He was well aware that the idea of the evolution of the species would be conceptually difficult for the average Jew to swallow. After all, didn't the scholars of the Middle Ages talk of creation *ex nihilo*, wherein a world is spontaneously brought into the full bloom of being? How can this idea hold up in light of an evolutionary explanation of nature? R. Kook addresses this clearly:

> The masses were not capable of understanding evolution as a complete and inclusive idea and could not [therefore] relate it to their spiritual world. The problematic aspect which weighs so heavily on the masses isn't the incompatibility of the biblical verses or of traditional texts with the idea of evolution. This type of work [of explaining the verses of Genesis or rabbinic texts on creation] is quite easy. [After all] everyone knows that metaphors and riddles dominate these areas which are cosmic secrets ... But [the problem is] how to relate to the idea of evolution all of the wealth of spiritual ideas developed by the masses which are based on the idea of [creation]ex nihilo and which [was taught since it] saves the mind from floating into areas too removed from understanding,.... This needs a great deal of the light [of pedagogical explanations].[129]

The problem that the masses have with evolution is neither scriptural nor rabbinic, but conceptual. For the masses were never exposed to the kabbalistic concepts of emanation but instead were taught that Genesis describes the story of creation from nothing to full bloom. This was done for educational reasons, to keep the masses from thinking that the world was eternal as Aristotle had said, or created from primordial matter as Plato had said. Therefore the masses were taught that this was wrong. But the act of creation was not necessarily instantaneous. There could have been a gradual sequence of events, and this actually accords better with the concepts of kabbalah than the standard philosophic concept of creationism.

A FINAL THOUGHT

As a last point of this essay, It is necessary to point out how Jewish religious thinking on Evolutionism differs from its Christian counterparts.[130] Christian thinkers, and all those who rely only on the Biblical account of creation, are presented with two options: the fundamentalist approach of the six days of creation, or some type of synthesis with evolutionary theories. There are two such possible syntheses—a special creationism (i.e. each day is a long period of time) or a gap theory (i.e. fossils found are part of an earlier creation).[131] On the surface, the rabbinic thinkers mentioned above seem to be taking the road of synthesis: they seek reconciliation, either using the Doctrine of the Sabbatical Worlds as a sort of gap theory; or, like Rabbi Kook, they offer a non-literal reading of the text. But in fact they only appear to be compromising between the tradition and evolutionary theory. The legitimate authority of the oral traditions to interpret the Biblical text is a fundamental Jewish belief. These traditions, usually from the classical period of the Mishnah and the Talmud, are considered by many as binding even in areas that do not concern Jewish law. They are considered by all as authoritative interpretations of the text. Therefore, rabbis who utilized these sources to create syntheses between new theories of cosmogony and the Bible were doing nothing untraditional; they were simply reinterpreting traditional sources in the light of new information. What thinkers like Rabbi Lipschutz did with the Doctrine of the Sabbatical Worlds, Rabbi Kook did with kabbalistic concepts of emanation and historiosophy. Ancient texts and ideas were used to create reconciliation without stepping out of the fold.[132] It is only at first glance, therefore, that one finds Orthodox thinkers preaching seemingly liberal views of reconciliation.

In conclusion, the rabbinic authorities quoted, living in the nineteenth and early twentieth centuries, saw the geological discoveries of their day as a challenge to be dealt with, but never as a threat. Some, such as Rabbis Lipschutz and Benamozegh,[133] actually greeted these discoveries with great enthusiasm, seeing them as a confirmation of the ancient midrashim which spoke of the worlds that predated our own. Others, such as Rabbis Gefen, Hirsch and Kook, saw them as a challenge, but felt that they had created a perfect synthesis between the new theories and authentic Jewish traditions. The concept of evolution was seen as a greater challenge than the geological discoveries, but even so was dealt with as a problem that lent itself to a satisfying solution. At times, as in the writings of R. Kook, evolutionary theory was greeted with great enthusiasm as a way to illuminate ancient kabbalistic doctrines. Rabbi Herzog,[134] writing in the mid-twentieth century, displayed the discomfort that many later rabbinic figures were to have with evolutionism. This discomfort was caused not just by the challenge which evolutionary theory posed to biblical exegesis, but by the fact that it was considered the flagship of secular scientific thought, which was trying to fight all organized religion. Eventually, some of the rabbis of the second half of the twentieth century began, like their Christian co-religionists, to see the theory of evolution as a threat; and as Orthodox Jews entered the arena of secular studies, many of them entered the battle against evolution, arguing, this time, not from a biblical or Talmudic point of view, but rather from a scientific standpoint,[135] looking to those who opposed evolution as their comrades in arms. Was this a superfluous battle on territory not their own? Why were the syntheses drawn up by Rabbis Lipschutz, Benamozegh, Hirsch, and Kook so quickly forgotten? Obviously, as R. Kook already pointed out, the answer to this question has more to do with politics and society than it does with exegesis.

CHAPTER 17

The Resurgence of Religion in the Late Twentieth Century and Judaism's Unique Contribution to a Moderate and Meaningful Life

I assume that some readers are chuckling here, saying to themselves: "Okay, religion can give someone meaning in life, but it doesn't seem to contribute to moderation. After all, there are ample examples of radical and fanatical religious sects and personalities preaching extremist fundamentalist ideas. If anything, John Lennon's 'Imagine' song, which speaks of the abandonment of religion as a road to peace, seems much more of an appropriate statement." My short answer to this serious question is that extremism is a psychology and not a philosophy. Moderate-minded people will understand the most extreme of ideas metaphorically or in a moderate way. Extremists, whether religious or not, will always find reasons to be extreme. In Chapter 8, I presented Maimonides' theory of morality. In it, he speaks of Judaism as teaching moderation in all aspects of life. Judaism believes in the moral way and in a balanced route, as do other religions; but, as R. Judah Halevi wrote in his Kuzari, the belief that God can be in contact with Man is "the root of faith as well as the root of heresy." Religion and faith are potent concepts. They can unlock hidden powers within mankind. Things that have this high energy can be used for good or for evil. If used for good they can transform the world to be a better place for all; if used for evil they can destroy everything in their path. Extremists look for things that are high energy, since they need these results. In a doctoral thesis written in the sociology department of Bar-Ilan university a decade ago, a young sociologist interviewed would-be or unsuccessful Moslem suicide bombers as well as their leaders in Israeli jails. She was surprised at how few of the would-be suicide bombers used religion to justify their actions and even more surprised that none of the "senders" acted out of religious motives but rather acted out of political ones, even if they employed religious arguments to recruit their emissaries. There is a rise in fundamentalist groups active today worldwide, but their agendas seem to be controlled by politically-minded people more than truly religious figures. Even in the cases where politics does not seem to come into play, fundamentalism always covers up an inner lack of spiritual self-confidence.[1] When one understands the power of organized religion it is not surprising to understand why former Romanian securitata agents found themselves among the clergy of the church. Confession is very revealing of secrets, and real-estate and money are still prominent aspects there. My point is not a condemnation of organized religion but that I am aware of how easy it is to abuse this power. After all, even in biblical times, idolatry was most rampant during the prophetic period. When there is the possibility of great spiritual power then there is the possibility of great spiritual corruption as well. One gives room for the possibility of the other.

Different people look for different things in organized religion. Some look for structure, some for companionship, some for an organized society, others for meaning in their lives—and some are seeking God. I am not being facetious, just realistic. I cannot stand in judgment of human needs, but they are multiple. Even if I feel that meaning, spirituality, and God are the most important things, I cannot disregard the fact that others find different things in religion that they value. The power of being human is locked in the soul. Religion teaches us to unlock these powers, but the use of these powers must be done carefully in order to build and not to destroy. Therefore the moral basis of religion must always be stressed and reason must always walk hand in hand with revelation. We live in a generation where people are looking for meaning in a world dominated by machines, markets and globalization. The individual wants to find identity, meaning and hope. These are things that science cannot fabricate. We can only educate against the corruption of the most meaningful power known to mankind. A. J. Heschel once said that religion asks the ultimate questions of human existence and that these questions are always relevant. No matter what flaws human leaders may have, religion represents an authentic spiritual quest natural to all men.

Judaism has a special message in the realm of moderation. It does not believe in the battle of body and soul. Both were created by God and human beings need them both in this world. The Torah says: "Be Holy" (Lev., 19:1), which is interpreted as meaning to act in holy and spiritual ways even while involved in the most mundane of acts in this world. Man was not created an angel; however, he or she has the capacity to transform their world into something sanctified and meaningful.

It has been my wish in this book to present a different perspective on Judaism and on religion, one of reason and revelation, of God and Man in a moral partnership caring for society and the world. For those who have internalized this message, I bid you go from "strength to strength" and God bless with the blessings of Zion and Jerusalem.

APPENDIX ONE   *Development of the Oral Torah*

100 BCE-200 CE

Mishnah — Tannaic scholars — editor — R. Judah Hanassi — President of the Sanhedrin- written in Hebrew in the Galilee

200 CE-until 500 CE

Gemmarah — Amoraic scholars — editors — Ravina and Rav Ashi- written in Aramaic- in Babylonia
(Also Jerusalem Talmud written in the Galilee)
The Mishnah and Gemmarah together are referred to as the Talmud. This period is called the classic period of rabbinic literature (*Hazal's* literature)

500 CE-600 CE

Sevora'im — edited the Talmud in Babylonia

600 CE-1000 CE

Ge'onim in Babylonia — Responsa in Jewish Law, explanations, history, counted *mitzvot*.

1000 CE-1500 CE

Rishonim — The first Rabbis of the new formed communities outside of Israel and Babylonia — Condensed the Legal issues of Talmud.

R. Isaac Alfasi, Maimonides, R. Asher.

Biblical exegesis — Rashi, Ramban, Seforno, ibn Ezra, Radak.

Talmudic commentaries — Rashi, Tosafot, Ramban, Me'iri, Ritva, Rashba, R. Nissim.

1500 CE-1800 CE

Achronim — Later Rabbis — Code of Jewish Law — R. Joseph Caro (Safed 16th Century) and R. Moses Isserles (Remah — Cracow 16th cent.) Maharal of Prague.

Talmudic commentaries Biblical commentaries Rabbinic Responsa

Midrashim of the Tannaic era: Halakhic and Aggadic (non-legal)
Mekhilta on Exodus Midrash Rabbah
Torat Kohanim on Leviticus Midrash Tankhuma
Sifra on Numbers
Sifrei on Deuteronomy

Braitha — Tannaic sayings left out of Mishnah (R. Hiyya and R. Oshaya)
Tosefta — another Tannaic corpus left out of the Mishnah

The World of Maimonides: An Unorthodox Modern History of an Orthodox and Modern Thinker

Who was Maimonides and why does everyone seem to know his name? Maimonides, known by his Hebrew acronym Rambam (Rabbi Moses Ben Maimon, 1135-1204) was born in Cordoba, Spain. Beginning in the year 711, Spain became a country dominated by two religions, Islam in the south and Christianity in the north. The Jews, for once not in the line of fire between two struggling sovereigns, experienced at first relative freedom. This is reminiscent of the story of the Jewish man walking in Belfast who was approached by a gunman. "Catholic or Protestant?" shouted the gunman. The nervous Jew replied, "Jewish." The bewildered gunman scratched his head and then in a moment of heightened intellect asked, "Jewish Catholic or Jewish Protestant?" In Spain during those days, not being a member of either category was a definite benefit, and Jews advanced up the social ladder on both sides of the Iberian peninsula. This era we refer to as the Golden Age of Spain. As the Muslims entered Western Europe en masse for the first time, they were interested in adopting European intellectual culture as their own. They asked the Jews to translate Greek works in medicine, philosophy and science into Arabic, as this was an age in which all three religions in Spain were struggling to understand their positions vis a vis Greek intellectual culture. This brought about a borrowing of ideas among Muslims, Jews and Christians. Despite this feeling of open cultural sharing, the social climate changed rather quickly. Within decades of the Muslim conquest, the Christians began the Reconquista of Spain from the North. This was eventually an effective operation, and by the mid-eleventh century the Muslim caliphates were struggling to preserve their rule. That's when they called in the Almohads for help. The Almohads, like the Hezbollah of Lebanon today, were fanatic Muslims ready to give their lives for jihad. Upon conquering Cordova from Christian hands in 1148, they wondered why there were so many Jews in such high positions. The Jews were offered forced conversion to Islam, death or exile. Maimonides' family was among those who chose exile, and for ten years the family roamed Spain before settling in Morocco. After leaving Morocco, Maimonides lived briefly in Israel before moving to Fostat, Egypt, in around 1168. In 1169, Maimonides' brother David, the family businessman and provider, drowned at sea after his boat to India sank in a storm. To support himself and his brother's family, Maimonides took on the role of physician to the Grand Vizier Al Qadi al Fadil and then to Sultan Saladin, after whose death he remained a physician to the royal family. In 1171, he was appointed Nagid, or head of the Jewish community, in Egypt.

Maimonides' first work was his commentary to the Mishnah, which he wrote in Arabic around the age of 23. This commentary is considered important unto this day. I always tell my students that they should not belittle their ideas due to their young age, since many of the most famous intellectuals in history made major discoveries at a young age, even if their ideas ripened and changed as time went on. Rambam's other major works include his *Guide for the Perplexed*, his major philosophic work, written in Arabic when he was fifty-two, and his *Book of Mitzvot*, also written in Arabic. His monumental work on Jewish law, the fourteen volumes of the *Mishneh Torah*, Maimonides wrote in a clear Hebrew easily understood by a modern-day Israeli reader.

Maimonides' ideas were not always easily accepted by his peers. He was under constant attack from the rabbis of Provence and differed on certain issues with Spanish rabbis as well. Maimonides, however, was never afraid to hold his ground and defend his opinion. As a rationalist, he attempted to find the synthesis between reason and faith. Some of the main issues of contention were:

A. The Writing of the *Mishneh Torah*

The Talmud is a monumental accomplishment discussing and clarifying the details of Jewish law. This work was produced over hundreds of years and contains the teachings of hundreds of rabbis. However, the Talmud is not user-friendly. If one needs a practical guide in how to keep the Shabbat, the Talmudic tractate of Shabbat, which takes over a year to study properly, is anything but helpful. The first attempt to isolate the legal decisions in Halakha (Jewish law) was done in the eleventh century by R. Isaac Alfasi. Alfasi summarized all the legal discussions of the Talmud and made sure they all came to a conclusion. This meant that after one read the 157 folio pages of the Talmud on Shabbat, he could then read the Alfasi's 68-folio-page legal summary of the laws of Shabbat based on the Talmud. This was definitely a step in the right direction toward a practical aid, but it was still far from a code of law. Maimonides made a bold move when he created the first code of Jewish law. In his *Mishneh Torah*, he breaks Jewish law into 14 categories, takes all the literature from both the Babylonian and Jerusalem Talmuds, and creates a single code — without the help of a computer. This required a thorough knowledge of the rabbinic sources and a perfect memory for all of them. The result was a user-friendly codex with chapter headings and structure. It is so carefully organised that Maimonides himself writes that through it one can know the laws of the Talmud without reading the Talmud directly. Despite how clever this seems to a modern-day reader, the rabbis of Provence, especially Abraham Ben David (the Raavad) of Posquiere, objected vehemently to this work and saw it as a sacrilege that someone would write a legal code to supplant the Talmud. This was not Maimonides' intention, but innovation is not easily accepted.

B His Ideas on Anthropomorphism in the Bible

The first part of Maimonides' *Guide for the Perplexed* deals with the issue of anthropomorphism, i.e. the physical attributes the Bible describes God as having. The Bible speaks of the hand of God smiting Egypt's cattle, or the eyes of God watching over the land of Israel. Does God have a hand or an eye? Maimonides goes to great length to explain these as metaphors. A hand, for example, represents ability, eyes represent providence, a throne represents kingship, etc. Maimonides goes as far as to claim that one who thinks that God does have a body is a sinner. The Raavad attacked Maimonides mercilessly on this point as well. The actual meaning of his attack is an interesting discussion by itself. Joseph Albo, of fifteenth-century Spain, explains this controversy as whether it is justified to call one a sinner after he reads the Bible and thinks that God has a body. Albo states that according to Raavad this Man might be philosophically mistaken, but that is not a sin.

C His Ideas on the Resurrection of the Dead

Maimonides in his commentary to the Mishnah tractate Sanhedrin discusses the notion of the end of days. He gives just a few lines to the idea of the resurrection of the dead. This brought the rabbis of Provence to claim that he didn't actually believe in resurrection. To combat this claim, Maimonides then wrote another work called *The Treatise on the Resurrection*, in which he discusses his views at length and denies the accusations. (It's hard to be Jewish when there are so many rabbis around).

D. His Ideas on Miracles

Maimonides in his commentary to the Mishnah tractate Avot, which speaks of ten miracles that God prepared between the sixth day of creation and the first Sabbath, explains this to mean that miracles are not a breach of nature but part of nature. God decided in advance when and where He would do a miracle, and these exceptions to the laws of nature were imbedded within the laws themselves. As a rationalist, Maimonides thus saves God from appearing to change his mind, for philosophers saw changes of mind as demonstrating a lack of perfection. The rabbis of Gerona, like Nachmanides, opposed this notion, which seems to limits God's ability to decide when and where he wants to change the laws of nature.

E. His Ideas on Prophecy

Maimonides develops a whole theory of prophecy in his introduction to the Mishnah, in his *Mishneh Torah*, and in the *Guide*. He explains that Moses was the greatest of prophets, as the Torah states, before and after him. This statement, of course, saves Judaism from anarchy. After all, the Torah itself was received through the prophecy of Moses. Therefore, if in theory there could be a prophet on the level of Moses, that would mean that the Torah could be changed. It is thus philosophically necessary that Moses stands alone in his prophetic capabilities. Maimonides explains, based on Numbers (12:4-9), that there are four differences between the way Moses received prophecy and the way other prophets did. First, Moses saw clearly and directly, and the other prophets received their prophecy through angels and therefore in riddles. Second, Moses received prophecy at any time whereas the other prophets received it only at certain times. Third, Moses was not startled by prophetic episodes, whereas the other prophets fell and lost their bodily strength during them. Last, Moses received his prophecy while awake, whereas the other prophets received theirs in a dream-like state. This last notion was contested by the students of Nachmanides. Did all other prophets truly receive prophecy in dreams? It's true that Jacob was dreaming when he saw the angels on the ladder and heard God speaking, but this the Bible clearly points out. Is it true, however, that Abraham was dreaming when he hosted the angels in his home as well? Was Jacob's fight with the angel in a dream, and if so, why was he limping after the angel struck his thigh? It's of interest that Gersonides in fourteenth-century Provence comes to Maimonides' defense and claims that even if Jacob dreamed about an angel striking him he would have still limped due to psychosomatic suggestion. This did not convince Rabbenu Bahya or the other followers of Nachmanides.

No great thinkers will ever be totally accepted in his lifetime, and so was it with Maimonides. The above were only examples of a few of the intellectual controversies he had to face.

Brief Biographies of Well-Known Jewish Thinkers

Gersonides (1288-1344)

Rabbi Levi Ben Gershom was born in Provence and lived most of his life in Orange. We know little of his biography, other than that he may have married a distant cousin. Gersonides is the enfant terrible of Jewish Philosophy. His major philosophic work, *Milkhamot Hashem*, or *Wars of the Lord*, was nicknamed "Wars Against the Lord" by his opponents. Hasdai Crescas and Isaac Abarbanel both wrote lengthy criticisms of his work, which meant they saw him as a worthy opponent. Gersonides was a super-rationalist who attempted to create synthesis between faith and reason, though his opponents claimed he compromised faith in order to reach his goal. His ideas influenced a broad spectrum of thinkers including Leibnitz and Spinoza, and his diverse works include a book on mathematics entitled *Maaseh Hoshev* and one on logic entitled *Sefer Hahekesh Hayashar*. His writings on astronomy are to be found in his *Wars of the Lord* and were translated into Latin for a non-Jewish audience during his lifetime. He was in fact a distinguished astronomer, finding fault with the Ptolemaic astronomy of his day and inventing an astronomical apparatus called Jacob's Staff, used to measure the height of the stars above the horizon. A crater on the moon was named Rabbi Levi after him.

Gersonides takes a non-conventional stand on issues of Divine Providence, prophecy, creationism and more. His commentary to the book of Job expresses many of his ideas on Divine Providence. He was well-versed in Halakha, but none of his works in this area have survived. His commentary to the Torah, however, has survived and is well regarded. For more information, see *The Stanford Encyclopedia of Philosophy* at: http://plato. stanford.edu/entries/gersonides/.

Hasdai Crescas: (1340-1411)

Rabbi Hasdai Ben Yehuda Crescas was born in Barcelona. He was a disciple of the great Talmudic scholar Rabbenu Nisim ben Reuven, and among his students we find R. Isaac ben Sheshet and R. Joseph Albo. He was a wealthy man, but had a trying life. His son was murdered in 1391 for believing in Judaism, and he himself was imprisoned in 1378 for a brief period on false accusations. He was referred to as the Rabbi of Saragossa.

Crescas's philosophic work *Or Hashem, The Divine Light,* includes an important chapter refuting Aristotle's physics. In this sense he anticipated Isaac Newton by centuries. Harry Wolfson devoted an entire book to this issue in 1929.Crescas also wrote a polemical book on Christianity defending the Jewish faith, entitled: *Bitul Ikarei Hanotzrim.* Crescas in *Or Hashem* takes a more faith-based position than Maimonides' or Gersonides' rationalism. He believes that in the end, reason cannot bring one to faith and cannot be the basis of faith, even if it can clarify issues of faith. As an anti-Aristotelian, Crescas attempted to create a unique route to faith. For more information, see *The Jewish Encyclopedia* at: http://www.jewishencyclopedia.com/view. jsp?artid=876&letter=C)

Judah Halevi (1075-1141)

R. Judah Halevi was a gifted poet and philosopher as well as a physician. He was born in Tudela or Toledo, Spain. While travelling to Andalus, he impressed Moses ibn Ezra with his poetry, and the two became friends. The period of stability, discovery, and high culture in Spain during his youth was disrupted by the invasion of the Almoravids, a fanatical Islamic sect from North Africa, in 1090. After the Almoravids took control of the petty kingdoms of al-Andalus, and in response to the fall of Toledo to the Christian armies of Alphonso VI, Jewish life in Granada and beyond began to deteriorate rapidly. Halevi left Granada in search of a more secure situation and eventually settled in Toledo, where his reputation as both a poet and physician preceded him.

Not long after 1108, the year his patron in Toledo, Solomon ibn Ferruziel, was murdered, Halevi began to move from city to city, travelling with his friend and younger colleague, Avraham ibn Ezra, the grammarian, biblical exegete, and Neo-Platonic philosopher, and relative of Moses ibn Ezra. According to legend, Halevi's daughter eventually married Avraham ibn Ezra's son. Halevi's books of poetry are used in the liturgy on the 9th of Av, which commemorates the destruction of the Temple.

Halevi's book, *The Kuzari*, was originally entitled *A Book of Refutation and Proof on Behalf of the Despised Religion*. The book's final title is based on the historical Khazar kingdom. The Khazars were a semi-nomadic Turkic people who established one of the largest polities of medieval Eurasia, with a capital city called Atil and territory comprising much of modern-day European Russia, western Kazakhstan, eastern Ukraine, Azerbaijan, large portions of the northern Caucasus (Circassia, Dagestan), and parts of Georgia, the Crimea, and northeastern Turkey. At some point in the last decades of the eighth century or the early ninth century, the Khazar royalty and nobility converted to Judaism, and part of the general population may have followed. The extent of the conversion is debated. The tenth-century Persian historian ibn al-Faqih reported that "All the Khazars are Jews." Notwithstanding this statement, some scholars believe that only the upper classes converted to Judaism; there is some support for this in contemporary Muslim texts. Despite the possibility that the conversion might have been due to political considerations of neutrality in a world dominated by Byzantium and Islam, Halevi claims that the conversion happened after the king had a dream in which an angel told him that his intentions were good but his practises were bad. Subsequently, a Jewish scholar convinced the king of the truth of Judaism. Halevi proceeds to elaborate on the discussion between the king and the Jewish scholar. The book is an anti-philosophical work and an attack on philosophic Judaism. Halevi believes that only revelation can be the true basis of belief, and all rational proofs are but partial. Therefore, he attempts to present Judaism from a more historical encounter between God and the people of Israel. Despite his criticism of philosophy, he displays a wealth of philosophical knowledge in the fifth part of the Kuzari. The book is quite Zionist in the sense that the Jewish scholar eventually goes to Israel. Halevi himself made aliya to Israel and may have died there. For more on the Kuzari, see http://plato.stanford.edu/entries/halevi/

Moses Hayyim Luzzatto (known as Ramchal, 1707-1746)

Ramchal was born in Padua and was well versed in Talmud and Jewish law. However, he is known primarily for his kabbalistic works as well as for his ethical work, *Mesilat Yesharim, The Path of the Just*. At the age of 20 he immersed himself in kabbalistic study and even experienced a "maggid," an angelic being that would speak to him while he was in a dreamlike state. Jekuthiel Gordon, a member of Luzzatto's kabbalistic circle, wrote this account in a letter: "There is here a holy man, my master and teacher, the holy lamp, the lamp of God, his honor Rabbi Moses Hayyim Luzzatto. For these past two and a half years a 'maggid' has been revealed to him, a holy and tremendous angel who reveals wondrous mysteries to him... The angel speaks out of his mouth but we, his disciples, hear nothing. The angel begins to reveal to him great mysteries. Then my master orders Elijah to come to him and he comes to impart mysteries of his own. Sometimes Metatron, the great prince [and angel], also comes to him as well as the Faithful Shepherd [Moses], the patriarch Abraham, Rabbi Hamnuna the Elder, and That Old Man and sometimes King Messiah and Adam... To sum up, nothing is hidden from him. At first permission was only granted to reveal to him the mysteries of the Torah but now all things are revealed to him." Publicising Luzzatto's maggid was detrimental to him. The rabbis of Venice blamed him for being a follower of Shabtai Zvi, the false messiah, and despite the defense he received from his rabbi, R. Yeshayahu Bassan, all of Luzzatto's works on kabbalah were confiscated and by way of compromise were kept in the safekeeping of Rabbi Bassan. Only *Mesilat Yesharim* was printed in his lifetime. Luzzatto eventually left for Amsterdam in 1735, and moved with his family to Acre, Israel, in 1743. He died of a plague in 1746 at the age of 39. He is buried in Tiberias near the grave of Rabbi Akiba.

Luzzatto's major works are: *Klach Pitchei Hokhma*, his interpretation of the writings of Isaac Luriah, the famous Kabbalist from sixteenth-century Safed known as the Ari (the lion); *Da'at Tevunot*, a two-part work which explains his theory of history and its connection to the writings of the Ari; *Derekh Hokhma*, a treatise on what a student should study; *Derekh Tevunot*, a work on Talmudic logic; *Kina't Hashem Zeva'ot*, an attack on Sabbatian ideology; and *Zohar Tinyana*, a continuation of the Zohar which he is said to have received from the Maggid. Another work, *Derekh Hashem, The Way of God*, is a sort of philosophical lexicon of terms of Jewish belief from a kabbalistic perspective.

Years after Luzzatto's death, the Vilna Gaon praised Ramhal as being one of three people who understood the writings of the Ari. He helped publish Luzzatto's commentary to the *Idrah Rabbah*, which was entitled *Adir Bamarom*. Luzzatto, as a man of the Renaissance, wrote poetry for weddings, authored a play called "The Story of Samson," and crafted treatise on public speaking. For a list of his works, see http://en.wikipedia.org/wiki/Moshe_Chaim_Luzzatto.

Notes

INTRODUCTION

1   Klonimus, *Hovat Ha-Talmidim*, pp. 88-89. R. Klonimus argues that even though saintly actions can purify the body, without the training of the intellect in matters of religion and life, eventually all the other faculties will be affected as well.
2   Maimonides, *Guide*, pp. 523-524.
3   See also Lamm, *Faith*, pp. 5-6, 26-28.
4   Vital, *Shaar HaHakdamot*, p. 5b.

CHAPTER 1

1   Kohlberg, "The Adolescent," pp. 1051-1086.
2   Kohlberg, "The Adolescent," pp. 1079-1080.
3   See Maimonides, *Guide*, introduction, p. 7. The metaphor of the lightening flash is taken from Avicenna. See Pines, "The Limitations of Human Knowledge," p. 89.

4   See, for example, Russel, *A History of Philosophy*, Introduction, p. xiii. For further discussion, see Heidegger, *Philosophy*. Heidegger is really asking what the goal of philosophy is.

5   See Maimonides, *Higayon*, chapters 6, 7, and 8.

6   This is called logical deduction since one can induce the result concerning the particular from the general rule. However, one can then ask how one knows that general rule? Wasn't it reached by induction, i.e. looking at particular cases and assuming a general rule? For example: Do I really know that all men are mortal? Have I met them all?

7   The Jews translated these Greek works into both Arabic and Hebrew. They also eventually translated the works of the Muslim philosophers into Hebrew. This brought about the unusual reality that there are manuscripts of Avicenna's writings that have survived in their Hebrew translations (for instance in the Near East manuscripts room of the Bibliotheque Nationale in Paris) but not in the original Arabic.

8   After Averroes in the fourteenth century, fundamentalist trends in Islam put an end to the possibility of philosophy in the Islamic countries.

9   This was discovered by Solomon Munk in 1846, based on Hebrew fragments of the original work quoted by Shem Tov ben Joseph Falaquera. See Sirat, *Jewish Philosophy*, p. 5.

10 See Maimonides, *Guide* II:15, pp. 289-293.

11 See Fackenheim, "The Revealed Morality," p. 62.

12 See Halevi, *Kuzari*, part 1, p. 67 and Maimonides, "Ma'mar Tehiyat Hametim," p. 372. This is contrary to Kierkegaard, who saw the Akeida story of Genesis 22 as a proof that religious belief and obedience stand in opposition to logic. See discussion on this issue in Korn, "Tselem Elokim," pp. 7-8, 24-26. Louis Jacobs tried to reinterpret Kierkegaard's position. See Jacobs, "The Relationship Between Religion and Ethics," pp. 52-54. See also Solomon Leiman's important critique of Jacobs' attempt to divorce religion from ethics: Leiman, "Critique of Louis Jacobs," pp. 58-60. See also Fackenheim, "The Revealed Morality," pp. 65-81.

13 For more on this literature see appendix.

14 On this matter I have to take issue with Colette Sirat, who writes: "The history of Jewish philosophy in the middle ages is the history of the effort of Jews to reconcile philosophy (or a system of rationalist thought) and scripture." (Sirat, *Jewish Philosophy*, p. 5) This might be correct to a certain extent concerning Philo, who lived before the redaction of the oral tradition, but it is not correct for those coming later. It is not just "scripture" that is the basis of the philosophers' beliefs but rather the whole Jewish traditional understanding of scripture as developed in Talmudic literature.

15 As Feldman wrote: "Indeed, the history of Jewish philosophy is in one sense the story of how the Jewish religion has been successfully reformulated in terms of changing philosophical fashions. We have the platonic Philo, the Aristotelian Maimonides, the Leibnitzian Mendelssohn, the Kantian Hermann Cohen. What is important in this ever-changing story is, however, the common attempt to understand Judaism philosophically." Feldman, *Wars of the Lord*, p. 53.

16   For instance: Shem Tov Ben Joseph Falaquera (fourteenth century), Isaac Albalag (late thirteenth century), Isaac Ben Abraham ibn Latif (thirteenth century). For a detailed list, see Sirat, *Jewish Philosophy*.

17   Here I agree with Sirat that Spinoza did not write Jewish philosophy (See Sirat, *Jewish Philosophy*, p. 4). He was Jewish and was an important philosopher, but his discussions did not center on the arena of Jewish philosophy. In the same way, Henri Bergson was an important philosopher of Jewish descent but did not write Jewish philosophy.

18   I heard this orally from Prof. Chaim Soloveitchik.

19   After all, King David says that a man lives three score and ten years. Psalm 90:10.

20   See, for example, *Encyclopedia Judaica*, vol. 13, p. 409.

21   Philo is essentially a commentator on the Torah using neo-Platonic thinking who did not write a comprehensive independent work of Jewish philosophy. See Sirat, *Jewish Philosophy*, p. 7.

22   For more on the Kalam, see Sirat, *Jewish Philosophy*, pp. 15-17.

23   Maimonides, *Guide*, Introduction, pp. 235-239.

24   See also Wolfson, *Crescas*.

25   See Halevy, *Kuzari*, Part I, p. 63.

26   Literally eternal Israel, this is actually a connotation for God. See I Samuel 15:29.

CHAPTER 2

1   See, for example, Exodus 9:3.

2   Deut. 11:12.

3   Isa. 66:1.

4   Dan. 9:18

5   Maimonides, *Guide* I:1, p. 22.

6   Ibid. p. 21.

7   Ibid. pp. 21-22.

8   Ibid. p. 22.

9   Ibid. p. 22. Rambam goes on to claim that the reason idols were called "*Zelamim*" (images) was due to the idea they represented and not their outward form.

10   Here Rambam uses the term "form" in an Aristotelian sense. If matter is the substance of an object, then "form" is its defining form or character. For instance, the substance of a chair might be wood or plastic, but its defining form is something that can be sat upon. If it cannot be sat upon it is not a chair. In the same sense, a human being is made of matter—the body, and form—and the intellectual soul, which is its defining character.

11   Maimonides refers to the intellect as the "Divine Honor (*Kavod*)" (commentary to the mishnah, Haggigah 2:1), which is a term he uses to denote God's presence, the *shekhina*, as well.

12   Albo, *Ikkarim*, part 3, 1, pp. 197-199.

13   See Ovadia Sforno on Genesis 1:26.

14 See, for example, www.sparknotes.com/psychology/psych101/emotion/section1.
html and http://en.wikipedia.org/wiki/Two_factor_theory_of_emotion

CHAPTER 3

1 *Guide* I:2, pp. 23-24.
2 Ibid. pp. 24-25.
3 See also Pines, "Truth and Falsehood," pp. 95-158. I do not think we can compare
the two categories to Aristotle's differentiation between theoretical and practical
knowledge (See Pines, p. 144) nor can we say that Maimonides is discussing
the superiority of truth over good (Pines, pp. 100-101). These categories in
Maimonides need to be understood in the context of his discussion as he uses
them in this chapter, the way Pines explains it on the bottom of page 149.
4 See Copleston, *A History of Philosophy*, vol. 1, p. 129. See also Cornford, *Socrates*,
p. 37. Concerning Aristotle's position, see Aristotle's *Nicomachean Ethics*, 1144b.
See also a discussion on this in Burnyeat, "Aristotle," pp. 70-72.
5 Maimonides, *Guide* III, p. 54. See also Safran, "Maimonides and Aristotle,"
pp. 152-156.
6 For a summary of Kohlberg's stage theory, see: http://en.wikipedia.org/wiki/
Kohlberg%27s_stages_of_moral_development
7 Gigerenzer attacks Kohleberg, claiming that even if there can be philosophic
deliberation in moral issues, moral reasoning on a day-to-day basis is based
on gut feelings that can only be rationalised after the fact. In my view
morality is both rational and intuitive. The examples Gigerenzer uses are all
from the "mefursamot" or agreed-upon moral norms, whereas Kohlberg's work
was all concerning the absolute moral issues. See Gigerenzer, *Gut Feelings*,
pp. 188-191.
8 Yalkut Shimoni 3:28.
9 Compare to Gersonides, fols. 14b-16b.
10 Talmud, Baba Metzia 62a. Soncino translation.
11 http://faculty.plts.edu/gpence/html/kohlberg.htm
Kohlberg's Heinz case: Heinz Steals the Drug
In Europe, a woman was near death from a special kind of cancer. There was
one drug that the doctors thought might save her. It was a form of radium that
a druggist in the same town had recently discovered. The drug was expensive
to make, but the druggist was charging ten times what the drug cost him to
make. He paid $200 for the radium and charged $2,000 for a small dose of the
drug. The sick woman's husband, Heinz, went to everyone he knew to borrow
the money, but he could only get together about $1,000, which is half of what
it cost. He told the druggist that his wife was dying and asked him to sell it
cheaper or let him pay later. But the druggist said: "No, I discovered the drug
and I'm going to make money from it." So Heinz got desperate and broke into
the man's store to steal the drug-for his wife. Should the husband have done
that? (Kohlberg, 1963, p. 19).

CHAPTER 4

1   See Rashi's commentary to Genesis 1:26.
2   Hagigah 12a. See also Genesis Rabbah 3:6 and Shuchat, *The Creation*, pp. 123-129.
3   See Nahmanides on Genesis1:14.
4   Genesis Rabbah 5:9
5   Rashi on Genesis 1:14.
6   Ibid.

CHAPTER 5

1   The Talmud relates a story of how Rabbi Akiba's daughter was told by an astrologer that she would die from the bite of a serpent on her wedding day. The Talmud relates that due to an act of charity which she did, she was saved by inadvertently killing the snake. This would imply that the snake was there, as the astrologer had said, but that her act of charity had saved her from a possible tragic outcome.
2   Maimonides, *Mishneh Torah*, Book of Knowledge, Laws of Teshuvah, 5:1.
3   As righteous as Moses but not a prophet on the level of Moses. See Maimonides, *Mishneh Torah*, Book of Knowledge, Yesodei Hatorah, 7:6.
4   Lit., or wise or dumb, but I translated according to the understanding of the Hagahot Maimoniot.
5   Maimonides, *Mishneh Torah*, Book of Knowledge, Laws of Teshuva, 5:2.
6   Maimonides, ibid, 5:3.
7   Commentary to the Mishnah, introduction to Chapter Helek.
8   I have mentioned above that no traditional Jewish scholar would ever say, "The Rabbis (*Hazal*) of the Talmud said this but I say otherwise," since *Hazal* are the pillars of our tradition and through them do we know of the early sources.
9   Brakhot 33b.
10   Maimonides, *Responsa*, pp. 309-310.
11   Ibid.
12   Moed Katan 18b.
13   See Rashi's commentary to Genesis 1:26.
14   For Maimonides, an obligatory war is either a war to gain the land of Israel or a war of defense. A non-obligatory war would be an economically or politically motivated war.
15   Rashi's commentary to Genesis 1:26.
16   He does so, for instance, when the Bible talks of God in corporeal terms. Maimonides even goes as far as to claim that in theory, the first verse in Genesis stating that God created the heavens and the earth could have been interpreted metaphorically if necessary, but that creationism is too important a concept to relinquish. *Guide* II, p. 25.
17   Rashi's commentary to Genesis 1:26.
18   Avot 3:19.

19   Maimonides, *Mishneh Torah*, Book of Knowledge, Laws of Penitence, 5:5.

20   Maimonides brings five aspects in which God's knowledge is different than human knowledge. See *Guide* III:20, pp. 482-484.

21   Gersonides, *Wars of the Lord*, pp. 188-190.

22   Ibid., p. 191.

23   Ibid., p. 293.

24   All the pre-Copernican Jewish rationalists, except for Maimonides, saw astrology as a science and not just a belief system.

25   Isaac Bar Sheshet Perfet (the Rivash, 1326-1408) criticizes Gersonides on this point, saying that if God does not know beforehand what a person will do but only knows of it after it is done, God then acquires knowledge of something He did not know before — which would show change in God as well as imperfection. The Rivash tries to give his own explanation, which is that God knows both what the person will choose and why, but does not force it (Responsum no. 118).

26   Hasdai Crescas dealt with this issue differently (Crescas, *Or Hashem* iv, p. 5), with an unconventional description of human free will.

27   *Guide* III:15, pp. 459–461. See also Aristotle, *Physics VI*, 10, 241b, 4-8.

28   Wolfson points out that Maimonides differs with the philosophers also on the question of whether God can know the future. Possibly Maimonides did not see this as something notable, since it does not include a physical interaction with our world or a change in the range of perceived logic but just an argument for an additional ability in God's knowledge. See Wolfson, *Kalam in Jewish Philosophy*, p. 199.

29   Commentary to the Mishnah of Avot, 5:6.

30   Reines reached a different conclusion, based on Strauss' concept of exoteric and esoteric Rambam. See Reines, "Miracles," pp. 260-262.

31   Albo, *Ikkarim*, part one, chapter 22.

32   Al-Farabi has a similar notion which he refers to as the exclusion of the middle. A thing cannot both exist and not-exist simultaneously. This would apply to God as well.

33   Teshuvot HaRashba, vol. 1, p. 216. (My translation.)

34   *Guide* III:15, p. 460.

35   I heard this example in the name of the late R. Yehudah Ashkenazi.

36   See for example *Guide* II:2, p. 252.

37   See also Davies, *Physics*, p. 136.

38   Ibid.

39   Ibid. p. 137.

40   See Armstrong, *The Case for God*, p. 266.

41   Ibid. p. 141.

CHAPTER 6

1   That is why all doctorates in universities today are called Doctor of Philosophy even if their studies are in literature or physics.

2   Hippocrates.

3   Maimonides, *Eight Chapters*, pp. 363-364.
4   Ibid. pp. 158-159.
5   Ibid. p. 159.
6   Ibid. pp. 159-160.
7   Ibid. p. 160.
8   Alfarabi, *The Perfect State*, p. 171. The exact source from which Maimonides took his cue can be found in Alfarabi, *Selected Aphorisms*, p. 15.
9   http://bmpt.bseu.by/english/history.htm
10   Maimonides, *Eight Chapters*, chapter two.
11   Ibid.
12   Makkot 15b.
13   I am not claiming that excommunication was never tried in Jewish circles, only that it was rare.

CHAPTER 7

1   See, for example, Cordovero, *Pardes*, 40b, Shaar Erkei Hakinuim, "*Razon.*" Gikatila seems to differ on calling *Hokhma* the will (*Razon*) However, he calls Keter the origin of will (see Gikatila, *Shaarei Ora*, pp. 94b and 106a).
2   In the kabbalistic writings of the Vilna Gaon this is represented by Keter, the highest sefirah, the *razon*, and Daat, the invisible sefirah of the Tree of Life, representing the *behirah*. See *Siddur HaGra*, p. 64b, 73a, in the commentary of Rabbi Naftali Hertz Halevi, Imrei Shefer.
3   About 150 cm. Based on archaeological findings, this appears to be the average height of Roman soldiers in that period.
4   Erubin 4b.
5   Erubin 48a.

CHAPTER 8

1   Nicomachean Ethics book II, chapter 4, in McKeon, *Aristotle*, p. 956.
2   Ibid chapter six, p. 959.
3   *Eight Chapters*, chap. 4.
4   Ibid.
5   Ibid.
6   Ibid.
7   Ibid.
8   Ibid.
9   Ibid. Twersky, *Maimonides Reader*, p. 370.
10   Ibid. p. 371.
11   Ibid. p. 372.

CHAPTER 9

1 Book of Jubilees 23:18.
2 Maimonides, *Guide* II:27, pp. 332-333.
3 Twersky, *Maimonides Reader*, p. 402.
4 Twersky, *Introduction to Helek*, p. 404. (My translation.)
5 Ibid. p. 410.
6 Ibid.
7 Ibid. p. 411.
8 Ibid.
9 Moody, *Life After Life*, pp. 5-6.
10 Moody, *Life After Life*, pp. 35-36.
11 Chopra, *Life After Death*, pp. 37, 43. See also pp. 257-258 and www.near-death.com.
12 Moody, *Life After Life*, p. 89.
13 Sutherland, *Reborn in the Light*, p. 39.
14 Ibid. p. 239.
15 Halevi, *Aseh Lekha Rab*, II, pp. 36-52.
16 Ibid. pp. 413-414.
17 Ibid. p. 416.
18 Ibid. p. 411.
19 Ibid. p. 416.
20 For example, Saul in I Samuel 10:1.
21 See I Samuel 16:1.
22 For example, Elisha in I Kings 19:16.
23 Ex. 29:7.
24 Gen. 28:18, 31; 13:14, 35.
25 Lev. 14:10.
26 King Cyrus is referred to this way even without his knowledge. See Is. 45:1.
27 Ps. 105:15; Chron. 16:22.
28 Is. 11:1; Hosea 3:5.
29 Twersky, *Maimonides Reader*, p. 414.
30 Maimonides, *Mishneh Torah*, Shoftim, Hilkhot Melakhim, 11:1.
31 Ibid. 12:2-3.
32 Ibid. 11:3. See also Maimonides, "Ma'amar Tehiyat Hametim," p. 369-371.
33 Twersky, *Maimonides Reader*, p. 415.
34 Ibid.
35 Maimonides, *Guide* II, pp. 332-333
36 See: http://www.universetoday.com/12648/will-earth-survive-when-the-sun-becomes-a-red-giant/
37 Twersky, *Maimonides Reader*, pp. 415-416.
38 Ibid. p. 414.
39 Maimonides, *Igrot*, "Igeret Tehiyat Ha-Metim," pp. 349-350. My translation.
40 Ibid. p. 359, p. 364.
41 Ibid. p. 376.
42 Ibid. p. 373.
43 Ibid. p. 391.

CHAPTER 10

1   Kook, *Orot HaKodesh* II, p. 380-381.

2   Zohar I, 227a.

3   Ibid.

4   Ibid. See De Vidas, *Reisheit Hokhmah*, Shaar Hayirah, Chapter 12, p. 215.

5   Zohar I 218 quoted in De Vidas, *Reisheit Hokhmah*.

6   Ibid.

7   De Vidas, *Reisheit Hokhmah*. Shaar Hayirah, Chapter 12, p. 215.

8   De Vidas, *Reisheit Hokhmah*, Shaar Hayirah, Chapter 13, p. 270.

9   Ibid. p. 269.

10   Luzzatto, *Yalkut*, Maamar Ha-Hokhma, vol. 1, pp. 266-268.

11   Weiss, *Only Love*, pp. 11-14.

12   Ibid. p. 272.

13   Ramhal, *Maamar Ha-Ikkarim*; Luzzatto, *Yalkut*, vol. 1, "On Gan Eden and Gehinom," p. 224.

14   "I, and not an angel, I and not a seraph, I and not a messenger."

15   See Shuchat, *Olam Nistar*, introduction, p. 24.

16   See *Daat Tevunot*, Bnei Brak, 1975, vol. 1, p. 82-84.

17   It is of interest that the modern Jewish national movement called itself Zionism. Zion in Hebrew ציון is the numerical value of Joseph in Hebrew (יוסף) = 156.

18   Which follows that of the messiah of the house of Joseph, which is a more natural stage.

19   Kook, *Orot HaKodesh*, vol. 3, p. 637.

CHAPTER 11

1   This chapter was originally published in Scripta Judaica Cracovia, Published by Jagellonian University, Cracow, 2008.

2   Babylonian Talmud, Makkot 23b-24a

3   Mishnah, Ohalot, 1:8. Talmud Bekhorot 25a. The mystics can find much symbolism in these numbers since a woman lights two candles on the Sabbath eve, representing the male and the female. A candle (נר) equals 250. Two candles equal 500, which is the sum of the limbs in the male and female bodies.

4   It is of interest that the Talmud uses the solar and not the lunar year of 354 days. Since the Hebrew calendar incorporates both the solar and lunar calendar in its 19-year cycle, it sees both as legitimate. Interestingly enough there is an alternative tradition that the 365 negative commands parallel the nerves (*gidim*) in the human body. No tradition can be found in our sources which enumerates these nerves. I find it of interest, however, that an ancient Chinese tradition states that there are 365 acu-points to be found on the nerve junctions of the body. (Acu-points are based on the classical book of Chinese medicine called *The Yellow Emperor's Canon of Internal Medecine*.)

5   The Decalogue (*aseret hadibrot*) is wrongly translated into English as the "ten commandments." It should be translated as the "ten utterances," as in the Greek "Decalogue." There is a dispute as to how many commands are actually contained within these ten statements.

6   Ex. 20:2-6; Deut. 5:6-11.

7   For example, Deut. 5:11.

8   Deut. 5:20-24.

9   See Nachmanides, *Commentary to the Torah*, Ex. 20:7. See also Heschel, *Torah Min Hashamayim*, vol. 1, pp. 31-32. Heschel sees this as a controversy between the academies of Rabbi Ishmael and Rabbi Akiba.

10   For example, Deut. 4:1, 4:40, and 8:11.

11   This work is ascribed to R. Shimon Kaira (841 CE).

12   Written in 1250 CE.

13   Crescas, *Or Hashem*, pp. 9-10.

14   Nachmanides' Commentary to Sefer Hamitzvot, p. 206, positive mitzvah one.

15   *Sefer Mitzot Gadol*, positive mitzvah one.

16   Maimonides, *Eight Chapters*, chapter two, p. 365.

17   For example, it says in Exodus concerning the Paschal offering: "You shall not leave any of it until morning and the remaining parts should be burned in fire." Accordingly, if one should leave part of the Paschal lamb until morning and not burn it, they would be committing a passive transgression which could not be punished by a human court.

18   Maimonides, *Sefer Hamitzvot*, introduction, criterion number 4.

19   In his introduction to his translation of the *Guide for the Perplexed*, Samuel ibn Tibbon writes that a translator needs "to know the language that the book was written in, to understand its investigations as well as the hidden and revealed issues therein, and to transfer all these issues of the book without changing them into the language he wants to translate it to; this is what translation is about." Maimonides, *Guide*, ibn Tibbon ed., pp. 1a-2b (my translation).

20   Maimonides, *Mishneh Torah*, Book of Knowledge, Yesodei Hatorah, chapter one, 1:6, pp. 43-44.

21   Maimonides, *Guide* I, p. 50. I used Freidlander's translation here since I found it preferable. See Maimonides, *Guide*, Friedlander ed., p. 6. Rawidowicz points out that in the *Sefer ha-Mitzvot* Maimonides uses the term "prime cause" to describe God, whereas in his Halakhic work *Mishneh Torah* he refrains from such Aristotelian terminology. See Rawidowicz, *Iyyunim*, vol. 1, pp. 354-355.

22   Maimonides, *Guide*, III:51, p. 618. Friedlander ed., p. 384.

23   This is an example of how Maimonides' legal writings and philosophic writings can explain each other. See on this topic Hartman, *Maimonides*, pp. 28-65. See Abarbanel, *Rosh Amana*, pp. 60-61, 70-71, who argues that Crescas misunderstood Maimonides. Maimonides, when speaking of a *mitzvah* to believe in God, was not referring just to the existence of a first cause but to the belief in a perfect God with absolute existence. I believe that our explanation is well supported from cross references and therefore more fitting.

24   See Lane, *Arabic-English Lexicon*, vol. one, book 1, p. 2105, eighth form.

25   See Kafih, *Sefer Hamitzvot*, p. 58, note 1. See also Hartman, *Maimonides*, p. 49 and notes 50 and 51 there.

26   See Shuchat, "Demuto shel Avraham," pp. 193-195.

27   Maimonides, *Mishneh Torah, Book of Knowledge*, Hilkhot Avodat Kokhavim, chapter 1:3. Translation by O'Levy, Immanuel M., 1993.

28 Maimonides, *Guide*, Freidlander ed., II:39, p. 231 (Pines ed. p. 379).
29 Ibid.
30 Genesis Rabbah, Vilna Edition, 39:1. (My translation.)
31 Crescas, *Or Hashem*, Hebrew, Treatise one, third principle, chapter 56, (page 27b). (My translation.)
32 See Halevi, *Kuzari*, I:13. See also Lobel, *Between Mysticism and Philosophy*, pp. 68-71.
33 See Shuchat, "Demuto shel Avraham."
34 See, for example, Maimonides, *Mishneh Torah*, Book of Knowledge, Fundamentals of Torah, 2:8; 3:9.
35 See Maimonides, *Guide* II:1, p. 246.
36 While Kant himself attempts to create an idealized form of Protestantism in the hopes of describing a rational form of religion based on reason and morality (in his *Religion Within the Limits of Mere Reason*. Cambridge: Cambridge University Press, 1998), Kant's philosophical criticism of metaphysics had much more of an influence on bringing about an era of philosophic enquiry divorced from metaphysical enquiry. See also, Agus, *Jewish Identity*, pp. 37-81. Interestingly enough, Hassidic thinking in the eighteenth and early nineteenth centuries also saw faith as beyond the realm of intellectual enquiry without being aware of Kant's writings. See *Derekh Mitzvotekha*, 93-94.

CHAPTER 12

1   "There are only three modes of proving the existence of God, on the grounds of speculative reason." Kant, *Critique of Pure Reason*, p. 406.
2   See Gilson, *Modern Philosophy*, p. 62.
3   See Kant, *Critique of Pure Reason*, p. 413, and Gilson, *Modern Philosophy*, p. 64.
4   In Hume's words: "Your appeal to past experience decides nothing in the present case; and at the utmost can only prove that that very object, which produced any other, was at that very instant endowed with such a power; but can never prove, that the same power must continue in the same object or collection of sensible qualities. Should it be said, that we have experience, that the same power continues united to the same object, and that like objects are endowed with like powers, I would renew the question, why from this past experience we form any conclusion beyond those past instances, of which we have had experience." Hume, David, *A Treatise Of Human Nature*, book one, part three, sec. 3. Quoted by Gilson, *Modern Philosophy*, p. 261.
5   Bertrand Russel was not the first to think of this problem even though he gives his readers this feeling. See Russel, *The Basic Writings*, p. 587.
6   See Maimonides, *Guide*, II:20, 23, and 25.
7   "The track it pursues, whether rational or sophistical, is at least natural, and not only goes far to persuade the common understanding, but shows itself deserving of respect from the speculative intellect." Kant, *Critique of Pure Reason*, p. 413.
8   Ibid. p. 416.
9   Even though he questions even step three, he adds that it needs the ontological argument as a basis, which really means that he is arguing that the cosmological proof cannot prove an infinite and perfect being as the prime cause.

[10] "This argument always deserves to be mentioned with respect. It is the oldest, the clearest, and the most in conformity with the common reason of humanity." Kant, *Critique of Pure Reason*, p. 423.

[11] I remain close to Kant's model. Ibid. p. 425.

[12] Ibid.

[13] Ibid. pp. 430-431. This he expands in Kant, *Future Metaphysics*.

[14] Kant, *Critique of Pure Reason*, p. 433. It is of interest that the debate over intelligent design in evolution has again reopened the question of the physio-theological argument. See Monton, *Seeking God in Science*, who argues as Kant did in his time that one can hold the view of intelligent design without assuming a deistic position (p. 41).

[15] Halevi, *Kuzari*, I:13.

CHAPTER 13

[1] See, for instance, McCarthy, "Postmodern Pleasure and Perversity," pp. 104-107.

[2] Quoted in Davies, *Physics*, p. 100.

[3] Zukav, *The Dancing Wu Li Masters*.

[4] Worthing, *God, Creation and Contemporary Physics*, pp. 203-204.

[5] See, for instance, Gigerenzer, *Gut Feelings*, p. 19.

[6] Ibid. pp. 4-5.

[7] Ibid. pp. 94-95.

[8] Wundt 1912/1973 "On Artificial Intelligence," in Copeland, B., *The Essential Turing: Seminal Writings in Computing Logic Philosophy Artificial Intelligence and Artificial Life Plus the Secrets of Enigma*. Oxford: Oxford University Press, 2004. Quoted in Gigerenzer, *Gut Feelings*, pp. 102-103.

[9] Gigerenzer, *Gut Feelings*, p. 103.

CHAPTER 14

[1] This chapter was published originally as an article entitled: "The Maturation of Jewish Monotheistic Theology," **Studia Hebraica** 5 (2005) Bucharest University.

[2] I thank Prof. Moshe Idel for pointing this out to me.

[3] Maimonides, *Mishneh Torah*, Laws of Idolatry 1:1.

[4] Genesis Rabbah 38:13.

[5] Sanhedrin 63b.

[6] Hayyim Volozhin, Nefesh Hahayim, Part 1, chapter 1.

[7] Halevy, *Kuzari*, 4:1.

[8] Even though the midrash ascribed this figure to Shem son of Noah (Nedarim 32b), the biblical text must always first be understood according to its simple meaning. "Ein mikra yozeh midei pshuto."

[9] See Pritchard, *Ancient Near East*, vol. 1, pp. 94-95.

[10] I would like to thank Prof. Shalom Paul for pointing this out to me.

[11] Genesis Rabbah, 91:5.

12   I have always wondered if Pharaoh Akhenaten might have been the pharaoh of the Joseph story. Was this exclusively sun-worshipping king, an anomaly to the pagan rulers of Egypt, a man working under the influence of his understanding of monotheism? See Freud, *Moses and Monotheism*. Here I take issue with Freud and take the exact opposite view of who influenced whom. However, I do not know if there is any way to reach an unequivocal conclusion here.

13   *Tikunei Zohar*, Vilna 1827 ed. P. 19a on Patah Eliyahu.

14   See Exodus 3:15-16 and 18, and 4:31.

15   See Exodus 8:6, 9:14 and 16, and 10:2, as well as 14:4.

16   Halevi, *Kuzari*, part I, p. 97.

17   Ex. 32:1.

18   Ex. 32:4.

19   See Fackenheim, "The Revealed Morality," p. 62.

20   Deut. 4:15.

21   Ex. 33:15.

22   Ex. 9:3.

23   Deut. 11:12.

24   Ex. 24:10.

25   Isa. 66:1.

26   I am referring to the midrash that God created the world from his garment, which Rambam condemns (*Guide* II:27).

27   The midrash which speaks of an order of time that predated the world is seen by Rambam as puzzling. Possibly due to the authoritative status of this corpus of midrash he adds nothing further to his criticism.

28   Sefer Hamada, Hilkhot Teshuva, 3:7

29   Sefer Ha-Ikkarim. I, p. 2.

30   R. Abraham Ben David of Posquiere (Raabad), in Maimonides' *Hilkhot Teshuva*, 3:7.

31   It has been argued that the Raabad held a material view of the Divine qualities. (See, for example, Agus, *The Writings*, p. 197.) I believe this is a misunderstanding of the Raabad's position. It is my opinion that his argument with Maimonides on the point of anthropomorphic descriptions of the Deity in the Bible was related to how the kabbalists understood the meanings of these descriptions and not whether the Deity in actuality bore physical qualities.

32   See the Vilna Gaon's commentary to the *Code of Jewish Law*, Yoreh De'ah, 179:13. Also see my article, Shuchat "Denuto shel Avraham," pp. 196-203.

33   See, for example, Agus, *The Writings*, pp. 184-186.

34   Ibid. p. 377.

35   See Shneur Zalman,*Tanya*, 83a. There were those who falsely attributed this opinion to the Vilna Gaon. See my aticle, Shuchat "Perush Hagra," p. 267, note 15.

36   *Tikunei Zohar*, 122b.

37   *Zohar III*, Ra'ayah Meheimna, 225a.

38   For more on the Talmudic concept of Shekhina, see: Auerbach, *Hazal*, pp. 29-52, Scholem, *Pirkei Yesod*, pp. 259-307, Tishbi, *Mishnat ha-Zohar*, vol. 1, pp. 219-231; and Halamish, *Kabbalah*, p. 111.

39   Maimonides, *Guide* I:27, p. 57. Abarbanel in his commentary to the *Guide* calls it a miraculous created light.

40   Saadiah, *Emunot ve-De'ot*, part two, 10, pp. 103-104.

41   See Halevi, *Kuzari II*, pp. 4, 7, 8.

42   The Maharal of Prague, a contemporary of R. Hayyim Vital, who probably was unfamiliar with his writings, addresses the same issue in his *Nezah Israel* (Jerusalem 1971, Hebrew Ed.) chapter 3, p. 16. The Maharal's concept of the created existence and the element of completion, "mashlim," is a philosophic concept close to the Lurianic idea of the *"igul"* and the *"kav,"* in the sense that it addresses this very issue.

43   Vital, *Eitz Hayyim*, 11b.

44   "The second investigation is close to the question of what is above and what is below, what is before and what comes after...therefore we cannot investigate or expound upon this in any profound fashion, however we will explain, God willing, by way of chapter headings peeking through the cracks without going into great depth." Vital, *Eitz Hayyim*, I (Igulim ve-Yosher), 1:1.

45   This is the term used by Pachter, "Bein Acosmism le-Theism," pp. 139-158, and Ross "Shnei Perushim," pp. 153-169. However, it is not certain that the Hassidim deny objective existence to reality. See, for example, R. Yehiel Safarin of Kamarno, *Ketem Ofir*, on the scroll of Esther: pp. 4 and 12-13.

46   Shneur Zalman, *Tanya*, p. 78a.

47   "For the revealed zimzum was only in relation to the [created] receivers, but from God's point of view there was no change, for the light remains contained in its source." See *Derekh Mitzvotekha*, p. 51a.

48   See Tikunei Zohar, 122b.

49   See Ross, "Shnei Perushim."

50   R. Elijah Ben Solomon (Vilna Gaon), "Hakdama le-Sod ha-Zimzum," quoted in Shuchat, "Perush Hagra," p. 288, including note 2 in the article.

51   Kook, *Igrot Haraayah*, vol. 1, letter 44, p. 48.

52   Kook, *Arpelei Tohar*, p. 45.

53   For more on Maimonides' negative theology see: Manekin, "Belief, Certainty, and Divine Attributes"; Wolfson, "Maimonides on Negative Attributes," pp. 195-231; Davidson, "Metaphysical Knowledge"; and Birnbaum,"Bahya and Maimonides."

CHAPTER 15

1   This chapter was originally printed as an article entitled: "Reflections on the Popularity of Mysticism in the West Today: A General and Jewish Perspective," Studia Hebraica 4 (University of Bucharest) (2004): pp. 332-340.

2   E-idra@yahoogroups.com

3   Kant, *Future Metaphysics*, pp. 79-80.

4   See, for example, Southgate, *Postmodernism in History*, pp. 62-74. As she writes, "Certainly skepticism is the philosophy with which postmodernism is most closely associated, and we can at least concede that the length of skepticism's history gives a good indication of the depth of post modernism's roots."

5   Armstrong, *The Case for God*, p. 264.
6   For a discussion on postmodern thinking about rationalism in the 1980's, see Bertens, *The Idea of the Post Modern*, pp. 114-137.
7   See Ben-David, *Scientific Growth*, pp. 545-551.
8   Ibid. pp. 521-531 and pp. 551-558. Ben-David puts the move from criticism against science to anti-scientism at about 1968, and sees the social impact of the anti-Vietnam war movement among students as a major catalyst for these feelings. See also Merton, "The Sociology of Science," pp. 111-113.
9   This belief in the omnipotence of science helped lead to a mistrust in scientism in general. See Ben-David, *Scientific Growth*, p. 555.
10 See Handlin, "Ambivalence in Responses to Science," introduction, pp. xii-xxii.
11 See also Southgate, *Postmodernism in History*, pp. 82-87.
12 Eliade, *Myth of the Eternal Return*, pp. 90-91.
13 Prophetic Kabbalah is the term used by Scholem, *Major Trends*, p. 119.
14 Scholem, *Major Trends*, chapter two. Blumenthal, Elior and Shaeffer have all written extensively on this literature.
15 See Idel, *Abraham Abulafia*, chapter one.
16 Ibid. p. 27.
17 Huss, "All You Need is Lav."
18 Ibid. p. 5.
19 See Shuchat, "Lithuanian Kabbalah," pp. 195-199.
20 Huss, "All You Need is Lav," pp. 11-12. Huss writes: "The Kabbalah Centre's apparent simplistic and superficial way of presenting kabbalistic signifiers integrated with other cultural and religious themes should be understood as typical postmodern pastiche, which reshuffles and re-constructs previous cultural elements."
21 Ibid. p. 12. This seems to be a general trend in western postmodern mysticism.
22 Lyotard, *The Postmodern Condition*, pp. 50-51.
23 See also McCarthy, "Postmodern Pleasure and Perversity," p. 102: "This view instates a new mysticism and a new form of pleasure seeking, acted out through the unrestrained dance of capital and desire in the social."
24 Jameson, *Postmodernism*, p. 9. See also p. 6. Huss mentions this quote in "All You Need is Lav," p. 12.
25 Fromm, *Escape From Freedom*, p. 36-37.
26 Ibid. p. 254.
27 Ibid. p. 255.
28 Ibid. pp. 255-256.
29 Ibid. p. 270.
30 Jameson, *Postmodernism*, pp. 15-16.
31 Ibid. p. 51.
32 For sources, see Shuchat, "The Historiosophy of the Vilna Gaon," pp. 128-129.
33 Shneur Zalman,*Tanya*, Shaar Hayihud, 78a.
34 Ibid. 6a.
35 Jameson, *Postmodernism*, p. 25.
36 Jerusalem Talmud, Shabbat, chapter I, Halakha 3. See also *Shir Hashirim Rabah*, (Vilna Edition), 1:9, and *Zohar Hadash* vol. 1, 76a.

CHAPTER 16

[1] See "Did the Kabbalists Believe that the World was Created in Six Days?" Badad 22 (2009). (Hebrew)

[2] Armstrong, *The Case for God*, p. 250.

[3] Ronald Numbers discusses this. See Numbers, *Darwinism Comes to America*.

[4] Armstrong, *The Case for God*, p. 275.

[5] I would like to thank Professors Yemima Ben Menahem, Alessander Guetta and Gad Freudenthal for their helpful insights and remarks.

[6] I am discussing thinkers who are interested both in reaching a synthesis between science and tradition as well as a common motif that is employed by them, the Doctrine of the Sabbatical Years. There are other nineteenth- and early-twentieth-century thinkers who do not fall under these criteria. R. Meir Leibush, Malbim (1809-1879), who does not discuss our main motif and only hints at evolutionism, I leave out. I leave out as well Naftali Halevi (1840-1894), an orthodox maskil who published a short essay on evolution and the Torah called *Toledot Adam*. He did not mention our motif and was not in a rabbinic position as were the others. For further information on his work see Cherry, *Evolution and Jewish Thought*, pp. 129-134. Cherry also discusses both orthodox and non-orthodox thinkers of the nineteenth and twentieth centuries on pp. 92-190. I found it rather curious that he left out both R. Lipschutz and R. Gefen from his quite comprehensive discussion of evolution. He seems also to have missed the importance of the Doctrine of the Sabbatical Years for this discussion.

[7] See: Robinson, *Judaism Since 1700*, pp. 288-289. Robinson claims that Jewish attitudes to the theory of evolution in the nineteenth century ranged from fierce opposition to acceptance. I will demonstrate that in the nineteenth century there was a more accepting attitude among rabbinic authorities toward scientific cosmology, which turned into opposition only in the second half of the twentieth century.

[8] See for example Maimonides, who incorporated the idea of God being the cause of all into the belief in God's existence. Maimonides, *Hakdamot*, p. 141. See also *Guide to the Perplexed*, II:27. Maimonides sees the creation of the world as a principle of Judaism but not its demise. Much has been written on Maimonides and creationism. For further reading, see Maimonides, *Guide*, Schwartz edition, vol. 1, p. 346, note 1 and p. 341, note *. See also Shapiro, *The Limits of Orthodox Theology*, pp. 71-77. Leibowitz, "Briat Ha-Olam be Emunato shel ha Rambam," pp. 71-78.

[9] Also known as Fourth Ezra or Propheta Ezra, chapter 5:30-31.

[10] Enoch II (also called the Slavic Enoch), 11:81.

[11] Sanhedrin 97a.

[12] Genesis Rabbah 3:7. I have followed the Soncino translation with some changes.

[13] Genesis Rabbah 9:2. See also Kohelet Rabbah 3 on the verse in Kohelet 3:11 and Midrash Shoher Tov on Psalm 34.

[14] For Biblical quotes I followed *Tanakh: The Holy Scriptures, The New JPS Translation According to the Traditional Hebrew Text*, Philadelphia: JPS, 1999.

15 Ibn Ezra's commentary to the Torah, Lev. 25:2. Ibn Ezra means to say that just as humankind has a Sabbath day for rest, so too the end of each cosmic cycle is a rest for the whole world and therefore referred to as "the Lord's Sabbath."

16 Nahmanides, Gen. 2:3: "For the six days of creation parallel [lit. are] all of the history of the world, for its existence will be [for] six thousand years. That is why they [the sages] said: God's day is a thousand years [Genesis Rabbah 19: 8]." Nachmanides, *Commentary to the Torah* vol. 1, pp. 30-31.

17 Nahmanides, *Commentary to the Torah*, vol. 2, pp. 166-167.

18 See notes 12 and 13.

19 A contemporary of ibn Ezra, R. Abraham Bar Hiyya argues that the world must have an end if it was created. One of the possibilities he mentions is 49,000 years. However, he does not connect this to the notion of the sabbatical years. See Bar Hiyya, *Meggilat Ha-Megaleh*, p. 10. Israel Weinstock argues that the basis for the Doctrine of the Sabbatical Years is hinted to already in the book of the Bahir. G. Scholem differs on this point. (See Weinstock, *Be-Maagalei Ha-Nigleh VeHa-Nistar*, p. 159, note 28). Scholem takes issue with Weinstock on a few counts. (See in this book in the Scholem Library a handwritten note taking issue with Weinstock. Catalog No. 6190.1, pp. 158–159.) On the development of the Doctrine of the Sabbatical Years in Jewish philosophy, see Weinstock, ibid. pp. 177-241.

20 R. Bahya B. Asher, a contemporary of Isaac of Akko and a student of the Rashba, uses the same phrase, attributing it to "the scholars" (*Hahmei Hamehqar*). See his commentary to Lev. 25:10 in Rabeinu Bahya, *Commentary to the Torah*, vol. 2, p. 565.

21 Isaac of Acre, *Meirat Eynaim*, pp. 230-31. (Lev. 25:2)

22 Ibid. p. 130

23 The exact dates of his lifetime are unknown.

24 Recanati, *Levushei Or Yeqarot*, 68b.

25 Ibid.

26 Ibid.

27 Maimonides, *Guide for the Perplexed*, II:27, pp. 332-333.

28 Biographical dates for R. Bahya are unavailable, but his commentary to the Torah was written in 1291.

29 See Lev. 25:34

30 Rabeinu Bahya, *Commentary to the Torah*, Lev. 25:8, p. 564.

31 Ibid. Lev. 25:2, p. 564.

32 Avodah Zarah 5a.

33 Hayyat, *Commentary to Ma'arekhet Ha-Elohut*, p. 188b

34 Concerning the authorship of this work, see Scholem, *Mehqarei Kabbalah*, pp. 171-176. Scholem takes the position that the author was of Nahmanides' circle.

35 *Ma'arekhet ha-Elohut*, 187b.

36 For a comparison between the *Sefer ha-Temuna* and Christian mysticism, see Scholem, *Origins of Kabbalah*, pp. 460-475.

37 See *Kiriat Sefer* 31 (1957), p. 392: "Since this world, the sabbatical [*shmita*] that we are in, is from the *sefira* of strength [*gevurah*], as you can see, for all the punishments in this world come from fire as they [our sages] of blessed memory said [Jerusalem Talmud Sanhedrin 10:3] that the flood [of Noah] was of boiling water and so too was Sodom and Gemorrah's punishment in fire." (My translation).

38 *Ozar ha-Hayyim*, Ginzburg collection ms. 775, 87a. Later in the work he adds 250 years to represent the "quarter."

39 Ibid. 88a-b.

40 Abarbanel, *Commentary to the Torah* (Leviticus), pp. 158-159.

41 *Maggid Meisharim*, Parshat Behar, 111a.

42 Cordovero, *Pardes*. Shaar ha-Sha'arim, chap. 3, pp. 70a-71b.

43 Cordovero, *Shiur Qomah*, Chap. 83, pp. 79-83.

44 Cordovero, *Eilima Rabbati*, Tamar 1, chap. 13, 5b.

45 Vital, *Sha'ar Maamarei Rashbi*, 46b.

46 See Weinstock, *Be-Maagalei Ha-Nigleh VeHa-Nistar*, p. 230. Rav Naftali Bakhrakh (seventeenth century) writes: "This is contrary to those who hold that there were sabbatical [worlds] of kindness [*hesed*] and now it is the sabbatical of strength [*gevurah*]. All this is untrue. They heard from their Rabbis that God built previous worlds and destroyed them and they added to this the notion of the sabbaticals, but this is not true." Bakhrakh, *Emek ha-Melekh*, vol. 1, p. 58.

47 For more on this commentary, see Posner, "Ba'al Tiferet Yisrael," pp. 395-401.

48 In an interesting defense of modern medicine, R. Lipschutz interprets the Talmudic saying, "The best of Doctors are for Gehenna," to mean that a doctor who thinks that he is the best and does not take advice from his colleagues is destined for Gehinom. (Kidushin, chapter 4, commentary 77. See Posner, "Ba'al Tiferet Yisrael," p. 400). In another commentary, he quotes a doctor named Hovland in a work on microbiology. (Kidushin 4: 14, Posner, "Ba'al Tiferet Yisrael," p. 398).

49 *Or ha-Hayyim*, part three, 4a. Found in Tiferet Yisrael, Nezikin, end of vol. 1.

50 Ibid.

51 Ibid.

52 Ibid.

53 Ibid.

54 For more on Cuvier, see the *Dictionary of Scientific Biography*, vol. III, pp. 521-527.

55 *Or ha-Hayyim*, part three, 4b.

56 Haggigah 13b-14a.

57 The pre-Adamite theory was popular during the first half of the eighteenth century, more among Protestants than among Catholics. It supposed the existence of humans who predated the Adam of the Genesis story in order to find a synthesis between science and religion. For more information, see Livingstone, "The Origin and Unity of the Human Race," pp. 452-457.

58 *Or ha-Hayyim*, part three. R. Lipschutz was not the first to make a connection between the 974 generations and the Doctrine of the Sabbatical Years. This link can be understood from *Tikunei Zohar Hadash*. The Vilna Gaon, in his commentary to *Tikunei Zohar Hadash*, spells out the connection clearly but with a fundamental difference. He understands the Doctrine of the Sabbatical Years in the Lurianic fashion, identifying it as a metaphor for spiritual worlds and not physical ones. See *Tikunei Zohar Hadash Im Beiurei Hagra*, Vilna 1862, 27a.

59 *Or ha-Hayyim*, part three.

60 He appears to be unaware of evolution despite the fact that Lamarck published his *Philosophy of Zoology* in 1809.

61 Zobel, M. N., *Encyclopaedia Judaica*, vol. 4, pp. 462-463. For more on the writings of R. Benamozegh see Guetta, *Philosophie et cabbale*.

62 See Benamozegh, *Israel and Humanity*, introduction, p. 3.

63 Benamozegh, Eliyahu, *Eim la-Miqra*, 4b on Gen. 1:5.

64 The idea of a Divine day being 1000 of our years is based on Psalms 90:4. See above, text relating to note 39-40.

65 Bereishit Rabbah 3:7.

66 Benamozegh, *Eim La-miqra*, 5a.

67 Ibid.

68 Ibid. 5b.

69 Benamozegh, *Israel and Humanity*, pp. 176 and 180-182. He goes on to explain in some detail the Doctrine of the Sabbatical Years, connecting it to the midrashic idea of earlier worlds.

70 Ibid. p. 180.

71 Ibid. p. 181.

72 Benamozegh, "Il Mio Credo," found in *Teologia- Dogmatica E Apologetica*, vol. 1, Livorno 1877, pp. 276-277. The original is as follows: "Credo come insegna le Scienza che le forme animali sono apparse sulla terrasempre piu perfette, che sia per rivoluzioni o cataclismi come voleva l'anticageologia con Cuvier, sia per lenti evoluzioni come vuole la moderna con Lyell, Darwin ed altri, specie e generi sempre piu perfetti siansi succeduti per milioni di anni sulla faccia della terra. La forma sin ora piu perfetta e l'*uomo*. Ma la natura si fermera qui? Questo dav vero sarebbe strano. All'umanita presente, come ben dice Renan, un'altra piu perfetta Umanita dovra subentrare. Ma Renan ed altri qui si arrestano. Non dicono che l'*ordine* che regna nel mondo fisico deve pure regnare nel mondo morale, e che non c' e ragione per credere che quel Me quella *forza* che ha formato l'uomo attuale, non debba ascendere a formare l'uomo avvenire. Non dicono che essendovi monadi, atomi, che sono anche forze organizzatrici per se medesime, questa essendo indistruttibili (come tutto cio insegna la scienza), e inevitabile il credere che dovranno entrare a comporre l'uomo avvenire sulla terra rigenerata. Ora tutto cio dice l'Ebraismo, e questo chiama col nome (appunto perche tale e) di *Resurrezione*."

73 See also Lattes, *Ani Maamin Shel Filosof Yehudi*, p. 20.

74 Zeidman, "Harav Shimshom Raphael Hirsch," p. 115.

75 Katz, Simcha, *The Encyclopedia Judaica*, vol. 8, pp. 508-510.

76 Kaplan,"Torah U'Mada in the Thought of Rabbi Hirsch," pp. 5-31.

77 Ibid. p. 23.

78 Hirsch, "The Educational Value of Judaism" in *The Collected Writings*, vol. 7, p. 263.

79 "So many of the theories confidently advanced by science to disprove the Jewish concept of God and man are subject to change at any time. How many decades ago was the variety of human races known today cited as an argument against the Biblical account which traces the descent of all mankind to one single human couple? And yet, today's science would brand as an ignoramus anyone who would dare discount the thesis that all living creatures, not only man and orangutan, but also the elephant and the spider, the eagle, the lizard and the tapeworm, etc., etc., are descended from one single living creature." Ibid. p. 265.

80 "The reviewer himself admits that all we know about the earth is its surface, and that the relationship of this surface, so far as it is known to us, to the whole mass

of our planet is something like the relationship of the membrane that surrounds an egg yolk to the egg in its entirety...Could such a superficial knowledge, then, enable us to form a judgment 'according to the laws of thought' not only on the origins and sources of the membrane itself but also on the origins and sources of the 'egg-planet' as a whole, if you will, and the entire universe with all its heavenly bodies moving in the immeasurable expanse of space—in short the origins or sources of the world?" Ibid. pp. 299-300.

[81]   Ibid. vol. 7, p. 265.

[82]   Ibid.

[83]   Ibid. p. 264.

[84]   R. Hirsch seems to be referring to the Divine command whereby the earth is to bring forth all species (*min*) of trees and plants (Gen. 1:11).

[85]   Ibid.

[86]   Letter to R. Gefen printed in Gefen, *HaMemadim HaNevuah HaAdmetanut*, p. 8 of the introductory pages.

[87]   Ibid. p. 223.

[88]   "Inasmuch as space and time are a priori forms of human sensibility, the range of their application is extended only to things as appearing to us." Copleston, *A History of Philosophy*, vol. 6, II, p. 35.

[89]   Copleston, Ibid. p. 36. For the sake of objectivity, it must be said that space and time are the spectacles through which we see reality. We cannot remove these spectacles to check what is really there but that does not necessarily mean that they are wrong either. "It has often been pointed out that the argument from the a priori character of space and time to their subjectivity is not conclusive. It is always logically possible that what we perceive under the form of space and time is so ordered independently of our perception." Körner, *Kant*, pp. 37-38.

[90]   Gefen, *HaMemadim HaNevuah HaAdmetanut*, p. 226.

[91]   Ibid. pp. 226-227.

[92]   Ibid. p. 227.

[93]   Ibid. p. 235.

[94]   Ibid.

[95]   Ibid. p. 236. A more modern version of this idea was written based on the philosophy of Berkley. See Norwich, "The Physics of Prayer," pp. 14-19.

[96]   Ibid. p. 240.

[97]   Feldman, *Rav A. I. Kook*, p. xviii. For more on R. Kook, See also Yaron, Zvi, *Encyclopaedia Judaica*, vol. 10, pp. 1182-1187 and his book *Mishnato Shel Harav Kook*, Jerusalem 1993.

[98]   Hillel Zeitlin claims that R. Kook never took a text out of its original context to build up a new idea, and despite this, his writings appear to be total innovations. This is due to the fact that the innovation is organic to the text and not grafted from an idea foreign to it. Zeitlin, *Sifran Shel Yehidim*, p. 237.

[99]   Kook, *Orot HaKodesh 1*, p. 64.

[100] Kook, *Orot HaKodesh 3*, Introduction, p. 34.

[101] Kook, *Orot HaKodesh 1*, p. 63.

[102] Lecture at the inauguration of Hebrew University, Jerusalem, 1925, found in Kook, *Hazon HaGeulah*, pp. 265-271.

103 For more on R. Kook's approach to science and religion, see: S. Rosenberg, "Torah U-Madda," pp. 46-58. See also Yaron, "Dat U-Madda be-Mishnat Harav Kook," pp. 97-121.

104 See Kook, *Orot Hakodesh 1*, p. 51. See also Yaron, "Dat U-Madda be-Mishnat Harav Kook," p. 109, as well as my article, Shuchat, "The Debate Over Secular Studies," pp. 283- 294.

105 This doctrine was known even to those who disagreed with it, i.e., R. Moses Cordovero and R. Isaac Luriah. From a rabbinic point of view, an idea found in the writings of Nahmanides and R. Bahya remains legitimate despite the Ari's criticism.

106 Letter 91, quoted by Feldman, *Rav A. I. Kook*, P. 5.

107 Ibid.

108 Ibid.

109 Lit. "A man who shall offer for you an offering to the Lord."

110 Zohar, III (Lev.) 5a. The Aramaic reads:

"א"ר אלעזר: האי קרא כי הוה ליה למכתב, אדם כי יקריב קרבן לה'. מהו 'מכם'? אלא לאפוקי אדם הראשון דהוא אקריב קרבנא כד ברא קב"ה עלמא והא אקמוה. והכא 'מכם' כתיב, האי אדם לאפוקי אדם אחרא דלא הוה מכם."

111 This follows the interpretation of R. Shalom Buzaglo in his commentary, Mikdash Melekh, Zohar 2, 5a.

112 Ibid.

113 Kook, *Shemoneh Kvatzim*, vol. 1, p. 189.

114 *Seder Olam Rabbah*, also called Midrash Seder Olam, Jerusalem 1988 (based on the Vilna 1896 version).

115 In fact the Talmud says that the Jewish sages count from Tishrei because it is the beginning of the year and not because the world was created then. Rosh Hashana 12a according to Rashi. According to the opinion that the man was created on the first of Tishrei there is a custom to mark the creation of the world 5 days before on the 25th of Elul. See Divlizki, Ozar Nehmad, p. 36.

116 Feldman, Ibid.

117 See also Gvirtzman, "Be'ayat beri'at haolam," pp. 136-142, who discusses this connection between R. Kook and Nachmanides.

118 Nahmanides on Gen. 1:1.

119 Haggigah 2:1.

120 Feldman, *Rav A. I. Kook*, p. 7.

121 Ibid. p. 6.

122 See Cherry,"Three Jewish Responses to Evolution," p. 258.

123 Kook, *Orot Ha-Kodesh*, 2, p. 537.

124 Kook, *Sehmoneh Kevazim*, pp. 42-44.

125 For more on comparisons between R. Kook and Ramhal see Avivi, "Historia Zorekh Gavoha," pp. 709-771.

126 Luzzatto, *Da'at Tevunot*, pp. 39-40.

127 For a more thorough discussion of Ramhal's concept of history, see Avivi, "Historia Zorekh Gavoha," pp. 709-771.

128 For more on R. Kook's concept of historical development, see Ben-Shlomo, "Shlemut ve-Hishtalmut," pp. 289-309, esp. 296-309; and Gerber, *National Vision in Rabbi Kook's Philosophy*, pp 246-256.

[129] Kook, *Shemona Kevazim.*

[130] For a discussion of Christian approaches to evolutionism see: Bowler, P., "Evolution," in G. Ferngren, *The History of Science and Religion*, (pp. 458-465); Moore, J., "Geologists and Interpreters of Genesis in the Nineteenth Century," in *God and Nature: Historical Essays on the Encounter Between Christianity and Science*, R. Numbers and D. Lindberg ed., Berkley 1986, pp. 322-350; Dupree, A. H., "Christanity and the Scientific Community in the Age of Darwin," in *God and Nature*, ibid., pp. 355-360, and 362; Gregory, F., "The Impact of Darwinian Evolution on Protestant Theology in the Nineteenth Century," in *God and Nature* Ibid., p. 386. On the revival of creationism among religious thinkers, see: Numbers, Ronald, "The Creationists," in *God and Nature*, Ibid., pp. 391-423. See also Numbers, *Darwinism Comes to America.*

[131] Numbers, *Darwinism Comes to America*, p. 392.

[132] Traditional Judaism is an interface between the written and oral traditions. This is true to such an extent that if the oral tradition interprets the biblical text differently from the simple meaning in matters of Jewish law, we must follow the oral tradition's interpretation. That is why the counting of the omer commences from the second day of Passover and not from a Sunday, even though the Bible says: "And you shall count unto you from the morrow of the Sabbath" (Lev. 23:15), which the Talmud interpreted to mean the day after the Yom Tov and not the day after Saturday. The oral traditions from the classical period of Judaism, the period of *Hazal*, are the basis of Jewish law and thought. Therefore, every interpretation of the Bible based on such a source is legitimate.

[133] Even the Syrian rabbis who criticized R. Benamozegh's *Eim la-Miqra* for bringing in non-Jewish points of view didn't seem to have any problem with his liberal interpretation of creation as taking thousands of years. See "Zori Gilad," R. Benamozegh's response to the Syrian Rabbis, *Halevanon* 1871-72, vols. 14, 15, 16, 17, 18, 19, 20, 23, 24, 32, 36, 42, and 43.

[134] I will discuss his ideas at length in a forthcoming article.

[135] See for example Shneerson, *Emunah U-Madda*, pp. 89-99, where Rabbi Shneerson of Lubavitch argues against evolutionism as not being scientific and takes issue with anyone who attempts to argue that the six days of creation were anything but 24 hours each (p. 99). Korman takes a similar approach; see Korman, *Evolution and Judaism*. This is the approach taken today by modern Haredi Jewish outreach institutions like Arakhim and Aish Hatorah. The Modern Orthodox rabbis have mixed views today. Many have sided with Aviezer's position; see Aviezer, *In the Beginning*, which assumes that the 6 days were epochs and not literal. Aviezer's counterpart, Schroeder, in his *Genesis and the Big Bang* (NY, 1992), creates an interesting synthesis between the literary reading of the Bible and modern science and is considered more welcome in the ultra-orthodox circles.

CHAPTER 17

[1] Armstrong writes: "Every single fundamentalist movement that I have studied...is rooted in profound fear." Armstrong, *The Case for God*, p. 271.

Biliography

Abarbanel, *Rosh Amana*

Abarbanel, Isaac. *Rosh Amana*. Commentary by Menachem Kellner. Ramat Gan: Bar-Ilan University Press, 1993.

Agus, *The Writings*

Agus, Jacob. *The Essential Agus: The Writings of Jacob B. Agus*. Edited by Steven Katz. New York: New York University Press, 1997.

Agus, *Jewish Identity*

Agus, Jacob. *Jewish Identity in an Age of Ideologies*. Scranton, PA: Frederick Ungar, 1978.

Albo, *Ikkarim*

Albo, Joseph. *Sefer Ha-Ikkarim*. Jerusalem: 1960.

Alfarabi, *Selected Aphorisms*

Alfarabi, Muhammad. *The Political Writings: "Selected Aphorisms" and Other Texts*. Translated by Charles E. Butterworth. Ithaca, NY: Cornell University Press, 2001.

Alfarabi, *The Perfect State*

Alfarabi, Muhammad. *Al-Farabi on the Perfect State*. Translated by Richard Walzer. Oxford: Oxford University Press, 1985.

Armstrong, *The Case for God*

Armstrong, Karen. *The Case for God*. New York: Knopf, 2009.

Aristotle's *Nicomachean Ethics*

Aristotle. *The Basic Works of Aristotle*. Edited by Richard McKeon. New York, Random House, 1941.

Auerbach, *Hazal*

Auerbach, Efraim. *Hazal: Pirkei Emunot ve-De'ot*. Jerusalem: 1969.

Avivi, "Historia Zorekh Gavoha"

Avivi, Yosef. "Historia Zorekh Gavoha." In *Sefer Hayovel Le-Rav Mordecai Breuer, vol. II*, edited by Moshe Bar Asher. Jerusalem: 1992.

Bakhrakh, *Emek ha-Melekh*

Bakhrakh, Naftali. *Emek ha-Melekh*. Jerusalem: 2003.

Bar Hiyya, *Meggilat Ha-Megaleh*

Abraham Bar Hiyya. *Meggilat Ha-Megaleh*. Berlin, 1924.

Ben-David, *Scientific Growth*

Ben-David, Joseph. *Scientific Growth: Essays on the Social Organization and Ethos of Science*. Edited by Gad Freudenthal. Berkeley: University of California Press, 1991.

Ben-Shlomo, "Shlemut ve-Hishtalmut"

Ben-Shlomo, Yosef. "Shlemut ve-Hishtalmut be-Torat ha-Elohut Shel haRav Kook." *Iyyun* 33 (1984): a-b.

Benamozegh, *Eim la-Miqra*

Benamozegh, Eliyahu. *Eim la-Miqra*. Livorno: 1862.

Benamozegh, *Israel and Humanity*

Benamozegh, Elijah. *Israel and Humanity*, ed. by Maxwell Luriah, NY 1995.

Bertens, *The Idea of the Postmodern*

Bertens, Hans. *The Idea of the Postmodern: A History*. London: Routledge, 1995.

Birnbaum, "Bahya and Maimonides"

Birnbaum, Ruth. "The Role of Reason in Bahya And Maimonides." *Shofar* 19 (2001): 76-86.

Burnyeat, Aristotle

Burnyeat, M. F. "Aristotle on Learning to Be Good." In *Essays on Aristotle's Ethics*, edited by Amelie Oksenberg Rorty. Berkeley: University of California Press, 1981.

Cherry, *Evolution and Jewish Thought*

Cherry, Michael Shai. *Creation, Evolution and Jewish Thought*. PhD Dissertation, Brandeis University. Waltham, MA: 2001.

Cherry, "Three Jewish Responses to Evolution"

Cherry, Michael Shai, "Three Twentieth-Century Jewish Responses to Evolutionary Theory." *Aleph* 3 (2003): 247-90.

Chopra, *Life After Death*

Chopra, Deepak. *Life After Death*. New York: Harmony, 2006.

Cordovero, *Eilima Rabbati*

Cordovero, Moses. *Eilima Rabbati*. Levov: 1881.

Cordovero, *Pardes*

Cordovero, Moses. *Pardes Rimonim*. Jerusalem: Mossad Bialik, 1965.

Cordovero, Shiur Komah — Cordovero, Moses. *Shiur Komah*. Warsaw: 1883.

Copleston, *A History of Philosophy* — Copleston, Frederick. *A History of Philosophy*. New York: Doubleday, 1962.

Cornford, *Socrates* — Cornford, Francis Mcdonald. *Before and After Socrates*. Cambridge: Cambridge University Press, 1968.

Crescas, *Or Hashem* — Crescas, Hasdai, *Or Hashem*, Jerusalem: Sifrei Ramot, 1990.

Cescas, *Or Hashem*, Hebrew — Crescas, Hasdai. *Or Hashem*. Ferrara, Italy: 1555.

Davidson, "Metaphysical Knowledge" — Davidson, Herbert. "Maimonides on Metaphysical Knowledge." *Maimonidean Studies* 3 (1993): 49-103.

Davies, *Physics* — Davies, Paul. *God and the New Physics*. London, Simon and Schuster, 1983.

De Vidas, *Reisheit Hokhma* — De Vidas, Eliyahu. *Reisheit Hokhmah*, Shaar Hayirah, Chapter 12. Jerusalem: 1980.

Derekh Mitzvotecha — Schneersohn, Menahem Mendel (The Zemah Zedek). *Derekh Mizvotekha*. New York: Sichos in English, 1970.

Divlizki,*Ozar Nehmad* — Divlizki, Seraya, *Ozar Nehmad*. Bnei Brak: 1980.

Dictionary of Scientific Biography — *Dictionary of Scientific Biography*, edited by Charles Gillispie. NewYork: Charles Scribner's Sons, 1971.

Eliade, *Myth of the Eternal Return* — Eliade, Mircea. *The Myth of the Eternal Return: Or, Cosmos and History*. Princeton: Princeton University Press, 1974.

Fackenheim, "The Revealed Morality" — Fackenheim, Emil. "The Revealed Morality of Judaism and Modern Thought." In *Contemporary Jewish Ethics*, edited by Menachem Kellner. New York: Hebrew Publishing Company,1979.

Feldman, *Rav A. I. Kook* — Feldman, Tsvi. *Rav A. I. Kook: Selected Letters*. Maaleh Adumim: Ma'aliot Publications of Yeshivat Birkat Moshe, 1986.

Feldman, *Wars of the Lord* — Feldman, Seymour. *The Wars of the Lord*. Translated by Levi Ben Gershom. Philadelphia: Jewish Publication Society, 1984.

Freud, *Moses and Monotheism* — Freud, Sigmund. *Moses and Monotheism*. Translated by Katherine Jones. New York: Vintage, 1955.

Fromm, *Escape from Freedom* — Fromm, Erich. *Escape From Freedom*. New York: Farrar & Rinehart, 1941.

Gefen, *HaMemadim HaNevuah HaAdmetanut*

Gefen, Shem Tov. *HaMemadim HaNevuah HaAdmetanut.* Jerusalem: Mossad HaRav Kook, 1974.

Gerber, *National Vision in Rabbi Kook's Philosophy*

Gerber, Reuven. *The Development of National Vision in Rabbi Kook's Philosophy.* PhD Dissertation, Hebrew University. Jerusalem, 1991.

Gersonides, *Perush Al HaTorah*

Gersonides (Levi Ben Gershon). *Perush al Ha-Torah al Derekh Beur.* Venice: 1547.

Gersonides, *Wars of the Lord*

Gersonides, (Levi Ben Gershon). *Gersonides' Wars of the Lord, III, 3: On God's Knowledge.* Edited by Norbert M. Samuelson. Toronto: Pontifical Institute of Mediaeval Studies, 1977.

Gikatila, *Shaarei Ora*

Gikatila, Joseph. *Shaarei Ora.* Jerusalem: Mordechai Etyah, 1960.

Gilson, *Modern Philosophy*

Gilson, Etienne. *Modern Philosophy: Descartes to Kant.* NewYork: Random House, 1963.

Gigerenzer, *Gut Feelings*

Gigerenzer, Gerd. *Gut Feelings: The Intelligence of the Unconscious.* New York: Viking, 2007.

Gvirtzman, "Be'ayat beri'at haolam"

Gvirtzman, Gedaliah. "Be'ayat beri'at haolam vehamehkar hamada'i." In *Emunah Dat U-Madda, (Hackinus Hashenati Le-Mahshevet Hayahadut).* Jerusalem: 1966.

Guetta, *Philosophie et cabbale*

Guetta, Alessandro. *Philosophie et cabbale: essaie sur la pensee d'Elie Benamozegh.* Paris: Groupe L'Harmattan, 1998.

Halevi, *Aseh Lekha Rab*

Halevi, Hayyim David. *Aseh Lekha Rab.* Tel Aviv: 1978.

Halevi, *Kuzari*

Halevi, Judah. *Kuzari.* Translated by Judah Even-Shmuel. Tel Aviv: Dvir, 1972.

Ḥalamish, *Kabbalah*

Ḥalamish, Mosheh. *Mavoh la-Kabbalah.* Jerusalem: 1992.

Hayyat, *Commentary to Ma'arekhet Ha-Elohut*

Hayyat, R. Judah. *Commentary to Ma'arekhet Ha-Elohut.* Mantua: Meir of Padua and Jacob b. Naphtali, 1558.

Handlin, "Ambivalence in Responses to Science"

Handlin, O. "Ambivalence in the Popular Responses to Science." In *The Sociology of Science,* edited by Barry Barnes. Harmondsworth: Penguin, 1972.

Hartman, *Maimonides*

Hartman, David. *Maimonides: Torah and Philosophic Quest.* Philadelphia, 1977.

Heidegger, *Philosophy*

Heidegger, Martin. *What is Philosophy?* New Haven: Connecticut College and University Press, 1956.

Heschel, *Torah Min Hashamayim*

Heschel, Abraham Joshua. *Torah Min Hashomayim*. New York: Defus Shontsin, 1962.

Hirsch, *The Collected Writings*

Hirsch, Samson Raphael. *The Collected Writings*. Edited by Elliot Bondi and David Bechhofer. New York: Feldheim, 1992.

Huss, "All You Need is Lav"

Huss, Boaz. "All You Need is Lav." Originally published in German as "Madonna, die 72 Namen Gottes und eine postmoderne Kabbala," in the catalogue book of the exhibition 5+10 = Gott. Berlin: Jewish Museum of Berlin, 2004

Idel, *Abraham Abulafia*

Idel, Moshe. *Hahavayah Hamistit Esel Avraham Abulafia*. Jerusalem 1988

Isaac of Acre, *Meirat Eynaim*

Isaac Ben Samuel of Acre. *Meirat Eynaim*. Jerusalem: 1993.

Jacobs, "The Relationship Between Religion and Ethics"

Jacobs, Louis. "The Relationship Between Religion and Ethics in Jewish Thought." In *Contemporary Jewish Ethics*, edited by Menahem Kellner. New York: Sanhedrin Press, 1978

Jameson, *Postmodernism*

Jameson, Frederick. Postmodernism, or, The Cultural Logic of Late Capitalism. Durham: Duke University Press, 1991.

Kant, *Critique of Pure Reason*

Kant, Immanuel. *Critique of Pure Reason*. London: Everyman Publishers, 1991.

Kant, *Future Metaphysics*

Kant, Immanuel. *Prolegomena to any Future Metaphysics*. Indianapolis: Bobbs-Merrill, 1979.

Kaplan,"Torah U'Mada in the Thought of Rabbi Hirsch"

Kaplan, Lawrence, "Torah U'Mada in the Thought of Rabbi Samson Raphael Hirsch." In *Bekhol Derakhekha Daehu* 5, edited by Cyril Domb. Ramat-Gan: Bar-Ilan University Press, 1997.

Kohlberg, "The Adolescent"

Kohlberg, Lawrence, and Carol Gilligan. "The Adolescent as a Philosopher: The Discovery of the Self in a Post-conventional World." In *Daedalus* 100/4. Boston: MIT Press, 1971.

Korn, "Tselem Elokim"

Korn, Eugene. "Tselem Elokim and the Dialectic of Jewish Morality". In *Tradition* 31:2. New York: Rabbinical Council of America, 1997.

Körner, *Kant*

Körner, Stephan. *Kant*. London: Penguin Books, 1977.

Korman, *Evolution and Judaism*

Korman, Avraham. *Evolution and Judaism*. Tel Aviv: 1974

Kook, *Hazon HaGeula* — Kook, Abraham Isaac. *Hazon HaGeula*. NY: 1974.

Kook, *Igrot Haraayah* — Kook, Abraham Isaac. *Igrot Haraayah*. Jerusalem: Mossad Harav Kook, 1961.

Kook, *Orot HaKodesh* — Kook, Abraham Isaac. *Orot HaKodesh* I, II, III. Jerusalem: Mossad Harav Kook, 1963, 1964.

Kook, *Arpelai Tohar* — Kook, Abraham Isaac. *Arpelei Tohar*. Jerusalem: R. Zevi Yehuda Kook Institute, 1983.

Kook, *Shemoneh Kvatzim* — R. Abraham Isaac Kook. *Shemoneh Kvatzim*. Jerusalem: 1999

Lane, *Arabic-English Lexicon* — Lane, Edward William *Arabic-English Lexicon*. London: Williams and Norgate, 1877.

Lamm, *Faith* — Lamm, Norman. *Faith and Doubt*. New York: Ktav, 1971.

Lattes, *Ani Maamin Shel Filosof Yehudi* — Lattes, Dante. *Ani Maamin Shel Filosof Yehudi*. Jerusalem: 1953

Leibowitz, "Briat Ha-Olam be-Emunato shel ha-Rambam" — Leibowitz, Yeshayahu. "Briat Ha-Olam be-Emunato shel ha-Rambam." In *Briat Ha-olam ba-Madda ba-Mitos ba-Emunah*, edited by I. Mazor. Jerusalem: 1991.

Livingstone, "The Origin and Unity of the Human Race" — Livingstone, David N. "The Origin and Unity of the Human Race." In *The History of Science and Religion in the Western Tradition: An Encyclopedia*, edited by Gary B. Ferngren. New York and London: Garland Publishing, Inc., 2000.

Lobel, *Between Mysticism and Philosophy* — Lobel, Diana. *Between Mysticism and Philosophy*. Albany: SUNY Press, 2000.

Luzzatto, *Yalkut* — Luzzatto, R. Moses Hayyim, (Ramhal). *Maamar Ha-Hokhma, Be-Inyan Ha-Gilgul*. Yalkut Yediot Ha-Emet, 1965.

Lyotard, *The Postmodern Condition* — Lyotard, Jean Francois. *The Postmodern Condition: A Report on Knowledge*. Minneapolis: University of Minnesota Press, 1999.

Ma'arekhet ha-Elohut — *Mareches Elokus*. Attributed to Peretz HaCohen.Mantua: 1558.

Maggid Meisharim — Karo, R. Joseph. *Maggid Meisharim*. Jerusalem: 1960.

Maimonides, *Guide* — Maimonides, Moses. *The Guide of the Perplexed*. Translated by Shlomo Pines. Chicago: University of Chicago Press, 1963.

Maimonides, *Guide*, Ibn Tibbon ed. — *Guide for the Perplexed (Moreh Nevukhim*, Hebrew Edition). New York: Pardes, 1946.

Maimonides, *Guide*, Schwartz ed.	Schwartz, Moshe. *Moreh Nevukhim.* Tel Aviv: 2002.
Maimonides, *Higayon*	Maimonides, Moses. *Milot Ha-Higayon* (Hebrew). Jerusalem: Hebrew University, 1965.
Maimonides, *Responsa*	Maimonides, Moses. *Responsa (Teshuvot Harambam).* Edited by Abraham Freimann. Jerusalem: Mekitzei Nirdamim, 1934.
Maimonides, *Eight Chapters*	Maimonides, Moses. *Eight Chapters,* chapter one. Mordecai Dov Rabinovitch, ed. Jerusalem: 1961
Maimonides, *Igrot*	Maimonides, Moses. *Igrot ha-Rambam.* Edited by Mordekhai Dov Rabinovitch. Jerusalem: Mossad ha-Rav Kook, 1974.
Maimonides, "Eight Chapters"	Maimonides, Moses. "Eight Chapters." In *A Maimonides Reader,* edited by Isadore Twersky. New York: Behrman House, 1972.
Maimonides, "Mishneh Torah"	Maimonides, Moses. "Mishneh Torah. "In *A Maimonides Reader,* edited by Isadore Twersky. New York: Behrman House, 1972.
Maimonides, *Hakdamot*	Maimonides, Moses. *Hakdamot Ha-Rambam.* Edited by Yitzhak Shailat. Jerusalem: Ma'aliyyot Press, 1992.
Maimonides, "Maamar Tehiyat Hametim"	Maimonides, Moses. "Ma'mar Tehiyat Hametim". In *Igrot Harambam,* edited by Mordecai Dov Rabinovitch. Jerusalem: 1974
Manekin, "Belief, Certainty and Divine Attributes"	Manekin, Charles. "Belief, Certainty, and Divine Attributes in the Guide of the Perplexed." In *Maimonidean Studies* 1, edited by Arthur Hyman. New York: Yeshiva University Press, 1990.
McCarthy, "Postmodern Pleasure and Perversity"	McCarthy, Paul. "Postmodern pleasure and perversity: Scientism and sadism." In *Essays in Postmodern Culture,* edited by Eyal Amiran and John Unsworth. New York: Oxford University Press, 1993.
Merton, "The Sociology of Science"	Merton, Robert King. "The Sociology of Science: An Episodic Memoir." In *The sociology of science in Europe,* edited by Robert King Merton and Jerry Gaston. Carbondale, Illinois: Southern Illinois University Press, 1977.
Moody, *Reflections on Life After Life*	Moody,Raymond. *Reflections on Life After Life.* Harrisburg: Stackpole Books, 1977.

Moody, *Life After Life*
Moody, Raymond. *Life After Life*. New York: Mockingbird Books, 1975.

Nachmanides' Commentary
to Sefer Hamitzvot
Nachmanides' Commentary to Sefer ha-Mizvot, Frankel Edition. Jerusalem and Bnei Brak: 1995

Nachmanides' commentary to the Torah
Nahmanides, Moses. *Perushei Hatorah Le-Rabbi Moshe Ben Nahman,* edited by C. B. Chavel. Jerusalem: 1959-1960.

Norwich,"The Physics of Prayer"
Norwich, Kenneth, "The Physics of Prayer and the Origin of the Universe." *Conservative Judaism* 40-2. 1987.

Numbers, *Darwinism Comes to America*
Numbers, Ronald. *Darwinism Comes to America.* Cambridge: Harvard University Press, 1998.

Pachter, "Bein Acosmism le-Theism"
Pachter, Mordecai,"Bein Acosmism le-Theism: Tefisat ha-Elohut be-Mishnato shel R. Hayyim me-Volozhin." In *Mehkarim be-Hagut Yehudit.* Jerusalem: 1989.

Pines "Truth and Falsehood"
Pines, Solomon. "Truth and Falsehood Versus Good and Evil, A Study in Jewish and General Philosophy in Connection with the Guide of the Perplexed, 1, 2." In *Studies in Maimonides,* edited by Isadore Twersky. London: 1990.

Pines, "The Limitations of Human Knowledge"
Pines, Solomon, "The Limitations of Human Knowledge According to Al-Farabi, Ibn Bajja andMaimonides." In *Studies in Medieval Jewish History and Literature,* edited by Isadore Twersky. Cambridge, MA: Harvard University Press, 1979.

Posner, "Ba'al Tiferet Yisrael"
Posner, Akiva Barukh. "Ba'al Tiferet Yisrael u-Perusho Leseder Nashim." Shana be-Shana 4 (1963-5724)

Pritchard, *Ancient Near East*
Pritchard, James. *The Ancient Near East,* Vol. 1. New Jersey: Princeton University Press, 1958.

Qafih, *Sefer Hamitzvot*
Qafih. Joseph. *Maimonides' Sefer Hamizvot.* Jerusalem: 1971.

Rabeinu Bahya, *Commentary to the Torah*
Rabeinu Behayei Ben Asher. *Beur al-Hatorah.* H. D. Chavel Edition. Jerusalem: 1967

Recanati, *Levushei Or Yeqarot*
Recanati, Menahem. *Peirush al ha-Torah (Levushei Or Yeqarot).* Jerusalem: Mordechai Etyah, 1961.

Rawidowicz, *Iyyunim*
Rawidowicz, Simon. *Iyyunim Bemahshevet Yisrael.* Jerusalem: Reuven Mas, 1969.

Reines, "Miracles"
Reines, Alvin J. "Maimonides' Concept of Miracles." In HUCA 45 (1974).

Robinson, "Judaism Since 1700"   Robinson, Ira. "Judaism Since 1700." In *The History of Science and Religion in the Western Tradition,* edited by Gary Ferngren. New York: Garland Press, 2000.

Ross, "Shnei Perushim"   Ross, Tamar. "Shnei Perushim le-Torat ha-Zimzum." *Mehkarei Yerushalyim be-Mahshevet Yisrael* 2 (1982)

Russel, *A History of Philosophy*   Russel, Bertrand. *A History of Western Philosophy.* New York: Simon & Schuster, 1972.

Russel, *The Basic Writings*   Russel, Bertrand. *The Basic Writings of Bertrand Russel,* edited by R. Egner and L. Denon. London: Allen & Unwin, 1961.

Safran, "Maimonides and Aristotle"   Safran, Alexander. "Maimonides and Aristotle on Ethical Theory." In *Alei Shefer: Studies in the Literature of Jewish Thought Presented to Alexandre Safran,* edited by Moshe Hallamish. Ramat Gan: Bar-Ilan University Press, 1990.

Saadiah, *Emunot ve-Deot*   Saadiah Gaon. *Sefer ha-Nivhar be-'Emunot ve-Deot,* edited and translated by Yosef Kafih. Jerusalem: Sura, 1970.

Scholem, *Origins of Kabbalah*   Scholem, Gershom. *Origins of Kabbalah.* Princeton: Princeton University Press, 1987.

Scholem, *Major Trends*   Scholem, Gershom. *Major Trends in Jewish Mysticism.* Jerusalem: Schocken, 1941.

Scholem, *Mehqarei Kabbalah*   Scholem, Gershom. *Studies in Kabbalah,* edited by Y. Ben-Shlomo and M. Idel. Tel-Aviv: 1998.

Scholem, *Pirkei Yesod*   Scholem, Gershom. *Pirkei Yesod beHavanat haKabbalah U-Semaleha.* Jerusalem: Bialik Institute, 1976.

Sefer Mitvot Gadol   Moses Ben Coucy. *Sefer Mizvot Gadol.* Jerusalem: 1961 (Venician edition).

Shapira, *Hovat Ha-Talmidim*   Shapira, Klonimus Kalman. *Hovat Ha-Talmidim.* Jerusalem: 1960.

Shapiro, *The Limits of Orthodox Theology*   Shapiro, Marc B. *The Limits of Orthodox Theology: Maimonides' Thirteen Principles Reappraised.* London: Oxford University Press, 2004.

Sirat, *Jewish Philosophy*   Sirat, Collette. *A History of Jewish Philosophy in the Middle Ages.* New York: Cambridge University Press, 1985.

Shneur Zalman, *Tanya*   Shneur Zalman of Liadi. *Tanya.* New York: 1976.

Shneerson, *Emunah U-madda* — Schneerson, Menachem Mendel. *Emunah U-madda*. Kefar Chabad: 1977.

Shuchat, *The Creation* — Shuchat, Wilfred. *The Creation According to Midrash Rabbah*. New York: Devora Publishing, 2002.

Shuchat, "Demuto shel Avraham" — Shuchat, Raphael. "Demuto shel Avraham Avinu BeVeit Midrasho she Hagra: Emunah Sihlit Mul Emunah Hitgalutit." In *Avraham Avinu Avi Hamaminim*. Ramat Gan: 2002

Shuchat, "Perush Hagra" — Shuchat, Raphael. "Perush Hagra Me-Vilna Le-Mishnat Hasidim," *Kabbalah Journal* 3 (1998).

Shuchat, "Lithuanian Kabbala" — Shuchat, Raphael. "Kabbalat Litah kezerem Atma'i be-Sifrut Hakabbalah." Kabbalah Journal 10 (2004). J. Abram and A. Elkayyam, eds.

Shuchat "The Debate Over Secular Studies — Shuchat, Raphael. "The Debate Over Secular Studies Among the Disciples of the Vilna Gaon." *The Torah U-Madda Journal* 8 (1998-1999).

Shuchat, "The Historiosophy of the Vilna Gaon — Shuchat, Raphael. "The Historiosophy of the Vilna Gaon and the Influence of Luzzatto on Him and his Disciples." *Daat* 40 (1998, Hebrew).

Shuchat, *Olam Nistar* — Shuchat, Raphael. *Olam nistar b'mamaday ha-zman*. Ramat Gan: Bar Ilan University Press, 2008.

Siddur HaGra — *Siddur HaGra - B'Nigleh Ve'Nistar*. Jerusalem: 1971.

Southgate, *Postmodernism in History* — Southgate, Beverly. *Postmodernism in History: Fear or Freedom*. London: Routledge, 2003.

Sutherland, *Reborn in the Light* — Sutherland, Cherie. *Reborn in the Light*. New York: Bantam Books, 1992.

Teshuvot HaRashba — *Shelot Ve-Teshuvot HaRashba*, part one, letter 418. Jerusalem: 1997

The Yellow Emperor — *The Yellow Emperor's Canon of Internal Medicine*. Translated by Wu Lian Sheng and Wu Qi. Beijing: China Science and Technology Press, 1997.

Tiferet Yisrael — Lipshutz, R. Israel. *Tiferet Yisrael Commentary to the Mishnah*. New York, 1969.

Tishbi, *Mishnat ha-Zohar* — Tishbi, Yishayahu. *Mishnat ha-Zohar*. Jerusalem: Mossad Bialik, 1957.

Vital, *Shaar HaHakdamot* — Vital, Hayyim. *Shaar HaHakdamot*, Introduction. Reprinted in *Eitz Hayyim*. Warsaw: 1890.

Vital, *Eitz Hayyim* — Vital, Hayyim. *Eitz Hayyim*. Warsaw: 1890.

Vital, *Sha'ar Maamarei Rashbi* — Vital, Hayyim. *Sha'ar Maamarei Rashbi*. Jerusalem: 1959.

Weinstock, *Be-Maagalei Ha-Nigleh VeHa-Nistar* — Weinstock, Israel. *Be-Maagalei Ha-Nigleh VeHa-Nistar*. Jerusalem: 1969.

Weiss, *Only Love* — Weiss, Brian. *Only Love is Real: A Story of Soulmates Reunited*. New York: Warner Books, 1996.

Wolfson, *Crescas* — Wolfson, Harry Austin. *Crescas' Critique of Aristotle: Problems of Aristotle's Physics in Jewish and Arabic Philosophy*. Cambridge, MA: Harvard University Press, 1929.

Wolfson, *Kalam in Jewish Philosophy* — Wolfson, Harry. *Repercussions of the Kalam in Jewish Philosophy*. London: Harvard University Press, 1979.

Wolfson, "Maimonides on Negative Attributes" — Wolfson, Harry. "Maimonides on Negative Attributes." In *Studies in the History of Philosophy and Religion*, Vol. 2, edited by I. Twersky and G. Williams. Cambridge: Harvard University Press, 1977.

Worthing, *God, Creation and Contemporary Physics* — Worthing, Mark William. *God, Creation and Contemporary Physics*. Minneapolis: Fortress Press, 1996.

Yaron, "Dat U-madda be-Mishnat Harav Kook" — Yaron (Zinger), Zvi. "Dat U-Madda be-Mishnat Harav Kook." In *Emuna Dat U-madda, Hakinus Hashenati Le-Mahshevet Yisrael*. Jerusalem: 1966.

Zeidman, "Harav Shimshon Raphael Hirsch" — Zeidman, Hillel. "Harav Shimshon Raphael Hirsch." In *Hokhmat Yisrael be-Eiropah*, edited by S. Federbush. Jerusalem: 1965.

Zeitlin, *Sifran Shel Yehidim* — Zeitlin, Hillel. *Sifran Shel Yehidim*. Jerusalem: Mossad HaRav Kook, 1979.

Zukav, *The Dancing Wu Li Masters* — Zukav, Gary. *The Dancing Wu Li Masters: An Overview of the New Physics*. New York: William Morrow, 1980.

Index

CPSIA information can be obtained at www.ICGtesting.com
Printed in the USA
LVOW07s0446010913

350443LV00002B/2/P